KIDS' GAMES

ALSO BY ELAINE MARTIN
Baby Games

KIDS' GAMES

Creative games and activities

A Parents' Guide to playing with your Three to Six-Year-Old

ELAINE MARTIN

RANDOM HOUSE

Published in Canada in 1989 by Random House of Canada Limited.

Canadian Catagloguing in Publication Data

Martin, Elaine
  Kids' Games

ISBN 0-394-22103-6

1. Games.   2. Amusements.   3. Parent and child.
I. Title.

GV1203.M37 1989   790.1'922   C89-094463-6

COVER AND TEXT DESIGN: Brant Cowie/ArtPlus Limited

TYPE OUTPUT: Tony Gordon Ltd.

ILLUSTRATIONS: Janet Wilson

COVER PHOTO: Peter Correz/Masterfile

Printed in Canada

CONTENTS

A Note to Parents

Dear Parent,

Your child brings his own individuality into our world. This means he has his own needs and interests, his own emotional intensity, and his own moods.

This book is my way of organizing some of the wealth of play materials available for your use with your child. His play is as individual as he is. He may be dramatic, adventurous, and outgoing. He may prefer to spend his time drawing intricate patterns, or cuddling quietly with you. At times he may hoot and holler around the vacant lot nearby, or spend hours searching bushes for ladybugs.

Don't limit yourself to the ages suggested for games. At one time your child may be entranced by one activity to the exclusion of all others. At another, he will flit from activity to activity, trying to find something that interests him. Your child will indicate his own preferences.

My neighborhood has many friendly children and parents who willingly shared their play experiences and ideas about what has worked for them. I have included all types of play experiences that have worked for me. Jenny and I love many of the games we have learned from our friends, at the playgrounds, and at school. Thus, I have been able to collect a wide range of games that have appealed to a wide assortment of children, with a wide variety of interests.

Not all of these games will appeal to your child. He will not like every game I have presented. Because he is unique, he wants to find his own patterns of play, his own favorite games, and do his own individual projects. There are times when he may be ahead or behind my purely arbitrary groupings of games. He may be able to throw and catch a ball accurately at four, or not until nearly six or even seven for games like Ordinary Movings (p 82).

There are games that may not interest him at the time I suggest that he might want to play for hours as his skills and interests grow. Some games may be personal family favorites, others may arouse a totally spontaneous reaction out on the playground. One day I was singing in my typically off-key fashion at the park, when suddenly I found myself in the center of a circle of moms all singing "Going to Kentucky" and doing the hootchie-kootchie. The children all clamored to join in the fun. What a great afternoon we all had trying different variations of the same games, and asking, "Did you ever play. . . ?" Try it at *your* playground!

The games children play are a huge part of the shared knowledge of their generation. They are also a wonderful way for us to spend "quality" time with our own child. Most of all, they're fun!

When you "coach" your budding athlete in the art of catching and throwing a ball, or skipping rope, or clapping rhythms and patterns with his hands, you give him lifelong skills. The songs he sings, the games he plays, the knowledge he acquires from card games, the poetry he learns, the science experiments he performs, the art projects he designs and builds, will all stand him in good stead for his future growth. Best of all, you will have fun playing together.

Please use this book as your guide to strengthening and deepening your child's — and your own — love of play, both together and with your ever-enlarging circle of friends and neighbors.

I am always seeking favorite BEST games. Please send me the play activities, songs, and games that you and your child totally LOVE. I invite your comments so that future editions can be even more fun. My address is: Random House of Canada Limited, 1265 Aerowood Drive, Mississauga, Ontario, Canada L4W 1B9.

Happy Playing!!

ELAINE MARTIN

SOURCE MATERIAL

ANY OF THE SONGS and rhymes in *Kids'
Games* are traditional folk material. I
discovered many of them at our playground, and Jenny has brought some of them
home. When I have been able to find the name
of the author of material, I have included it.

I have indicated the specific locality or country of origin where it is possible. When specific
origin of material is not known, I have indicated
where it appears widely.

Children's songs and rhymes are from the oral
tradition. I have made every effort to ensure that
I have not infringed on any copyright in the
songs and games I present. Because I learned most
of the games at the playground, if I did inadvertently quote material not in the public domain,
please accept my apologies.

A Note on His and Her

Since kids come as both girls and boys, the use of
the male and female pronouns will alternate with
each chapter.

PROLOGUE

KIDS' GAMES FOR GROWNUPS

CHILDHOOD IS the fascinating time of seeking truth, wisdom, knowledge, and understanding in a never-ending quest. Few grownups understand the world we live in. We don't even know which questions to ask!!! Your child NEVER STOPS. "Is my fish dead or real?" "Why don't we remember tomorrow?" "I came from you, Mommy, and you came from Granny. Granny had a mommy. Are people infinite?" "Where is the end of the universe?" "Why is there a rainbow?" "What makes lightning?"

Your child's unique spirit and creativity come from deep within. When she creates understanding through her play, she gains an open window through which she can view her world and gain new achievements. She is learning and growing through every one of her play experiences.

Play Requirements

There are very basic requirements for play with your child. Heed them or Black Peter (p 162) will record your infractions in his red record book and carry you off in his sack next Saint Nicholas Day.

A. You need to learn when to step back and let your child learn from her own experiences. You know how to tie your shoes and cut along a line; she is learning. Coming to her rescue, because it's faster if you do it, doesn't help her learn. You need to learn how to tread the very fine line between support, encouragement, approval, and help, and bossiness, perfection, interference, and meddling. Let her be "boss" about what she's doing, at least part of the time, as she learns to climb to the top of the slide or work out the sharing of toys.

B. We all make mistakes. Part of being human is our ability to learn from our mistakes. Be tolerant of your child's errors and encourage her to learn from them. For instance, appliqué, paste and paper overlay, magic tape, or piles of stickers, often provide more opportunity for creative expression than the original concept you envisioned. Use both your mistakes and those of your child as opportunities for growth, without nagging.

C. NEVER, EVER coerce your child to do any play activity that "spooks" her, or that she insists she does not want to do. How can you deal with this fear? You may want to remove her from frightening situations, to deal with them at a less threatening time. You may want to let her watch and choose to participate at her own pace. You may want to talk it through, saying something reassuring like: "Dinosaurs lived millions of years ago, and they are extinct. These are pretend dinosaurs that we are visiting at the museum today. They are not alive and they will not hurt you. Do you want to hold my hand, or let me hold you, while we look at them?" If the issue is critical to your life style; for instance, if you own a cottage and are in boats all the time, you may want to consider Red Cross swimming lessons to help overcome her fear of the water. Cuddly hand puppets are not nearly as threatening as a Punch and Judy show. A clown at a circus or on television is easier to deal with than a clown nose-to-nose at her birthday party. Often, what "spooks" your child now will be her very favorite play when she has had a little time and maturity to resolve her fears in her own way.

D. Humiliation does not lead to self-confidence or growth. Rid your vocabulary of words and phrases such as "bad," "stupid," "scaredy cat," "because I said so," "I told you so," "it doesn't look like that to me." When it's possible, let your child attempt to resolve complex things herself. When it is necessary to intervene, do so without censure. Avoid comparison of your child with anyone else, whether it is for what she made or for what she did.

E. Be honest with your frank, open praise and remarks. Comments can include: "I was proud of the way you shared the slide with Ian." "Perhaps next time you can ask Caitlin for a turn, instead of pulling her off." "What a *great* triceratops, I love the colors you used. It looks so happy with that wonderful smile. I don't think the brontosaurus is quite as interesting. Were you, maybe, painting just a little bit too fast?" Always include suggestions and alternatives without insisting she do it your way. For instance, "What a wonderful rocket. Would you like to have some red and yellow ribbons to tie on for streamers?"

Safety _____

Your child needs the safest possible play world. Monitor all play areas to ensure her safety. Pick up broken glass, watch out for animal feces. Check ropes, swings, slides, and all playground equipment for safety, even at well-used playgrounds. If your child has long hair, make sure you tie it back before she plays so it won't get caught. Pediatricians recommend absolutely NO riding of trikes or bikes on the street until at least age eight, so if your child has a bike or trike, ensure that she has a safe place to ride. Make sure your home is child-proofed.

THE BUDDY SYSTEM

Take along a "buddy" when your child shares interests with her friends. Everybody feels better when they have a friend, and your child is no exception. Whether you are camping, at the playground, playing Hide 'n' Seek, going on a trip to the museum, walking back and forth to school, swimming, going to the corner store, or just playing outside, a buddy ensures there is always someone to get help fast if something goes wrong. Of course, the "buddy system" never eliminates the need for responsible adult supervision of all play.

Home and Family _____

Your home and family are the sacred center of your child's universe. They provide her with a springboard to the rest of the world, as well as a sanctuary when it is required. Never underestimate how important both are to her.

YOUR CHILD'S NEST

Your child needs a special place at home that is exclusively hers. She may have her own room. If she shares a room, make her a special nest somewhere within the house. This place will be her own private comforting retreat when experiences are overwhelming. There are times she may retire there on her own, and other times when you need to separate her from unpleasant situations. Her nest should contain comfortable, child-sized furniture or cushions, her favorite books, a few of her special comforting toys, and some of her favorite artwork.

YOUR CHILD'S ROOM

Your child's room needs to reflect her interests and personality, as well as be a pleasant place to live. Perhaps she has special pets living there: fish, a gerbil, a bird, a hamster, mice, or an ant farm. Put up a bulletin board or blackboard for important artwork, invitations, family pictures, maps, collectibles and posters. Let her change her decor as her interests change, perhaps by changing posters from dinosaurs to star maps.

Her room needs to be organized for a minimum of stress for both you and her. Even if it takes your child hours to tidy up her room, YOU should be able to tidy it in ten or fifteen minutes. If it takes longer, reorganize. Your child should have some say in the overall level of tidiness or messiness of her own space, at least some of the time. Toy organization, accessibility of clothes, and ease of finding favorite books has to be a "given" at your own level of sanity. Use open shelves, drawstring bags, cookie tins, and bins to organize all the bits and pieces. Small, cloth zipper suitcases are absolutely great for keeping all the pieces of one type of activity together.

WORKSPACE

Your child needs her own flat, easily scrubbable workspace where she can be creative with a minimum of supervision. A table or flat desk would be suitable for playdough and artwork when she is very young, and for her pencil and paper work later on. Cover her desk with newspapers when she is being messy.

PHYSICAL ACTIVITY

Your child probably loves being active and stretches her limits daily. She balances as she walks along the edge of a wall or curb. She would rather run than walk. She skips along ahead of you, and climbs to great heights on the playground equipment. One of her greatest delights may be emulating an orangutan going hand over hand, bouncing up and down on a mattress, or hanging by her knees from playground equipment.

Join her in her physical activity and work on your own fitness level! Participate in family sports: bicycle along a bicycle path, swim together at the pool, jog around the track or around the block. Do YOU have a favorite sport? Coach her in whatever it may be. Get her a baseball mitt and a Tee Ball set if you like baseball. Show her how to kick a soccer ball. Put a basket-ball net at child height on your garage and practice shooting baskets together. Do you dance? Be sure to dance together. Spend several long sessions a week at the playground. You will both be energized by the time you are active together.

FAMILY STORIES

Every family has its "you wouldn't be here but for this" type of story. It might tell how Mom and Dad met. It might tell how Great, Great,Great,Great Grandpa was hung outside his church back in the old country, so the family moved to a new country.

It might tell how great Gram was one ship away from taking the Titanic when she came to this country. It might tell how Grampie was a soldier, or how Great, Great Grandmother walked to Quebec to find her stepson and bring him back home after his mother died. Search out the old stories from other family members, write down any you remember, do the research necessary to dig out your family anecdotes, and pass them along to your child. Don't lose your family records; they're priceless.

FAMILY REUNIONS

Does your family have reunions? They might be weddings, christenings, funerals, anniversaries, bar mitzvahs, or just large get-togethers of the extended family. Do go, and take your child. Take your camera, take a tape recorder (especially wonderful for figuring out relationships and having the source handy), and perhaps a video camera.

FAMILY RELATIONSHIPS

Your child is busy figuring out how everyone fits together in a family. Mommy and Daddy may be husband and wife. Daddy's brother is Mommy's brother-in-law, and her uncle. Nanny is my grandmother. She's Daddy's mother, and Mommy's mother-in-law. She's Katie's grandmother, too. But Katie's mother and father aren't my mother and father. No wonder it's confusing! Talk about who everyone is, and if you get confused, just listen to Michael Cooney singing "I'm My Own Grandpa" on his *Pure Unsweetened Live Family Concert* album, Alliance Records.

FAMILY TREE

Kinship and lineage are fascinating. Start a family tree for your child, with her at the base. Track branches to mom and dad, mom and dad's brothers and sisters, mom and dad's parents, their brothers and sisters, their parents, and on and on back. There are reference sources and public records to help you in your search when memories, visits to graveyards, letters to distant relatives, documentation, and the family Bible fail to provide you with the knowledge you are seeking. Who knows, you may even find some bright lights or interesting skeletons in your child's ancestry. By contacting distant members of your family you may find pearls of family wisdom and unearth special memories.

SPECIAL MEALS

Wonderful family memories are created around special meals. Serve favorite foods, dim the lights, turn on music, light candles, and use your special dishes. Share good feelings, give compliments, remember happy occasions, plan an outing. Now is the time for your child to learn the social graces she will need later on.

One of the rites of passage in our family was the first time a child was allowed to eat in the dining room at a formal meal. Usually the children ate separately, in the kitchen. I still have never eaten a meal in Aunt Eleanor's dining room!

ART PORTFOLIO

Establish a special place to save prized pieces of your child's artwork. As she grows and develops, so does her art. You may want to purchase a special art portfolio from an artists' supply store, or simply use a file folder or scrapbook. Keep drawings, special greeting cards, report cards, awards from field days, certificates for completing music class or Tee Ball. Frame and hang several truly wonderful pieces of her art.

CREATE YOUR SPECIAL RITUALS

Create magic times together. Draw a treasure map to lead your child to a special treat. Create a meal with all her favorite foods, and have a "princess party." Go on long, lovely walks together. When her teeth start loosening, have the tooth fairy ingrained as part of this rite of passage. Wish on wishbones, wish on stars. Tell fortunes (p 41). Welcome Santa Claus, Saint Valentine, and the Easter Bunny, and perhaps a fairy godmother who will bring her presents at certain times of the year, "just because."

SPECIAL DAYS

Go special places together as a family. Take pictures and create special memories that will last a lifetime. Where to go? Contact Boards of Tourism or Chambers of Commerce in towns or cities close to where you live. Draw up a list of possible places to visit, and see which ones fit your family's interests. Some possibilities:

- Climb a mountain
- Dip nets in a marsh
- Go on a boat cruise
- Attend a children's concert
- Roam through a museum or children's museum
- Visit an art gallery
- Go cross-country skiing
- Relax on a beach
- Visit a planetarium or observatory
- Visit an aquarium
- Go to the birthplace of a famous person and talk about that person
- Visit historical villages, museums, forts, parks
- Take a bus tour of your own city
- Attend a circus
- Hike around the zoo
- Watch a sporting event
- Visit a scenic landmark
- Take a "bird walk" with a naturalist
- Hike around conservation areas
- Go camping

KEEPING HER RECORD

Take plenty of pictures and mount them in albums. Record her first Tee Ball practice. Take a video along to her first dance recital or school concert. Tape-record the concert and send it to grandma. Keep a journal, a line or two a day, of significant events in her life. Or just scribble on a family calendar; when she went on her first sleepover at a friend's house, when she had chicken pox, who was at her birthday party, when she lost her first tooth.

HER EXPRESSION OF HER LIFE

Encourage your child to record her feelings and experiences. A journal is a great record for her. Lace together some blank pages for her drawings. If she asks, you write her story on the back of her picture. Read back her comments and add more if she continues. If you have a tape or video recorder, have your child sing a song or tell a story, and let her play it back. At about age five, give your child an inexpensive camera and photo album for her pictures. Write down the stories that go with the pictures she takes. All of this will be a treasure to her as she grows.

About Play

Many of the activities that interest your child now will interest her for years. You expand her interests and knowledge by supplying complex information and materials for her. Your child may be interested in dinosaurs, wild animals, birds, farm animals, her neighborhood, the ocean, marshes, insects, the zoo. I have gone into a specific interest in depth in the "Facts Around a Theme" chapter, using space as an example of how to cover a topic in depth. Your child may suddenly expand one topic into another. For instance, an interest in space can lead to questions about weather, or dinosaurs. A fascination with dinosaurs can arouse curiosity about reptiles or archaeology. Follow your child's interests wherever they lead, and expand your own knowledge.

INDIVIDUAL DIFFERENCES

At times, your child will persist at an activity until she masters it. At other times, she will be unwilling to attempt an activity that she thinks might be too difficult, or that she might not be able to do perfectly. Her physical development makes a big difference in her abilities. Most three-year-olds aren't able to jump rope at all; by five-and-a-half some children have mastered Double Dutch. Let your child choose her own level of play. Something that is too challenging for her now may captivate her later.

PLAY DIFFERENCES — BOYS AND GIRLS

Before first grade there is very little difference in how children play and what games they find appealing. Small boys may tend to be noisier and play with cars and trucks more than small girls. Small girls may dress up slightly more often than small boys. The boys like skipping rope. But play seems to be based on the interests of the friends your child plays with. For instance, Jenny searches for bugs and creepy crawlies with Jordan. She has tea parties with Dan and Norah. She and Clare build massive constructions with blocks, and Clare is no slouch at turning over a rock either. Jesse, Ethan, Clare and Jenny play for hours in Sherwood Forest, a small ravine near the playground; sometimes the girls even get to be Robin Hood. When Jordan wanted to invite only boys to his birthday party, he insisted that Jenny and Clare be invited, too. "What do you mean they're not boys?" Let your child experience all the possibilities in her play. The routine will soon change.

THE MAGIC OF PLAY

Your child believes in the magic of play. There is perhaps nothing on earth as enduring and universal as the games children play. Rules, songs, and jingles evolved everywhere, with local variations and through misunderstandings of the words. The same rhymes are recited in far-flung corners of the world as children skip, clap, or bounce balls. Rules of games are handed on from child to child, as well as from parent to child. Children play tag, hide 'n' seek, skipping, or clapping games the same way their grandparents and great grandparents did.

RITUAL MAGIC

Do you still avoid stepping on cracks? Ritual, wishing, telling fortunes, good and bad luck, are all a large portion of your child's play. Tell fortunes by: skipping, wishing on a star, believing in the tooth fairy, wishing on a milkweed or dandelion fairy, finding a four-leaf clover, making a wish before blowing out the candles, keeping your last penny, rubbing a horseshoe, drinking the "money" (small bubbles) quickly on a drink, finding a coin and giving it to a friend, or breaking a wishbone.

Of course, you avoid spilling salt (if you do, throw a pinch over your left shoulder), walking under ladders, letting a black cat cross your path, five-leaf clovers, and most especially, stepping on a crack.

WINNING

Your child needs the opportunity to win and lose according to the luck of the draw, as well as through the development of skill and cunning. By winning and losing at random, she learns that good and bad luck are a part of life. She also learns that skills increase with practice. If you know how to play a game, any game, according to the rules, it is much more fun. You win some, you lose some, and you are able to influence the outcome of events some of the time. Of course, as you play together you stack the deck so that she wins fairly frequently. Build up her self confidence and skills before you engage in anything competitive. Competitive team sports and the message of winning at all costs belong with much older children or with grownups, who are able to handle winning and losing on an adult level.

CONTENT OF RHYMES AND JINGLES

Don't listen too closely to the songs, rhymes, chants, taunts, and nonsense verse that your child brings home from the playground. Some of what you hear may be gross, macabre, rude, or totally unintelligible. Your child is learning how to play with language. She loves the way words fit together, she loves the innuendo and impact she is able to create. She is learning about the power of words.

By all means, establish your house rules about rudeness and profanity. Calling Great Aunt Winnifred a poo-poo head is definitely *not* allowed. But try to be flexible about some of the gruesome, violent, yucky language, even if it is sometimes offensive to adult sensibilities. "Never Laugh When a Hearse Goes By" (p 77), the "Frog Sandwich" joke (p 58), and even the traditional "Three Blind Mice" (p 54) are all examples of material that have survived through many years because they have deep underlying messages about life for your child. They may be about scary, evil, or naughty characters but your child loves them, even though they are not "nice." Playground songs and rhymes survive because they express your child's feelings and fears in a form that is manageable for her.

Remember, too, that although some jingles are risqué and downright rude, many more include some most evocative poetic language:

Turn back, turn back, thou scornful knight, and rub thy spurs, they are not bright (p 108);
Not last night, but the night before, twenty-four robbers came knocking at my door (p 77);
There she stands a lovely creature, who she is I do not know. (p 60).

Play and Your Child's Creativity

Your child delights herself when she plays creatively, solving problems in new ways, and creating something from nothing. What most adults regard as garbage takes on new life through your child's eyes as she builds a moon city from tin cans, old boxes, and all the bits and pieces of junk she can find.

Encourage your child's curiosity, excitement, wonder, and originality. Do everything you can to keep her wonderful imagination flourishing. Creativity makes us all feel more alive!

THE ARTS

The visual arts, drama, storytelling, dance and music all need to be a natural part of your child's life. The more opportunities she has to experience and investigate arts processes, the more opportunities she has to express her own feelings and ideas. The arts help your child discover her world and give her an appreciation of her own uniqueness.

Never demand an exact imitation of either a process or an outcome. Let her express herself. Let her figure out how things go together. Show her how things CAN go together, not how they MUST go together.

MUSIC

Most children between the ages of three and six are not interested in being part of a quiet audience. They want to experience music with their whole bodies, and they want to perform. Sing together with your child every day. Sing skipping jingles, nursery rhymes, circle games, popular songs, old favorites, and whatever musical fragments pop into your mind as you go about your daily routine. Hold hands and sing together as you skip along the street.

Share your own musical loves with your child. If you adore classical music, introduce her to the music of the great composers. If you love folk music, attend concerts or festivals where the audience participates. Listen to bagpipes, pan pipes, salsa, hillbilly, reggae, rock, Maori, country and western, ballroom dance music; whatever you enjoy. Take her to see children's performers like Sharon, Lois & Bram; Raffi; Kim and Jerry Brodey, and Michael Cooney when they perform in your area.

STORYTELLING

Tall tales, folk legends, and native legends are all meant to be TOLD. Share the tales from the oral tradition, from Beowulf to Anansi, with your child. When you tell them, remember that descriptions should be brief and colorful, and that you must leave the essential magic, without embellishing or explaining what happened or why; otherwise, the magic disappears. Share the stories you love, preferably on a warm night under the stars or in a cozy corner.

One day Nanabush did something very bad . . .
Once, a great huntress of Africa . . .
Pecos Bill could rope a streak of lightnin' . . .
Long ago, in the old time, there were giants who . . .
[STORYTELLER] *Crick crack*
[AUDIENCE] *Break my back*

HER NATURAL WORLD

The natural world is a fascinating and mysterious place for your child. Her inherent curiosity is aroused by time spent outdoors, watching an insect, pouring over a field guide looking for the bird that comes to her feeder, watching the clouds as they form, roll by, and dissipate. The processes and daily transformations of the creatures and plants around her, the night sky, and the weather add to her knowledge of where she fits into the world. By sharing these experiences, you are able to communicate a sense of the value and fragility of our environment and of our responsibility to preserve and protect our world.

INTELLECTUAL CONCEPTS

Expand your vocabulary with your child so she can internalize the concepts we use to organize and label our world. The alphabet, the months of the year, the hours of the day, are all part of traditional skipping and clapping games. Use the words below, naturally, in play and in everyday conversation.

- Some, a few, many, none, zero, less than, more than, fewer, as many as
- First, second, third, fourth, fifth . . .
- In order, join, member, pair
- Alike, different, similar, same as, equivalent
- Thick, thin, small, large, big, heavy, light
- Few, many, less, great, most, least, biggest
- Above, below, behind, before, after, top, middle, bottom, high, low, around
- Near, far, inside, outside, up, down, here, there
- Morning, afternoon, evening, day, night, soon, never
- Week, month, year, day, hour, second
- Today, tomorrow, yesterday, future, history, past, ahead
- Early, late, long ago, far away, now, old, new, young
- Fast, fastest, slow, slowest, slower, faster
- Hot, cold, cool, warm, shivery, chilly, melting
- Long, short, narrow, wide, tall
- Measure, length, width, depth, breadth, distance
- Feet, inches, miles, yards, millimeters, centimeters, kilometers, meters
- Here, there, everywhere.

Play and Your Community _____

Most neighborhoods are full of resources for you and your child to utilize. Take the time to investigate your neighborhood and the surrounding communities. Make a list of programs and activities, investigate classes for children, and find the resources that best fit your interests. You might find:

- Drop-in centers
- Playgrounds
- Parks
- Nature trails
- Wilderness areas
- Day camps
- Library programs
- Recreation centers
- Swimming pools
- Wading pools
- Play groups
- Nursery schools and kindergartens

YOUR PUBLIC LIBRARY

Your library can be one of your best resources. It introduces her to the wonder of limitless books, and may also offer activities for children. If yours doesn't, get involved and start some. Crafts, story time, music and dance classes, Saturday afternoon movie matinees, storytelling, puppet shows, and live entertainers are all available in library programs in our city. In addition, some libraries have a piano where individuals can practice, some have parent-child drop-in centers, some have toy lending, record lending, and movie or videotape lending, many have community meeting rooms. Most of the programs and facilities are free.

ACTIVITY BAGS

Make a series of bags to take along with you whenever you go out with your child. If you are taking public transportation, the bag could include a snack, a juice box, and something to do — an activity book, favorite books to read together, pencil crayons, or flash cards. If you are on your way to the wading pool, take along towels, fruit, cold drinks, a water squirter, a bubble ring and solution, and some paper and crayons for "quiet time." Depending on your child's interests, you may want to create a Tee Ball bag, a swimming bag (shampoo, bathing suit, water toys, towel, comb), a park and playground bag, or a travel-in-the-car bag (favorite tapes, easy snacks, miniature toys).

HER FRIENDS

Your child requires opportunities to play with friends. Provide occasions where she can meet and make friends who share her interests. She may develop friendships through your friends and neighbors, playgroups, daycare, music classes, Tee Ball, gym, children she meets at the park or playground, or at school. She may have one special friend who loves to dress up and another who loves to turn over rocks in the garden and investigate what's living there. Encourage her to play with other children, both individually and as part of a larger group.

OUR GANG

We are blessed with a large, friendly, mostly safe neighborhood. We have collectively made up a few "street" rules for the children who play on our street.

- You always let your parents know where you are. "We are playing at Chris's house."
- If you leave Chris's house, you phone home and say where you are. "We are going to Natalie's house now. We will be playing inside."
- You NEVER, EVER go inside a house without phoning home.
- You ALWAYS stay inside specified boundaries.
- There is always at least one adult monitoring the children when they are playing outside. (This is a great chance to have a cup of tea and a chat with neighbors.)

HOUSE RULES

While you cannot control all the play in your neighborhood, you can control your own environment. You are, of course, allowed to have different rules from those of your neighbors. Here are some guidelines to help you establish your house rules for small visitors.

Who is going to tidy up afterwards?
- Everybody playing? The child who had visitors? Mom? Dad?

What kind of behavior can you tolerate? What won't you allow?

- "We do not allow that kind of language here. If I hear it again, you must go home."
- "If you hurt someone else on purpose, you must leave."
- "There is no running in our house. If you want to run, you play outside."
- "You are not allowed to break something that belongs to anyone else."
- "You may play in the yard or the driveway. You may *not* play on the street or sidewalk."

Feel absolutely free to ban children if you must. And listen to your child: "I don't want to play with Kyle. He smashed my block village."

SNACKS

Always check dietary limitations with parents before you feed any visitors. A peanut butter sandwich could be fatal to an asthmatic child. Many children have religious restrictions, allergies, or strong dislikes.

Children need quick and easy energy and lots of drinks, but endless trips to the fridge for food and drink is a bore, and can be expensive when you have a gang over to play. Our working plan is that water is available for everyone at any time. If it's snack time, I may provide chunks of apple, grapes, carrot and celery sticks, or something similar.

I save the juice, crackers, cheese, and fruit leathers for back-yard tea parties for invited guests. Often, everyone provides for her own child, with lots of sharing. Clare may have a banana, Jordan an apple, Ian some rice chips, and Jenny some vegetable sticks. I cut up everything and arrange it on one plate, and everybody shares.

Snacks (and tidying up) are often contentious issues among friends and neighbors. When you disagree with what's being offered, bring your own child into the house for her required fuel, in privacy.

YOUR NEIGHBORHOOD

Through the friends Jenny made, I was quickly able to establish my own friendships and become a member of a flourishing, dynamic neighborhood. I feel we have an extended family in our few city blocks. We have been able to organize, and petition politicians and administrators to help in making our community a better place for children to play and grow. We have gotten newer and better playground equipment and park activities, expanded evening swimming programs at the local pool, lights installed around our wading pool, stop signs installed at the corners, and Neighborhood Watch established.

Our neighborhood provides reassurance and a "sanity" mechanism. Every normal preschooler can drive every normal parent nuts once in a while, and it helps to know that our five-year-old whines just like every other five-year-old, that other children tell tall tales and take things that don't belong to them. Our neighborhood provides safety and security for our children too. They recognize homes and parents where they can go for help if they need it. We have had two instances of finding wandering children before the police arrived. Some parents criss-crossed the blocks with their cars, the rest mobilized a phone search.

We pool our talents. For a minifair at the playground, Ellen does the athletic events, Susan the puppetry, Candy the art, Maggi the face makeup, Linda the costumes, I do the bubbles.

Every Christmas Eve Susan has a neighborhood "Wiglia," the Polish wait for the birth of the child. The families all arrive early, five or six in the evening, and everyone brings a contribution to the potluck supper. We sing carols. St. Nicholas or Black Peter rings the doorbell and scampers away, leaving a sack on the porch with a gift for every child. By about eight or nine the party breaks up, and families go home to their private Christmas preparations.

Get involved with people in your community. When a thriving neighborhood exists, it creates something strong and beautiful.

By joining your child in her world of play, you rediscover your own ability to make new friends, and you become connected in your community. You experience a drive to explore, investigate, create, and discover. Both you and your child develop the precious gifts of intelligence and creative life. Your fun together creates a love that lasts forever.

CHAPTER ONE

THREE TO THREE-AND-A-HALF

Daddy!!! There's a Tyrannosaurus Under My Bed

 OUR THREE-YEAR-OLD is a delightful being. Loving, lovable, and fun to be with, he is learning what pleases and displeases you. Most of the time he does try to please. While he may get frustrated, his outbursts are over quickly. He talks at great length about everything under the sun.

His attention span increases as his interests develop. One day he may surprise you by spending an hour watching one insect. Another day he might spend as much time cutting and pasting. He prefers to choose his play himself and will not be coerced. He gets bored when he is doing what others want him to do, and charges from activity to activity, leaving chaos along the way. Try to allow him time with his own projects, without rushing him.

Your child has real fantasies and fears. He has trouble differentiating between what is make-believe and what is real in his day-to-day life. He might be convinced that a tyrannosaurus lives under his bed, and you will have to convince him that it is really a protective, friendly pachy-cephalosaurus instead.

Your child's best playmates are children his own age or slightly older. Younger children usually bore him, as he's already done what they are doing; he wants new challenges. He loves to pretend and to be silly.

Movement

Your child needs lots of active playtime. He is able to hop, walk on tiptoe, run, stop, start, turn corners, and go up and down stairs competently. He can jump about twelve inches off the ground. He can probably ride tricycles and climb on jungle gyms. He loves to balance as he walks along low walls. He loves games where make-believe is part of the action. Play many games to help his ever-improving coordination.

FOLLOW THE LEADER

The purpose of Follow the Leader is to imitate the leader. For the first few times, you be the leader, then let your child set the pace. Walk along, changing directions, moving two or three times to the left and then to the right. When your child is comfortable with the game add different motions: jumping, hopping, skipping, giant steps, baby steps, popcorn steps, kangaroo steps, and anything else you can think of.

SIMON SAYS

This game can include any number of players. You be Simon, or IT, for the first few times. Simon barks out orders to the other players. They follow only the commands preceded by "Simon says." For instance, when IT says, "Simon says rub your tummy," everybody rubs their tummies; "Simon says pat your head," everybody pats their heads. "Rub your tummy and pat your head" becomes an "out" for anyone doing the action, because Simon didn't say to do it. The last person "out" is the next Simon.

Dancing on the Mountain

Tune: "In and Out the Window"

(Perform the actions suggested by the words of the song.)

Chorus and First Verse:

Dancing on the mountain, dancing on the mountain
Dancing on the mountain, now everybody sing.

Verses:

Bend down and hold your motion, bend down and
* hold your motion*
Bend down and hold your motion, now everybody sing.

One foot up and hold your motion, one foot up and
* hold your motion,*
One foot up and hold your motion, now everybody
* sing.*

The other foot up and hold your motion, the other
* foot up and hold your motion,*
The other foot up and hold your motion, now
* everybody sing.*

Jump up and show your motion, jump up and show
* your motion,*
Jump up and show your motion, now everybody sing.

Turn around and show your motion, turn around
* and show your motion,*
Turn around and show your motion, now every-
* body sing.*

Other verses can include:

Stretch up and hold your motion . . .
Running on the mountain . . .
Skipping round the mountain . . .
Sit down and show your motion . . .
Kneel on one knee and show your motion . . .
Crawling down the mountain . . .
Clap hands and show your motion . . .
Pat your head and show your motion . . .
Lie down and show your motion . . .

Last Verse:

Rolling down the mountain, rolling down the mountain,
Rolling down the mountain, now everybody rest!

(Traditional, North America)

OPEN THE GATES

Open the Gates is a great game to play when you have several visitors. Two adults or older children agree secretly to be either "gold" or "silver." Then they join upraised hands to from a "gate." The rest of the players circle through the gate, in line, trying to get safely through before the gates fall down on "CHOP" (See the chant below). The captured player whispers his choice of "silver" or "gold," and gets behind the gate which represents his choice. After all the players are caught, the two sides have a tug of war.

The chant:

Open the gates as high as the sky
To let King George and his horses pass by.
Here comes a lantern to light you to bed,
Here comes a hatchet to CHOP off your head!

(Traditional, Great Britain)

Using Fingers _____

Your child is starting to gain manipulative control over his fingers. Fingerplays are fun for him.

Once I saw a Little Bird

Once I saw a little bird
(Extend one hand to make a bird
Go hop, hop, hop.
Hop the fingers of the other hand
So I said, "Little Bird,
to the bird,
Will you stop, stop, stop?"
Make "Stop" hand signal.)

I was going to the window
(Peer through pretend eyeglasses
To say, "How do you do,"
Pretend to shake hands,
But he shook his little tail
Wiggle thumb on "bird" hand
And away he flew.
Interlock thumbs and "fly" hands away.)

(Traditional, North America)

Clap Your Hands

(Suit the actions to the words, extending 1, 2, and 3 fingers.)

Clap your hands, clap your hands, 1, 2, 3,
Clap your hands, clap your hands, just like me.
Roll your hands, roll your hands, 1, 2, 3,
Roll your hands, roll your hands, just like me.
Shake your hands, shake your hands, 1, 2, 3,
Shake your hands, shake your hands, just like me.
Rub your hands, rub your hands, 1, 2, 3,
Rub your hands, rub your hands, just like me.
Wiggle your hands, wiggle your hands, 1, 2, 3,
Wiggle your hands, wiggle your hands, just like me.
(Traditional, North America)

Two Little Birds

Two little blackbirds sitting on a hill
(Both hands on top of head
One named Jack, the other named Jill
Lift one hand, then the other
Fly away Jack, fly away Jill
Fly one hand away, then the other
Come back Jack, come back Jill
Fly one back, then the other.)

Two little blackbirds sitting on a wall
(Both hands on shoulders
One named Peter, the other named Paul
Lift one hand, then the other
Fly away Peter, fly away Paul
Fly one hand away, then the other
Come back Peter, come back Paul.
Fly one hand back, then the other)
(Traditional, Great Britain, North America)

CROW

Crow is a great game when you and your child are waiting in a doctor's office or store. Try to catch your opponent's index finger as you form a fist. Your opponent tries to pull his finger away before it gets caught.

HOT POTATO

A small group of people sit in a circle. One player is IT, and he crouches in the middle with his eyes closed. A small ball, the "Hot Potato," is passed quickly from hand to hand around the circle in back of the players. IT shouts "Stop" and whoever is caught with the hot potato is the next IT. The faster the game is played, the more fun it is.

WHIZZERS

Whizzers, Bull Roarers, Whirligigs, or Buzz, are found the whole world over. All you need to make one is a two-holed button and a piece of thin, strong string, about four to five feet long. Lace the string through both holes of the button and tie it so it becomes one continuous cord. Move the button to the middle of the string and place the ends of the string over your child's hands. He makes the button spin by alternately pulling and relaxing the tension of the string. As the button spins, a whizzing or buzzing sound is created.

You may want to experiment with different types of string or cord to see which produces the best result. Some buttons can hurt if they hit your child's knuckles, so be careful of whizzing buttons until he masters the technique. Be sure to keep long hair tied back so it won't get caught in the winding string.

Although round buttons are traditional, you and your child can make oblong, square, cylindrical and propeller shapes out of pieces of wood. Sand them, drill two holes, lace the string, and listen to the sounds your different-shaped whizzers produce.

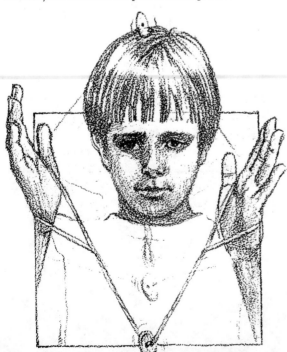

Indoor Games

Your child needs unstructured time with his toys. This is an age, perhaps more than any other, when he needs "props" to help him understand his experiences and the world around him through play.

He is playing with roles and occupations, so he needs to be able to dress the part. Make sure that his dress-up area has a full-sized mirror, so he can admire his reflection. He needs blocks to build cities, roads and towers. He plays at family living with child-sized kitchen appliances (overturned boxes are fine), dolls, carriages, and cleaning tools. He plays with trucks, building his own roads, bridges and tunnels. He loves airplanes, trains, garages, and anything to do with travel. He loves to build elaborate structures with interlocking bricks and construction sets.

PROPS FOR DRAMA

Your child needs stage props to make sense of his life. Chairs become trains, cars, or boats; a small table with a big blanket over it or a pile of cushions becomes a house, a tent, or a cave; an empty carton becomes a house, a fire station, a school, a fort, or a puppet theater. With play money, old receipts, bags, empty food containers, pretend food, a basket or cart, and perhaps a toy cash register, your child has a store. Kitchens can be made from boxes turned over to become appliances, pots and pans, beaters, spoons, shakers, cutlery, a toy phone, squirt and spray bottles, a small broom, and a sponge. To become a postal worker he will need stamps, old envelopes, a stamp pad, a bag for his mail, crayons, pencils, and paper.

DRESSING UP

Provide a dress-up box filled with some scarves, jewelry, old shoes and clothes to support his fantasy play. Items that support his role playing might include a foil-covered cardboard badge for a police officer or postal worker; some nylon netting or old curtain for a ballerina, a princess, or a bride; high boots and a raincoat for a fire fighter; a wild shirt for a punk rocker; hats for almost everyone. Go through your old clothes and pass on any that might support his play. Visit your local thrift shop or a garage sale for some glitzy evening wear, wild ties, hats, old purses and costume jewelry.

SUPPORTING DRAMA

Write stories together about your child's favorite occupations, and turn the stories into puppet shows or plays. Costumes and makeup are always fun.

LET'S PRETEND

Join in some of your child's pretending games. Pretend to be dinosaurs, police officers, doctors, dentists, pilots, truck drivers, teachers, waiters. Let his imagination take you both to a farm, to the beach, to a party, to Grandma's.

NOISE BOX

Create a noise box containing objects that make interesting sounds. Some ideas: a bell, a shaker, rhythm sticks, paper to scrunch, paper to tear, a whistle, sand blocks, wood blocks, a kazoo, a comb and paper. Make a sound with one of the objects and ask your blindfolded child: "What made the sound?"

IDENTIFYING SOUNDS

Tape-record the everyday sounds of food cooking, a favorite song, running bath water, a toilet flushing, an eggbeater or blender, a lawnmower, sirens, bird calls, animal sounds, footsteps. Play bits of the tape and ask your child, "What made that noise?" Then ask if he knows what was happening when the sounds were made. Replay short segments of the tape and ask which sound came first, second, and third. Keep adding to your tape as his familiarity with different sounds grows.

REPEAT THE SOUND

Collect a number of objects that make sounds; for example, a bell, a whistle, a comb, a timer, a toy. Start with three different sounds from three different objects and ask your child what sound each object makes. Ask him which sound he heard first, second and third, and ask him to make the noises in the same sequence. Then ask him to listen blindfolded. You can add new sounds that aren't connected to objects; hand clapping, foot stomping, tongue clicking, teeth chattering.

CHORES

Have your child help you with the chores. Talk about everything you do and how you do it. The knowledge he picks up now will pay dividends when he's older and knows where his dirty socks go, and how to set the table. Let him help whenever and wherever he can and praise his accomplishments. His favorite place is the kitchen where he can mix, measure, pour, scrub vegetables, wash the unbreakable dishes, and wipe the counter. Start a recipe file using symbols as well as words for his special recipes.

JUICICLES

One of Jenny's favorite pieces of kitchen equipment is an inexpensive plastic popsicle maker. I simply showed her how to carefully pour the fruit juice and stick in the plastic holders. We pop it in the freezer, and the popsicles are ready in a couple of hours.

SUPER JUICICLES

Blend together your favorite combination of juice and fruit, and add some fruit-flavored yoghurt if you wish. Plain yoghurt or buttermilk mixed with fruit and a bit of sugar or honey is as delicious as ice cream. Our favorites are fresh mango with buttermilk and honey, and banana bits with apple juice.

Outdoor Play _____

Your child needs outdoor play daily, weather permitting. How he spends this time depends on the people around him. He needs stimulation and challenge in what he does outside, and he needs friends to play with.

THE OUTDOOR BIN

We keep a large bin with outdoor toys close to the front door. That way, toys can be easily grabbed on the way out the door and dumped back on the way in, just as quickly. The contents of the bin are strictly for outside use. Depending on the season and your child's age and interests, your outdoor bin might contain:

- a jacks and ball set for the front steps
- two skipping ropes (regular length and Double Dutch)
- two identical hard bouncing balls
- a beach ball (deflated)
- a large playground ball
- a bag of marbles
- a round, flat hopscotch marker (hoptaw)
- bubble solution, well sealed, and wands
- a tennis ball
- a rotary lawn sprinkler, lawn shower, or flip-flop sprayer
- a tee ball, bat, tee, and baseball glove
- a joystick
- a roll-up magic carpet (plastic sled)
- a plastic bucket, shovels, sand toys, squirt bottles
- you may want to throw in a towel and bathing suit, or mittens and a hat

OUTDOOR TABLE

Your child needs a table outside for tea parties, artwork, and selling lemonade to the neighbors. You could use a child-sized picnic table or a portable inside table that can be carried outdoors. It's amazing to see what happens to an inside activity moved outdoors for a change.

JOYSTICK

A joystick is a very large bubble-making stick. It creates tremendous bubbles with a cord slider that is slowly moved back and forth. Joysticks are readily available in toy stores, or you can create your own. Secure a loop of about six feet of cord to one end of a three-foot stick. Tie about two feet of cord to a slider on the stick. Tie a weight to the middle of the other four feet of cord. Now dip the closed joystick into a pail of bubble solution, lift it carefully out, and slide the slider open and shut slowly. The results are best when there is little wind and the bubbles are blown in the shade. Dampened grass helps save the bubbles a little longer.

Joystick Bubble Solution

Mix together in a plastic pail:

    1 cup of strong, clear liquid dishwashing
       detergent (such as Joy, Sunlight, etc)

    1/2 cup thick vegetable oil (such as olive oil)

    2 tbsp rubbing alcohol.

Stir thoroughly, and add 10 cups of room temperature water. Save any leftover bubble solution for blowing regular bubbles.

PLAYGROUNDS

Your local playground can be your biggest asset in providing outdoor play and interesting companionship for your child. The ideal playground will provide ropes to swing out on and drop off, places to climb, slide, balance, go hand-over-hand, and tire walls to climb. It will probably terrify you out of your wits! Generally, you need to trust your child's ability to manipulate his body effectively and to get himself out of difficult situations. You might think he's in physical danger, but most of the time he really isn't. In a well-designed playground he can't fall far enough to hurt himself, even though the slides may seem as

high as Mount Everest to you. Unless he asks for help, or children start getting out of control, try to avoid interrupting his play.

TRICYCLES

The best place for your child to ride a tricycle is in a fenced paved play area or blocked driveway. Otherwise, allow him to ride his tricycle on the sidewalk, well away from traffic. Make it clear that he is NEVER to ride in the street and make sure that tricycle riding is always supervised. Tricycles are so low that drivers cannot see them or their riders. A large open basement or hall is a perfect place to ride tricycles indoors.

SKIPPING

While your child probably doesn't have the ability yet to do a true skip, he is probably galloping around quite well. Show him how to skip and encourage him to practice as you go out on your walks together. If he sees older children in your neighborhood skipping rope, he may want to try to copy them.

HIGH WATER

High Water is a jumprope game that even quite small children can enjoy. Two people, "enders," hold the ends of the rope still and flat on the ground. The jumper jumps over the rope. If there are several children, they take turns jumping. Then the rope is raised slightly and the children jump over again. Keep raising the rope until someone misses. Then, the rope goes back to the ground, and the person who missed becomes an ender. Three-year-old children can usually jump over a rope until it is about twelve inches from the ground. Scissors jumps, one leg going up before the other one, sideways, are allowed when the rope gets high. If only you and your child are playing, fasten one end of the rope to a door knob or fence to take the place of one ender. Once he gets used to jumping over a stationary rope, start wiggling the rope at one end to play "Snakes."

Music

Your child loves walking, jumping, marching, galloping, and slithering to music. Watch him move to his own spontaneous music and singing games, and encourage him by clapping or swaying. Put on favorite records or tapes and dance with him. Show him how to run, tiptoe, walk, and gallop to a simple drum beat.

INSTRUMENTS

Select simple percussion instruments that your child can manipulate himself. An inverted plastic ice cream container makes a great drum; bells or keys jingle when laced together; small plastic containers filled with dry popcorn or beans make shakers; two sticks or wooden spoons can be tapped together. Noisy random banging is not music. He will need favorite rhymes or songs to play along with. Katharine Smithrim and Bob McGrath's *Songs and Games for Toddlers*, available on Kids' Records or Golden Book Video, is a great introduction to music and instruments for your child.

SONGS

Your child's favorite songs will have repetitive choruses and many verses. Lots of actions make the songs you sing together great fun.

My Bonnie *

(Every time a word starts with the letter "B" you do something. For instance, if you are standing, you sit down; if you are sitting, you stand up. You can also devise hand motions, pointing to yourself for "my," waving your hands horizontally for "ocean," touching your eyes for "sea," touching your back for "bring back.")

Chorus:
Bring back, bring back, bring back my Bonnie to me, to me,
Bring back, bring back, oh bring back my Bonnie to me.

Verses:
My Bonnie lies over the ocean, my Bonnie lies over the sea,
My Bonnie lies over the ocean, oh, bring back my Bonnie to me.

Oh blow ye winds over the ocean, and blow ye winds over the sea,
Oh, blow ye winds over the ocean, and bring back my Bonnie to me.

The winds have blown over the ocean, the winds have blown over the sea,
The winds have blown over the ocean, and brought back my Bonnie to me.

(Traditional, Highland Scotland)

* Bonnie was the nickname of Charles Stuart, Bonnie Prince Charlie. Kim and Jerry Brodey do a great version of "My Bonnie" on their *Simple Magic* album, Kids' Records.

The Chickadee Song

(Fly your fingers away one by one as you sing this song)

Chorus:

Chickadee, chickadee, happy and gay
Chickadee, chickadee, fly away.

Verses:

Five little chickadees, no room for more,
One flew away, and then there were four.

Four little chickadees, sitting in a tree,
One flew away, and then there were three.

Three little chickadees, don't know what to do,
One flew away, and then there were two.

Two little chickadees, sitting in the sun,
One flew away, then there was one.

One little chickadee, can't have any fun,
He flew away, and then there were none.

(Traditional, North America)

Sharon, Lois & Bram do a lovely version of "Five Little Chickadees" on their *Mainly Mother Goose* album, Elephant Records.

Over in the Meadow

(Create your own actions for this one)

Over in the meadow in the sand in the sun
Lived an old mother turtle and her little turtle one.
"Dig" said the mother, "I dig" said the one.
And they dug and were happy in the sand in the sun.

Over in the meadow where the stream runs so blue,
Lived an old mother fish and her little fishies two.
"Swim" said the mother, "we swim" said the two,
So they swam and they leapt where the stream runs so blue.

. . . in a hole in a tree . . . old mother bluebird and her little birdies three . . . "sing"
. . . in the reeds on the shore, old mother muskrat and her little muskies four . . . "dive"
. . . in a snug beehive . . . old mother bee and her little buzzers five . . . "buzz"
. . . in a nest built of sticks . . . old mother crow and her little crows six . . . "caw"
. . . where the grass grows so even . . . old mother frog and her little tadpoles seven . . . "ribbit"
. . . by the old mossy gate . . . old mother lizard and her little lizies eight . . . "bask"
. . . by the old scotch pine . . . old mother duck and her little duckies nine . . . "quack"
. . . wee cosy den . . . old mother beaver and her little beaves ten . . . "dive."

(Traditional, Appalachian)

Raffi sings "Over in the Meadow" on his *Baby Beluga* album, Troubadour records.

Art

Your budding Picasso loves to create, construct, and build using a myriad of art supplies. He delights in discovering how to put together new materials in different ways. For instance, with some empty toilet tissue or paper towel tubes, tape and paper, he might create space rockets, binoculars, totem poles, musical shakers, or puppets. Provide inspiration and material, but let your child express his creativity freely.

ART STUFF

Begin to build an ever expanding collection of art materials for your child to use as he grows. In addition to crayons, markers, paints and paper, your collection will provide hours of happy construction and inspiration for him. Some ideas:

acorns	cotton cloth	gold and silver	paper tubes	stickers
aluminum foil	cotton swabs	thread	paste	straws
aluminum trays	crepe paper	golf tees	pastels, oil and chalk	streamers, crepe paper
apple seeds	dominoes	google eyes	pebbles	string
ballpoint pens	dowels	graph paper	pine cones	styrofoam
beads	dried beans	gravel	pipe cleaners	tape
bird seed	driftwood	greeting cards	pinking shears	thread
bobby pins	dried pasta	gummed papers	plasticine	tin cans, smooth
bottle caps	dried weeds	gummed stars	plastic boxes	inside
boxes, all sizes	dry cereals	hologram stickers	plastic jars	tissue paper
broken toy parts	egg cartons	jar lids	plastic eye droppers	tongue depressors
(no sharp edges)	egg shells	keys	plastic spray bottles	toothpicks
buckles	emery boards	kitchen utensils	plastic squeeze bottles	tree bark
burlap	empty pill bottles	kleenex	plastic tubs	velvet, velveteen
buttons	fabric crayons	lace	popcorn	scraps
candy wrappers	fabric markers	leather scraps	rickrack	vermiculite
carbon paper	fabric puff paint	magazines	ribbon	wallpaper scraps and
cardboard	fabric glitter paint	magic mylar dots	roll-on deodorant	samples
candles	fancy papers	magnets	bottles (clean)	watercolors
cellophane	faucet washers	meat trays, styrofoam	ruler	waxed paper
chalk, sidewalk and	feathers	metallic papers	sand	washable white glue
blackboard	felt	milk cartons	sandpaper	wine corks
charcoal	film cartridges	milkweed pods and	saw, small	wooden boxes
checkers	fishing line	fluff	sawdust	wooden ice cream
chestnuts	fishing lures, hooks	mylar papers	scissors	spoons
clean bones	removed	netting	screws	wooden matchsticks,
clothespins, wooden	floor tiles	nuts	seeds	non igniting
cloves	food colors	orange pits	sequins	wooden popsicle
coins	fringes	paint-sample chips	shells	sticks
combs	fur	paper	shoelaces	wood scraps
confetti	gift cards	paper bags	silver dragées	wood shavings
containers	gift wrap	paper clips	snaps	yarn
conté	gimp (plastic lacing)	paper cups	soap	other "junk"
cookie cutters	glitter	paper fasteners	sponges	
costume jewelry	glitzy stickers	paper muffin cups	spools, wooden	
cotton balls	glitzy stones	paper plates	stamp pad and stamps	
cotton batting	glowing stickers	paper punch	stapler	

And, for use by grownups only: art fixative, adhesive, rubber cement, shellac, acrylic paints, oil-based paints, varnish, urethane, and any materials containing solvents.

STAMPING

Mix some tempera paint in a shallow pan (a styrofoam meat tray is perfect), and cover your table with old newspapers. Place some absorbent paper, such as rice paper, construction paper, newsprint, or paper towel, on top of the newspaper. Gather together a variety of objects with interesting shapes or textures: nuts, bolts, half a vegetable, a potato masher, cookie cutters, tools, toys, a comb. Dip the objects into the paint and stamp them onto the absorbent paper. Show your child how to make single stamps, how to make tracks, how to "walk" the object across the paper, how to rotate the paper while he is stamping in one place, and then let him experiment.

ROLLER PAINTING

Carefully pry the balls out of roll-on deodorant containers, and wash both the balls and containers thoroughly. Fill these containers with thick tempera paint and replace the balls. Encourage your budding Rembrandt to use his rollers on both wet and dry paper to create different effects.

EYEDROPPER PAINTING

The plastic eyedroppers that come packaged with children's medicines can be used to syringe up small amounts of paint. Ask your child to squirt the paint onto wet or dry paper and show him what happens when you mix two or more colors in the eyedropper. Ask him to puff on any large drops of paint that don't soak in immediately. *Hint:* Powdered tempera paints mix best with warm water.

CUT AND PASTE

Give your child blunt-ended plastic-coated metal scissors and an old glossy magazine. Provide a large piece of paper or cardboard and a glue stick or paste so he can stick his own cutouts into a grand design.

ANOTHER ME

Find a HUGE piece of paper or Bristol board, and ask your child to lie down on it. Trace his outline with a felt marker. Have him color his picture of himself, adding his features, his clothes, his favorite toys, possibly even his pet. Display his picture on the door of his room.

LACING CARDS

Cut pieces of cardboard or clean styrofoam meat containers into simple shapes. Punch holes about an inch apart around the edge of the shapes. Have your child lace in and out of the holes in the card using gimp (plastic lacing), old shoelaces, or stiffened yarn or string (dip in melted wax or laundry starch and let dry). You may want to have him glue a picture onto his card before punching out the holes. Use contrasting lacing to create a special effect.

MAKE YOUR OWN WATERCOLOR BLOCKS

It's simple to make your own watercolor paint blocks. Simply squirt or mix a different tempera color into the bottom of each section of a styrofoam egg carton and allow the paint to harden over several days.

Word Play ————————

Words are tools for your child. His speech is becoming clearer now, and his vocabulary is growing daily; his thoughts astound you with their complexity and richness. When you talk with him, never use baby talk or imitate his mistakes in pronunciation. Talk about interesting new ideas, introduce new words, and above all, listen to his thoughts and ideas.

Your child may know colors, shapes, counting and the alphabet. His memory is improving, and he is inquisitive about the world around him. He needs to work out solutions to problems for himself. Never underestimate what he says or feels; deal with his complex feelings and unceasing questions openly, honestly, and patiently.

WRITING STORYBOOKS

Create your own storybooks together. Your child draws a picture and tells you the story. You write down what he says. You might want to start a story yourself: "If a fairy princess gave you three wishes, what would they be?" Show your child a picture of a group of children and ask, "What are they doing?" Ask your child to select a picture and tell you a story about it. Remember that a story has a beginning, a middle, and an end. Ask the questions Who? What? Where? When? Why? and How? and write down the answers. Lace the pages together or use brass paper fasteners to hold the pages. Add a cardboard cover decorated by your child. Your stories will create magical memories for you to share many times over.

I One the Sandbox
This much-loved joke is so old it has grey chin whiskers. You and your child alternate lines.

> *I one the sandbox.*
> I two the sandbox.
> *I three the sandbox.*
> I four the sandbox.
> *I five the sandbox.*
> I six the sandbox.
> *I seven the sandbox.*
> I eight the sandbox.
> *You ate the sandbox!!! Did it taste good?*

RECITATIONS

As you sing songs, recite poetry, and chant nursery rhymes, take turns reciting the lines. You say the first line, ask your child to say the second line, you say the third, and so on. It won't be long before all your favorites are memorized for instant use.

NONSENSE VERSE

Your child loves the magic that comes from traditional nonsense poetry and funny rhymes. There is wonderful poetry in Lewis Carroll's *Alice in Wonderland, Through the Looking Glass*, and *Taming of the Snark*; in Edward Lear's *Grumbolian Tales*, in Eugene Field's work, and of course, Mother Goose. Don't forget *Alligator Pie* and *Jelly Belly* by Dennis Lee (Macmillan) and all of the wonderful Dr. Seuss Books (Random House).

The Deaf Woman's Courtship
(Decrease the volume of the sound as you say this)

Old woman, old woman, are you fond of cooking?
Speak a little louder, sir, I'm very hard of hearing.

Old woman, old woman, are you fond of sewing?
Speak a little louder, sir, I'm very hard of hearing.

Old woman, old woman, will you darn my stocking?
Speak a little louder, sir, I'm very hard of hearing.

Old woman, old woman, will you let me court you?
Speak a little louder sir, I just begin to hear you.

Old woman, old woman, don't you want to marry
  me?
Oh, my goodness gracious me, I think that now I
  hear you.
(Traditional, Great Britain, North America)

Quiet Times _____

Your child often needs a transition time from strenuous play to naptime or bedtime. This is a great opportunity to recite some of his favorite nursery rhymes. He loves to listen to nonsense poetry and sing nonsense songs, and is starting to memorize his favorites. He loves looking at and listening to storybooks. Read together daily.

Fuzzy Wuzzy

Fuzzy Wuzzy was a bear.
Fuzzy Wuzzy had no hair.
Fuzzy Wuzzy wasn't fuzzy,
Was he?
(Traditional, North America)

Hey Diddle Dumpling

Hey Diddle dumpling, my son John.
He went to his bed with his stockings on;
One shoe off, and the other shoe on,
Hey diddle dumpling, my son John.
(Traditional, Great Britain, North America)

As I Was Going Out One Day

As I was going out one day,
My head fell off and rolled away.
But when I saw that it was gone,
I picked it up and put it on.
And when I got into the street
A fellow cried: "Look at your feet!"
I looked at them and sadly said:
"I've left them both asleep in bed!"
(Anonymous)

The House that Jack Built

You will be amazed at how quickly your child will join in with the endings of this marvellous repetitive tale. The story should be chanted, and can be repeated faster and faster once you know it.

This is the house that Jack built.

This is the malt that lay in the house that Jack built.

This is the rat that ate the malt that lay in the house that Jack built.

This is the cat that killed the rat that ate the malt that lay in the house that Jack built.

This is the dog that worried the cat that killed the rat that ate the malt that lay in the house that Jack built.

This is the cow with the crumpled horn that tossed the dog that worried the cat that killed the rat that ate the malt that lay in the house that Jack built.

This is the milkmaid all forlorn that milked the cow with the crumpled horn that tossed the dog that worried the cat that killed the rat that ate the malt that lay in the house that Jack built.

This is the beggar all tattered and torn that kissed the milkmaid all forlorn that milked the cow with the crumpled horn that tossed the dog that worried the cat that killed the rat that ate the malt that lay in the house that Jack built.

This is the parson all shriven and shorn that married the beggar all tattered and torn that kissed the milkmaid all forlorn that milked the cow with the crumpled horn that tossed the dog that worried the cat that killed the rat that ate the malt that lay in the house that Jack built.

This is the rooster that crowed in the morn that awakened the parson all shriven and shorn that married the beggar all tattered and torn that kissed the milkmaid all forlorn that milked the cow with the crumpled horn that tossed the dog that worried the cat that killed the rat that ate the malt that lay in the house that Jack built.

This is the farmer sowing his corn that fed the rooster that crowed in the morn that awakened the parson all shriven and shorn that married the beggar all tattered and torn that kissed the milkmaid all forlorn that milked the cow with the crumpled horn that tossed the dog that worried the cat that killed the rat that ate the malt that lay in the house that Jack built.

(Traditional, Great Britain, North America)

SHAPES

Cut out an assortment of cardboard shapes; squares, rectangles, diamonds, stars, circles, triangles, and ovals. Have your child draw around the shapes, using colored sidewalk chalk on a blackboard or sidewalk, or felt markers on paper. Talk about the shapes he makes, and where you find them around you. For instance, a triangle looks like a fir tree; a circle can represent a full moon or the sun; a square is like the flat side of a box, a rectangle looks like a window; a diamond is like a baseball field. Point out familiar shapes everywhere.

DOT-TO-DOT

With dot-to-dot exercises, your child learns how to change direction, and form patterns using a crayon, marker, or pencil. Use some self-sticking dots, stars, or stickers in a sequence that will make a shape on a large sheet of paper. You place two dots and ask your child to draw a line between them. Add a third dot, he draws that line, and so on. Place the dots so the direction changes, but avoid crossing lines to avoid confusion, at first. Gradually increase the length of the lines and the difficulty of the pattern. As he grows more familiar with the technique, use numbers or letters to indicate the sequence of dots that make up the pattern.

THE ANIMAL WORLD

Your child is fascinated by animals, both as make-believe friends and as creatures in nature. Make up short stories about his favorite animals or his pets. Read stories like *Petunia*, by Roger Duvosin (Alfred A. Knopf), that have animals as their characters. Sing songs like "Old McDonald" and "Over in the Meadow" (p 21). A book like *Gobble, Growl, Grunt* by Peter Spier (Doubleday) will get you started on making animal noises together. Take day trips to the zoo, conservation areas, or a farm, and watch nature programs on television together, like "Nature," "Wild America" or "National Geographic."

Growing Interests _____

Your child loves to sort, classify, collect, and organize sets of objects. Toy manufacturers and sticker-book sellers have capitalized on this need, but commercial collections can get expensive and take up valuable toy storage space with some very poor toys. Your child can satisfy his urge to gather like objects by collecting something simple like rubber bands, mermaids' tears, stones, pine cones, shells, buttons, old keys, foreign coins; the list goes on.

RUBBER BAND BALL

Everybody loves bouncing rubber balls. Why not make one of your own from rubber bands? Help your child collect the rubber bands he finds in his travels, and put them together. Scrunch up the first two or three elastics and tie them to form a lump core. Then, stretching the elastics until they hold, wrap them around the core as many times as necessary. The ball can be bounced, although you may have to collect and reapply some elastics. I've seen a rubber band ball eight inches in diameter at the tourist office in Sainte-Foy, Quebec. Perhaps you and your child can establish a new world's record! Don't forget that you can save string and aluminum foil to make balls, too.

MERMAIDS' TEARS

As you walk along beaches, especially ones with water-washed pebbles, you may notice smooth pieces of glass washed up along with the rocks. Jenny and Megan must have collected at least ten pounds of them on our morning walks along the boardwalk before nursery school. These pieces of glass are called mermaids' tears. They come in a wide range of colors, the rarest being true blues and reds. When mermaids' tears are put in a clear bottle, covered with water, and placed near a window they will glisten like gems in the sunlight. Bulbs love them as a place to grow during the winter, as the roots can burrow through the spaces. Baker's clay ornaments (p 40) have a gem-like quality when mermaids' tears are pressed in. Talk about the mermaids and why they were crying.

BANANA STICKERS

Jordan's refrigerator is covered with banana stickers. Have your child save the stickers from his bananas (or melons, or apples, or any other fruit), and mount them, on the refrigerator like Jordan, on a large piece of cardboard hanging in his room, or in a scrapbook. Look for the country of origin on a map or globe and talk about where bananas (or melons, or apples) grow.

STICKER BOOKS

Sticker books can be lots of fun, but try to avoid the ones near the checkout at your convenience store, or you will be hooked into buying innumerable packets of identical stickers. Either buy a self-contained sticker book, or make your own. Bind together some light cardboard with brass fasteners or use a photo album or scrapbook. Every time we're in a specialty store with interesting stickers, I'll buy a few or Jenny can spend her allowance. All of the "stamp" stickers that arrive in our junk mail are handed over to Jenny, as well as fruit stickers and party favors. Especially prized are the metallic fig stickers that arrive from the Middle East in the depths of winter, and the la-di-da seals and warrants on some tea containers. The bonus in collecting stickers is trading duplicates with friends.

FORTUNE COOKIES

Do you eat at Chinese restaurants? Save the fortunes from the cookies and make a collection. Have your child glue his fortunes onto the pages of a blank book and read them together once in a while.

MARBLES

Marbles make great collections. According to Jenny's grandpa, these are the traditional terms for classical marbles.

Biggies, Shooters, Boulders: Large glass marbles, plain or fancy.

Aggies, Agates: Opaque glass, varied colors. Once dibs, but now rarer. Also called alleys.

Crystals: Clear glass marbles, solid colors.

Cat's Eyes: Uncolored clear glass marbles with colored "cat's eyes" in contrasting colors in the center of the glass.

Dibs: Ordinary, everyday playing marbles. In Grandpa's day they were small, inexpensive clay marbles. A generation ago they were alleys or aggies; now, in most localities, "dibs" refers to cat's eyes.

Steelies: Once, ball bearings were used as marbles. Now they are an opaque glass with a metallic cast.

Ransom: If you lose a favorite marble while playing, you can ransom it back by paying for it with five dibs.

Hint: You may want to try a trick that I learned from my friend Jan. Every member of the family has a marble collection. If certain family standards aren't met, the person forfeits a specified number of marbles. For instance, a light left burning may warrant a two-marble fine, socks thrown under the bed instead of put in the hamper are worth five marbles, and so on. The culprit has to pay every member of the family the specified number of marbles.

COLLECTING AND SORTING

In a cookie tin or old shoe box, keep a collection of "sorting treasures" for your child. Keep all the pine cones, acorns, chestnuts, maple keys, rocks, bottle caps, can tabs, bread-wrapper tabs, fruit pits, rubber bands and paper clips that accumulate around the house and garden. Give him an old muffin tin or egg carton and ask him to sort out his materials according to shape, color, size, or material. Ask him how they are alike and how they are different. For instance, "Can you bring me everything in your box that is metal?" "Red?" "Circular?"

Remember, too, that your child can be a great help with the sorting you do around the house. He doesn't know it's not a game, so don't tell him! Ask him to help you separate the colors when you are sorting the laundry. Ask him to help you find his clothes or match socks when you are putting them away. Ask him to help you unpack the groceries and put together things that go in the cupboard, in the freezer, in the refrigerator, in the basement. He can sort screws and nails when you are tidying the workbench and blocks when you are putting toys away. "Bring me the squares, bring me the rectangles, bring me the red blocks, the blue triangular blocks, the large blocks."

THREE-AND-A-HALF TO FOUR 29

CHAPTER TWO

THREE-AND-A-HALF TO FOUR

"Daddy, Can I Help You, Mommy, Can I Help You, Daddy. . .?"

AGER AND ENTHUSIASTIC, your three-and-a-half-year-old wants to "help" with everything you do. She loves practicing familiar routines over and over, to get them all just right. She loves to play with her friends, with words, with her imagination, at the playground, and most especially with you. She tries hard to please you, and she does try to cooperate with others.

Give your child small versions of your own tools; a screwdriver, a small hammer, cookie cutters, a pot or pan for her own cooking, a small rake or broom for collecting leaves, an unbreakable teapot or pitcher to pour her juice into her own cup.

At times, she may be very fearful. She may be afraid of the dark, of being in new situations, of funny faces, or just of her own imagination. Provide plenty of calm reassurance.

Movement

Your child runs smoothly now, walks on tiptoe, balances on a low balance beam or wall, hops on both feet in one place, jumps high off the ground, and can probably ride her tricycle without bumping into everything. She loves to play catch with you. Sometimes she can be quite clumsy as her body muscles have been growing rapidly and aren't coordinated yet. Be sure that she gets plenty of active play daily to help her coordination. Dance together often.

Alice the Camel

Tune: "The Toe Bone Connected to the Foot Bone"
(Walk around the room, pretending to be camels, to the beat of the music. On "boom, boom, boom" bump bottoms. Hold up the number of fingers for the number of humps in subsequent verses, decreasing one each time.)

Alice the camel has ten humps
Alice the camel has ten humps
Alice the camel has ten humps
So go, Alice, go, BOOM, BOOM, BOOM!
. . . nine, . . . eight, . . . seven, . . . six, . . . five,
. . . four, . . . three, . . . two, . . . one.
Alice the camel has NO humps
Alice the camel has NO humps
Alice the camel has NO humps
Because Alice is a horse, of course!!!
(Traditional, North American Summer Camp)

George Washington Bridge

Tune: "Over the Waves"
George Washington Bridge
George Washington Washington Bridge
George Washington Bridge
George Washington Washington Bridge
George Washington Bridge
George Washington Washington Bridge
George Washington Bridge
George Washington Washington Bridge
(Traditional, United States Summer Camp)

If you have at least three people singing "George Washington Bridge" it becomes a great action song. Each person is assigned a part (or a group is divided into three parts). One part is George, the second part is Washington, and the third part is Bridge. When the word comes around in the song,

George Washington Bridge

the person jumps up, sings the word, and sits down. Needless to say, the Washingtons can be quite busy. The Travellers do "George Washington Bridge" on their *Merry-Go-Round* album, Elephant Records.

Rig-A-Jig-Jig

(Walk around the room for the verses, then grab your child's hands and dance together quickly, twirling and sliding across the floor, for the chorus.)

Chorus:

*Rig-a-jig-jig and away we go, away we go, away
we go*
*Rig-a-jig-jig and away we go, heigh-ho, heigh-ho,
heigh-ho.*

Verses:

*As I was walking down the street, down the street,
down the street*
*A pretty girl I chanced to meet, heigh-ho, heigh-ho,
heigh-ho.*

*Said I to her, "What is your trade?" heigh-ho,
heigh-ho, heigh-ho, heigh-ho*
*Said she to me, "I'm a weaver's maid," heigh-ho,
heigh-ho, heigh-ho.*

(Traditional, United States)

Sharon, Lois & Bram do "Rig-a-Jig-Jig" on their *Elephant Show* record, Elephant Records.)

SALLY WATERS

Sally Waters is a great party game. IT is Sally Waters, who sits in the center of the circle formed by the other players. They join hands and dance around during the first two lines. During the second two lines the circle stands still, and Sally runs around the inside of the circle in the directions pointed by the group. In the fourth line Sally chooses a partner. During the second verse, Sally and the chosen player hold hands and dance together inside the circle, while the players in the ring circle around them. Sally blows a kiss and leaves, the partner becomes the next Sally.

Rise Sally Waters, rise if you can!
Rise, Sally, rise, Sally, choose your man.
*Choose, choose from the east, choose, choose from
the west,*
Choose, choose the very one that you love the best.

Now they are married, I wish you good joy,
First a girl, and then a boy,
Seven years now after, and seven years to come,
Take her and kiss her and send her off home.

(Traditional, Great Britain)

In and Out the Windows

(A group of players forms a circle, hands joined and arms upraised, as IT weaves in and out under the upraised arms. In the second verse IT selects a partner, they join hands and skip around the inside of the circle. There are now two ITs to select partners for the third verse. This continues until everybody has a partner.)

Go in and out the windows, go in and out the
windows
Go in and out the windows, as we have done
before.

Now stand before your partner, now stand before
your partner
Now stand before your partner, as we have done
before.

Go round and round the village, go round and
round the village,
Go round and round the village, as we have done
before.

(Traditional, Great Britain, North America)

Using Fingers _____

Your child's dexterity may be erratic because her finger muscles are still developing. Activities like stringing beads, scribbling, drawing, and doing art and craft work help your child use her hands and fingers. Play lots of finger games and make shadow puppets to help her strengthen her fingers.

Here is the Church

Here is the church,
    (Lace fingers together, pointing downwards,
Here is the steeple,
    Index fingers extended if the steeple
    is at the front of the church, baby
    fingers extended if the steeple is at the back,
Open the doors,
    Spread thumbs open,
See all the people?
    Turn hands upright, showing fingers
Here is the parson
    Index finger of one hand
Walking upstairs.
    walks up extended fingers of other hand.
And here he is,
Saying his prayers.
    Fold hands.)
(Traditional, North America)

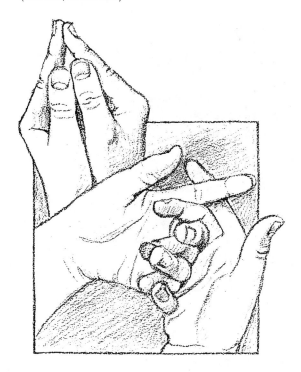

Mr. Thumb

Mr. Thumb, Mr. Thumb
>(Form fists, thumbs inside

Where are you?
Here I am, here I am
>Extend thumbs and intertwine

How do you do.
>in "thumbshake")

(Traditional, North America)

Go through each of the fingers in turn: Peter Pointers, Tall Men, Ruby Rings, Babies Small, and Fingers All, extending each pair and wiggling them.

I Shut the Door

I shut the door and lock it tight
>(Make a fist with one hand, insert
>index finger of other hand in fist and turn

And put the key out of sight
>Hide finger behind back

I found the key to open the door
>Index finger in front again

And turned and turned and turned some more
>Index finger in fist, turning

And then I opened up the door
>Open pretend door)

(Traditional, North America)

My Hat, It Has Three Corners

My hat, it has three corners
>(Join thumbs and index fingers to form a triangle,

Three corners has my hat
>Place on top of head

If it did not have three corners
>Raise 3 fingers, raise other 3 fingers

It would not be my hat.
>and shake head.
>Join thumbs and index fingers and place on head
>again.)

(Traditional, North America)

SHADOW PUPPETS

Project a light onto a wall in a darkened room. When you place your hands in front of the lamp, you can form animal-shaped shadows on the wall. Start with simple shapes and see if you and your child can invent more. Perhaps you can add sound effects and make a puppet play from the characters you form?

Rabbit: Thumb tip meets ring and baby fingers to form head. Index and middle fingers extend to form ears. Wiggle the ears.

Duck: Index fingertip is flexed to touch the second joint of the middle finger. Thumb touches ring and baby fingertips. Wiggle middle and index fingers up and down, so duck will quack.

Giraffe: Index and baby fingers are extended upwards, thumb touches the middle and ring fingers. Flex and twist to move head, wiggle horns.

Swan: (two hands) Extend one arm with wrist flexed, four fingers straight, thumb underneath to make the bill. At the elbow bend place the other hand, with all fingers extended, to form the wing.

Elephant: (two hands) Both wrists flexed down, one hand over the other, lower hand forming trunk, upper hand forming head.

Bird in Flight: (two hands) Place forearms together, pointing upwards, lock thumbs, flap extended fingers.

Dog: (two hands) Forearms together, place one hand against thumb joint, and put fingers down. Two thumbs up for ears, drop baby finger for mouth.

Stegosaurus: (two hands) Palms of hands placed flat together, fingers spread open. Alternate fingers intertwined, with tips about an inch apart to form the plates, thumbs flat together to form the head.

PAPER, STONE, OR SCISSORS

Paper, Stone, or Scissors is a quiet game that can also be used to determine who is IT for another game. You need three players, each holding one hand behind his back. On the count of three, everyone brings out his hand in his chosen position: fist (stone), flat (paper), or index and middle finger extended (scissors). The object is to guess what the other two players are going to do and best them. Scissors cut paper, so scissors win over paper. Paper wraps stone, so paper wins over stone, and stone smashes scissors, so stone wins over scissors.

Indoor Play _____

Through observing and recreating everything she experiences, your child is trying to make sense of her life. Dramatic play enables her to express her emotions, create her own stories, and organize her ideas so she can share them with others. She wants to share her discoveries with you, so learn to listen.

Provide all kinds of puzzles for her to use: jigsaw, lotto, matching squares, block patterns; she will probably never need them more.

Pretend to be Animals

An elephant walks and swings his trunk
(Clasp hands, swing arms back and forth
An eagle flaps his great big wings
Arms flap up and down
A tall giraffe stretches his neck
Raise hands high, stretch neck, stick out tongue
A big hippopotamus winks and blinks
Blink eyes and sink to the floor
A kangaroo goes jumping about
Hop in a circle
A camel marches across the desert
March around
A snake goes twisting and slithering about
Slither across the floor on tummies
And the little mouse tiptoes away.
Tiptoe, hands making mouse ears)
(Traditional, North America)

The Elephant

The elephant goes like this and that
(Arms swing as elephant trunk
He's terribly big
Arms open wide
He's terribly fat
Arms circle in front
He has no fingers
Wiggle fingers
He has no toes
Point to toes
But goodness, gracious what a nose!
Swing trunk again)
(Traditional, North America)

Sharon, Lois & Bram have recorded this on their *One Elephant, deux éléphants* album, Elephant Records, as part of their signature song.

GRID PUZZLES

Make your own wooden or Bristol-board tiles, approximately 2" x 2". Paste or paint on pairs of letters, designs, patterns, numbers, shapes, colors, or textures. Have your child match and organize the tiles. You could do the colors, the alphabet, the numbers from 0 to 9, shapes: circles, stars, diamonds, triangles, squares, rectangles.

DESIGN MATCHING PUZZLES

Create two identical pictures, perhaps cut from a magazine or a wallpaper sample book. Leave one of the designs intact. Mount the second design on a piece of thin cardboard and cut it into small pieces of different shapes. Ask your child to reassemble the design on top of the original, so they match.

NAIL BOARD

Give your child a piece of board, about 6" x 9", lots of small nails and a small hammer. Make dots about a half-inch apart around the edge of her board and have her pound her nails part way in on the dots, until they stick. Then give her elastics, colored wire, yarn, or string to wind from nail to nail to create a design or shape.

JACOB'S LADDER

A Jacob's Ladder is an easily made, old-fashioned sleight-of-hand toy found in many cultures. It is a series of rectangular tiles hinged together with cloth tape. When the top tile is tipped one way and then the other, the illusion is created of all the other tiles falling down, one at a time.

You need at least seven or eight 2 1/2" by 3 1/2" rectangular tiles, cut from wood paneling, masonite, wood, or thick cardboard. Wood or masonite is best, because it creates clicking sounds as the tiles "fall." Ask your child to sand all the edges so they are slightly round. You will need three pieces of half-inch wide fabric tape, such as hem binding or bias tape, about five inches long, for all but one of the tiles.

Horizontally, glue down one piece of tape in the middle of the left side of the tile, approximately 1/2" to 3/4" in from the edge. Glue two tapes on the right side of the tile, approximately 1/2" from the top and bottom. Make all the slats, except one, exactly the same, one tape sticking out at the left and two tapes sticking out at the right. Allow the glue to dry completely.

Turn the first tile over onto a table, with the tapes on the bottom of the tile. The single tape will be on the left, the double tapes will be on the right. Fold all three tapes up and over the top of the tile. Put the second tile on top of the first, with its tapes on the bottom. You now have two short tapes and one long tape underneath on the left, and one short tape and two long tapes on the right. Pull the short tapes tight and glue them to the top of the second tile. Then pull the long tapes across the second tile and add the third tile. Continue gluing and adding tiles until you get to the last tile, that has no tapes. Glue the short tapes from the preceeding tile to this tile. Let it dry thoroughly.

To make the Jacob's Ladder work, tip it back and forth.

Cooking

Familiarize your child with all aspects of cooking. Even when you're making something intricate, she can collect and pass the ingredients. When you prepare foods with your child, set out simple rules for safety.

1) Tie all long hair back or use a chef's hat.
2) Keep recipes and procedures simple.
3) Wash hands before and after cooking.
4) Keep everything clean as you go.
5) Refrigerate everything that needs it.

Develop a "cooking chatter" about the different types of healthy foods you eat. Talk about the taste, shape, texture, and color of all the foods you handle. Sample new ingredients together; cooking a food may be a great way to persuade a picky eater to try something new. Try to have your child do as much of the fetching, scrubbing, peeling (have her use a peeler, not a knife), sifting, beating, mixing, grating, grinding, and measuring as possible. Show her how to tear lettuce, shell peas, snap beans, scrub potatoes and wash apples.

Adults must handle the cooking and burners. Carefully show her how to use a vegetable peeler, keeping her fingers back from the area being peeled. She should not be using sharp knives until she is at least five. Write down all favorite recipes.

RAW VEGETABLE PLATTER

Most young children prefer the taste and texture of raw vegetables to cooked vegetables. A platter of raw vegetables and dipping sauce is particularly popular if your child has prepared it. Show her how to wash all the vegetables, peel carrots and cucumber, and break up cauliflower or broccoli. While you do the cutting, she can arrange the vegetables on a plate and mix up a dipping sauce. She can add a little ketchup and some herbs or spices or onion soup mix to plain yoghurt or sour cream.

PEANUT BUTTER

Does your child realize that peanut butter is made from peanuts and doesn't have to come out of a jar? Shell peanuts together, remove the skins, and sample a few. Put 2 cups of the shelled peanuts through your blender or food processor, or twice through a hand-crank meat grinder. If the peanut butter is very dry, you can blend in up to 2 tbsps of peanut oil.

FLIES ON A LOG

Separate and wash celery stalks. Smear the "logs" with peanut butter, cream cheese, or cheese spread and press raisin "flies" onto the spread. Add some sunflower seed "maggots," if you wish.

Outdoors _____

Your child is interested in exploring everything she sees. She loves following paths and trails. Point out prominent features and landmarks whenever you are out on your walks and be sure to mention that you reverse the landmarks on the way back, to find your way home.

SHARKEY

You need between two and five players to play Sharkey. IT is Sharkey. The other players sit on top of a wide, low slide or on a steep hill, with their feet hanging down. Sharkey tries to pull them down by grabbing their ankles and pulling hard. The players lock arms, grasp hands, or hold onto each other in any way that prevents Sharkey from pulling them down, but they cannot use their hands to hang onto anything but each other. The first person Sharkey pulls down becomes the next Sharkey. A word of warning: I loosened two of my teeth playing Sharkey; take it easy.

I Saw Esau

Recite "Esau" as you ride the seesaw at the park. You sit inside the hand grips in order to balance your child. Make sure she hangs on tight.

I saw Esau sawing wood,
And Esau saw I saw him;
Though Esau saw I saw him saw,
Still Esau kept on sawing.
(Traditional, Great Britain)

See, Saw Margery Daw

See, saw, Margery Daw,
Jacky shall have a new master;
Jacky shall have but a penny a day,
Because he can't work any faster.
(Traditional, Great Britain, North America)

POT, POT, JACKPOT!

Pot, Pot, Jackpot! is a city sidewalk game. Water and gas main shut-off valves, contractor's logos, storm-sewer grates and manhole covers are usually embedded in concrete sidewalks. As you move along the sidewalk, you shout "Pot!" or "Jackpot!" according to what it is that you step or jump on. We score five points for the shut-off valves and logos, and ten points for a manhole cover (the jackpot), but you should determine your own point count by the design of your sidewalks. Every pot or jackpot must be stepped or jumped on, no shortcuts. Be sure to include "If You Step on a Crack" (p 37) when you play Pot, Pot, Jackpot! Jenny and Jord are usually a block ahead of me whenever we walk anywhere together because they play Pot, Pot, Jackpot! Going onto the street, for any reason, is *never* allowed while playing this game; it is *only* played on the sidewalk. Every 100 points earns a marble or sticker.

IF YOU STEP ON A CRACK

As you walk down the sidewalk you NEVER step on cracks. Of course, you know why: *If you step on a crack, you'll break your back*, or *If you step on a crack, you'll break your MOTHER's back*. There's another version for sibling rivalry: *If you step on a crack, you'll break your back. If you step on another, you'll break your BROTHER's!* Just in case you inadvertently step on a crack, remember, *Step on a line, and you'll be fine!* The casting lines for concrete sidewalks don't count as cracks.

HINT FOR SKIPPING

If your child hasn't learned how to skip yet, hold her hand and skip together towards a specific spot. Your child will pick up your rhythm and movement patterns as you move along.

JUMPROPE HORSIE

A single-length jumprope makes perfect reins for playing Horsie. You be the horse. Place the middle of the jumprope at the back of your neck. One side of the rope goes forward over a shoulder and under the same arm. Do the same for the other side. The jumprope becomes the reins, and your child the driver. Run around. Make sure that your child understands she is never to cross the reins or put them around her neck.

TAG

Tag is one of the greatest games of childhood. One player is IT and tries to touch another person, who then becomes IT. There are zillions of variations that add to the fun. Part of the fun, of course, is taunting IT, while trying to get as close as possible without being caught. The favorite taunt in our playground is *Na-na-na, boo boo*, done with a little hootchie-kootchie dance. Here are some more:

Charlie Over the Ocean
Substitute IT's name for "Charlie."

> *Charlie over the ocean*
> *Charlie over the sea*
> *Charlie caught a big fish*
> *Can't catch me!*
> (Traditional, Great Britain, North America)

Hee, Hee, Hee
> *Hee, hee, hee,*
> *You can't catch me!*
> (Traditional, North America)

Cowardly, Cowardly Custard
> *Cowardly, cowardly custard*
> *Couldn't run for mustard!*
> (Traditional, Great Britain)

Can't Catch You
Sometimes IT may want to play hard to get, and he retorts:

> *Can't catch you.*
> *That is true!*
> (Traditional, North America)

Music _____

W(hile) your child may not yet be singing in tune or to a beat, spontaneous singing is a major ingredient of her life. Simple rhythmical action games, skipping, sliding, slipping, clapping, slithering, shimmying, pointing and swinging to music are all part of her musical enjoyment. Let her generate her own movements to the music. If you give her too many complicated movements to do, she may forget to sing.

By all means, let her see the actions for songs as they are performed, but let her add the actions when they become hers. The path to musical understanding develops from listening and paying attention to the music, to singing, bouncing along, and tapping to simple percussive instruments, and then on to performing complicated rhythm patterns, actions, and dance steps. Only after these experiences with music, can formal musical training truly begin.

MUSICAL COACHING

In any song or game that suggests movement, your role should be to suggest a variety of movements so your child can build her own repertoire. Vary the routine, so that actions for a game or song don't become fixed. Gradually, your child will introduce new movements, both familiar and unique. As this starts to happen, it is time for you to withdraw from the actions, or follow her actions. Continue to help carry the melody and the beat of the song.

Where, Oh Where Has My Little Dog Gone?

Where, oh where has my little dog gone?
(Hands, palms up, near shoulders
Oh where, oh where can he be?
Swivel head, searching
With his tail cut short
Wiggle "tail"
And his ears cut long
Flip hands for "ears"
Oh where, oh where can he be?
Hands near shoulders again)
(Traditional, German Origin, North America)

Polly Wolly Doodle

(Invent your own actions)
Chorus:
Fare thee well, fare thee well
Fare thee well my fairy fay,
For I'm off to Louisiana
For to see my Susyanna
Sing Polly wolly doodle all the day.
Verses:
Oh, I went down south for to see my Sal,
Sing Polly wolly doodle all the day
My Sal she is a spunky gal,
Sing Polly wolly doodle all the day.

Oh, a grasshopper sat on a railroad track
Sing Polly wolly doodle all the day.
A pickin' his teeth with a carpet tack,
Sing Polly wolly doodle all the day.

Behind a barn, down on my knees
Sing Polly wolly doodle all the day
I thought I heard a chicken sneeze
Sing Polly wolly doodle all the day.

He sneezed so hard with the whoopin' cough
Sing Polly wolly doodle all the day
He sneezed his tail and his head right off
Sing Polly wolly doodle all the day.
(Traditional, Southern United States)

Fred Penner sings "Polly Wolly Doodle" on his *Special Delivery* album, Troubadour Records.

Oh, Dear, What Can the Matter Be?

Chorus and First Verse:

Oh, dear, what can the matter be?
Dear, dear, what can the matter be?
Oh, dear, what can the matter be?
Johnny's so long at the fair.

Verses:

He promised he'd buy me a fairing should please me,
And then for a kiss, oh he vowed he would tease me.
He promised he'd bring me a bunch of blue ribbons,
To tie up my bonny brown hair.

He promised he'd bring me a basket of posies,
A garland of lilies, a garland of roses,
A little straw hat, to set off the blue ribbons
That tie up my bonny brown hair.

(Traditional, Great Britain, Appalachia)

Sharon, Lois & Bram sing "Oh, Dear, What Can the Matter Be" on their *Mainly Mother Goose* album, Elephant Records.

Little Tommy Tinker

(Little Tommy Tinker can be sung as a round or catch, with the different parts joining in where indicated by the asterisks.)

Little Tommy Tinker
> (Sitting down

Sat upon a clinker*
He began to cry
> Rub eyes

Ma, Ma*
> Stand up and throw hands in air

Poor little innocent guy.
> for each "ma," sit down again)

(Traditional, Great Britain, North America)

Joshua Fit the Battle of Jericho

Joshua fit the battle of Jericho, Jericho, Jericho
Joshua fit the battle of Jericho
And the walls came tumblin' down.

You can talk about your king of Gideon
You can talk about your man of Saul,
But there's none like good old Joshua
At the battle of Jericho.

Joshua fit the battle of Jericho, Jericho, Jericho
Joshua fit the battle of Jericho
And the walls came tumblin' down.

(Traditional, Spiritual, United States)

Art

Give your child art materials that she can use without your assistance. Have markers, crayons, colored pencils, and an inexhaustible supply of inexpensive paper available at all times. Give her a supply of stickers and interesting bits of paper to glue together and a gluestick. Provide easy access to playdough and baker's clay.

When you are able to supervise, use more complicated materials such as tempera paints, finger paints and watercolors.

PLAYDOUGH

Here's the best playdough recipe I have found: Boil 1/2 cup of salt in 2 cups of water until the salt dissolves. Add food coloring, tempera powder, or water crayon, if desired, for color. Add 2 tbsps salad oil, 2 cups of sifted all-purpose flour, and 2 tbsps of either alum or cream of tartar (available at your drugstore). Knead the dough or process it in your food processor until you have an even consistency. Store in an airtight container or plastic bag. The dough will last for two months or longer if you store it in the refrigerator.

BAKER'S CLAY — SALT DOUGH

Sift together 4 cups of all-purpose flour and 1 cup of salt. Add 1 1/2 cups of cold water and mix well. Knead for at least ten minutes, or process with a steel blade in your food processor to bind the mixture so it will not fall apart when it is being used. Model the mixture as you would clay. Add any other art materials you like, and allow your creations to air dry. Large undecorated objects can be baked in a very slow oven (less than 200°F) for two or three hours. This dough can be frozen and defrosted, and keeps well in a sealed plastic bag. It is best made in advance and allowed to sit in a sealed package for a few hours. *Hint:* Make any holes before the clay dries.

STARCH AND SOAP FINGER PAINT

1 cup of laundry starch (not liquid) mixed with enough cold water to make a paste.
1 1/2 cups boiling water
1/2 cup soap flakes or powder (not detergent)
1 tbsp glycerine (available at your drugstore)
Coloring (tempera powder, poster paint, food coloring, water crayon)

Add the boiling water to the starch and cook it in a saucepan until glossy. Stir in the soap while the mixture is still warm. When it's cool, add the glycerine and coloring. This is a smooth, creamy paint. Store it in airtight containers.

STRING PAINTING

You will need pieces of string (try different thicknesses), paint mixed with white glue, and paper (try white, black, and colored). Dip the string in the glue and paint mixture. Drop it at random on the paper or form your own special shapes and designs. Your child may also enjoy painting in some of the areas outlined by the string.

CHALK PAINTING

Dampen glossy finger-paint paper to hold it to the table and help the paint run a bit. Add a teaspoon of yoghurt, buttermilk, or liquid laundry starch to the paper as a fixative. (Buttermilk or yoghurt will create more of a finger-paint effect than the starch, but both effects are worth trying.) Ask your child to draw through the liquid with brightly colored chalk. Try it with several types of paper, including damp paper towel. When you are finished, wash off the ends of the chalk. You can also allow the chalk to dry and scrape the ends off for "Splatter Chalk" (p 104).

CRAYON RESIST

Your child draws a picture on smooth, rough, or watercolor papers, using brightly colored, fluorescent, or metallic crayons. Then he paints a thin wash of transparent watercolor paint or ink over the crayon drawing with a large soft brush. *Hint:* For the wash, try using a color darker than the color of the crayons.

Word Play

Your child is in love with language. Her imagination is blossoming, and she starts her own stories: "What if . . ." and "Supposing . . ." She adores nonsense verse and silly stories. Be sure to introduce her to tongue twisters and the fun of telling fortunes.

TONGUE TWISTERS

Say any or all of the following quickly:
- Six thick thistle sticks
- Truly rural
- Six sticks
- A proper cup of coffee made in a proper copper coffee pot.

- She sells seashells at the seashore. The seashells that she sells are seashells for sure.
- Three buckets of black bugs' blood.

Be sure to recite Mother Goose rhymes like "Betty Botter," "Theophilus Thistle" and "Peter Piper" to keep your tongue in good working order, too.

FORTUNES

Every child is curious about the future. Will I get married? How many children will I have? What will my job be? What will I wear? What kind of house will I live in? Will I be rich? How many kisses? When will it happen?

Through the ages children have told fortunes in their play. They pull daisy petals, count cherry stones left on their plates, skip rope or bounce balls until they miss, as they chant their incantations. Good luck with the answers.

Occupations?

Tinker, tailor, soldier, sailor,
Rich man, poor man, beggar man, thief,
Doctor, lawyer, merchant, chief,
Royal Canadian Mounted Police.
(Traditional, Canada)

Soldier brave, sailor true,
Skilled physician, Oxford blue
Learned lawyer, Squire so hale,
Dashing airman, curate pale.
(Traditional, England)

A laird, a lord,
A cooper, a thief,
A piper, a drummer,
A stealer of beef.
(Traditional, Scotland)

Peerage, gypsy, medicine, law,
Divinity, trade, nothing at all.
(Traditional, Great Britain)

Lady, baby, gypsy, queen,
A girl in Playboy magazine.
(Traditional, North America)

Dress?

Silk, satin, calico, rags . . .
(repeat if necessary)

What Kind of Ring?

Diamond, emeralds, ruby, pearl . . .
(repeat if necessary)

What Kind of House?

Big house, little house, pig pen, barn . . .
(repeat if necessary)

How Will I Travel?

Airplane, rocket ship, coach, car, wheelbarrow,
Jag, Chevy, horse & carriage . . .
(repeat if necessary)

When Will It Happen?

This year, next year, sometime, never . . .
(repeat if necessary)

What Day of the Week?

Sunday, Monday, Tuesday, Wednesday . . .

At What Age Will I?

Five, twenty-five, fifty, never . . .
(repeat if necessary)

Will It Happen?

Yes, No, Maybe so . . .
(repeat if necessary)

DAISY PETAL PULLING

One I love, two I loathe, three I cast away,
Four I love with all my heart, five I love I say;
Six he loves, seven he don't, eight he'll marry me.
Nine he won't, ten he would but he can't
Eleven he courts, and twelve he tarries,
Thirteen he's waiting, and fourteen he marries.
That's what the daisies say.
(Traditional, American and British Folklore)

Sharon, Lois and Bram do a version of this as a song on *Stay Tuned*, Elephant Records. Of course, you can always say, *She loves me, she loves me not, she loves me . . .*

Quiet Times _____

While your child may not be napping regularly anymore, she still requires "timeouts" where she can recharge her batteries. This is a good time to read together quietly, play relaxing games, or cuddle up with a favorite toy. Your child might want to curl up with you and sing favorite lullabies or quiet songs.

Poor Adam

I'm so sorry for old Adam,
Just as sorry as can be,
'Cause he never had a mammy
For to rock him on her knee.

And he never had a daddy
For to tell him all he knowed,
And he never had nobody
To point out the narrow road.

And he never had no childhood
Playin' round the cabin door.
And he never had a mammy
For to snatch him off the floor.

And he never had a feeling
When he laid him down to rest
Of the 'possum and the taties
Tucked beneath his little vest.

And I've always had a feeling
He'd have let that apple be
If he'd only had a mammy
For to rock him on her knee.
(Traditional, American Spiritual)

Rick and Judy sing "Poor Adam" on their *Family Album*, J & R Records.

The Cowboy and the Lady

As I was a walkin' and a ramblin' one day
I spied a fair couple, a ramblin' my way.
One was a lady, and a fair one was she,
And the other was a cowboy, and a brave one was
he.

Oh where are you goin' my pretty fair maid?
Just down by the river, sit down by the shade.
Just down by the river, just down by the spring,
To the wildwoods, see the water, hear the
nightingale sing.

I'll go to Wyoming, I'll stay about a year,
Often I'll think of you, my little dear,
And when I return to you, it will be in the spring,
And we'll walk down by the river, and hear the
nightingale sing.

(Traditional North American Cowboy from an old English ballad)

Annie Laurie

Maxwelton's braes are bonnie, where early falls the
dew,
And it's there that Annie Laurie, gave me her
promise true.
Gave me her promise true, which I ne'er forgot will
be,
And for bonnie Annie Laurie, I'd lay me doon and
dee.

(Traditional, Scotland)

Growing Interests — Choosing IT

Virtually every chase, circle, jumping or hiding game requires an IT, the player who is going to do all the work. One of the most joyous rituals of childhood is deciding who is going to be IT. Sometimes the routine is simple, especially when being IT is not desirable. The oldest or the bossiest child simply says, "You're IT," and everyone scatters. At other times more complex methods are used, especially when being IT confers great status. Choosing IT is often a better game than the game itself. Most games provide for successive ITs in their structure, so IT is only found once in any play cycle. My favorite routine for finding IT is "Stella Ella Olla" (p 79), but it can take all day to finish! Here are some ways of finding IT.

KING COUNTER

King Counter is the basic countout on fists. Everybody puts in two fists, and one person counts around, reciting a rhyme such as *Eachy peachy pear plum, who is your best chum?* The last person can either say her own name or make a friend IT.

King Counter is used in many traditional games where outs occur, like One Potato or Bee, Bee, Bumblebee.

Train Train *(King Counter)*

Train, train, number nine,
Coming down Chicago line,
If the train goes off the track,
Do you want your money back? Yes or No?
Y-E-S spells "yes" and out you must go. (or)
N-O spells "no" so out you must go.
(Traditional, North America)

One Potato, Two Potato *(King Counter)*

(All fists in center. One player pounds the fists around the circle. On each MORE, that fist is removed and put behind the person's back. The last remaining fist is IT.)

One Potato, two potato
Three potato, four
Five potato, six potato
Seven potato, MORE.
(Traditional, Great Britain, North America)

Eenie Meenie Miney Mo *(King Counter)*

Eenie Meenie Miney Mo
Catch a tiger by the toe
If he hollers let him go
Eenie Meenie Miney Mo. You're IT.
(Traditional, North America)

Eenie Meenie Miney Mo
Put the baby on the po
When he's done, wipe his bum
Tell his mother what he's done! You're IT.
(Traditional, Great Britain)

Inky, Pinky, Ponkey *(King Counter)*
Inky, Pinky, Ponkey
Daddy bought a donkey
Donkey died, daddy cried
Inky, pinky, ponkey. You're IT.
(Traditional, North America)

Bee, Bee, Bumblebee *(King Counter)*
Bee, bee, bumblebee
Sting a man upon his knee
Sting a pig upon his snout
I declare that you are OUT!
(Traditional, Canada)

My Mother and Your Mother *(King Counter)*
My mother and your mother were hanging out
*   some clothes.*
My mother gave your mother a punch on the nose.
What color was the blood? Blue. B-L-U-E
That was the color of her blood. You're OUT.
(Traditional, Great Britain)

TOE TICKER

Everybody puts one foot into the center, and the toes are "ticked" around. Toe Ticker is usually used with the "You're IT" type of rhymes.

Round and Round the Butter Dish *(Toe Ticker)*
Round and round the butter dish,
One, two, three.
If you want a pretty girl,
Just choose ME!
(Traditional, Great Britain)

One, Two, Sky Blue *(Toe Ticker)*
One, two, sky blue,
All out, but YOU. You're IT.
(Traditional, North America)

NOT IT

Not IT is most often used when starting a game of Tag (p 37). The last person to shout "Not IT" is IT.

Not Because You're Dirty
When IT is *finally* arrived at, the rest of the players chant:
Not because you're dirty
Not because you're clean
Just because you kissed a boy (or girl)
Behind a magazine.
(Traditional, Great Britain, North America)

Other Ways of Finding IT
Other time-honored ways of finding IT include:
- Drawing straws. The short straw is IT.
- Flipping coins. One player calls "Heads" or "Tails." If his call matches the visible side of the coin, that player is IT.
- Odds or evens. One player calls "Odds" or "Evens." On the count of three each player extends one or two fingers. If the total of fingers matches the call that person is IT.
- Spinning a baseball bat or tennis racket. The player the handle points to is IT.
- Hand over hand. One player tosses a baseball bat, handle up to another player. Taking turns, each player goes hand over hand to the top. The first person able to cover the end of the handle is IT.

CHAPTER THREE

FOUR TO FOUR-AND-A-HALF

"Mommy, Where Do the Stars Go During the Day?"

OUR FOUR-YEAR-OLD is a confident, creative chatterbox! He wants to talk about everything he thinks and does. Listen, and praise his accomplishments and shining ideas. He demands your attention and inquires about everything, nonstop. He asks questions because he wants your attention, but also because he wants knowledge.

He loves playing with words, not only for the sounds, but for the responses they generate. Sometimes he will be a showoff with his language.

He can be moody, with quick shifts in feelings. When you give him too much direction he can be defiant; he wants to make his own decisions.

Make-believe and dress-up are essential parts of his play and he invents his own games. Provide scope for his dramatic play, his musical enjoyment, and his artistic expression.

Movement

Your child needs to get out daily, to run, roll, slide, climb trees or gym equipment, and monkey around. He is starting to catch a ball. He can hop on one foot and his galloping is getting regular; he is very close to being able to skip.

HOPSCOTCH (POTSY)

Hopscotch is a hopping-on-one-foot game that is nearly worldwide. Any number can play. A grid is drawn on pavement or scratched in the dirt with a stick. A player throws a hoptaw (marker) into a square to indicate which square he must hop over. Then he hops through the rest of the squares sequentially, without stepping on a line and without touching the other foot to the ground.

There are many ways to draw a hopscotch grid. Sometimes there are a couple of "even" squares where both feet can touch. Sometimes the numbers are placed in a straight line in one direction, sometimes they form a snail spiral, sometimes there are diagonal triangles to hop in the middle, sometimes there is a "home" area to rest on.

Show your child how to draw a grid with sidewalk chalk. Show him how to throw the hoptaw, perhaps a round, flat stone, into the numbered squares.

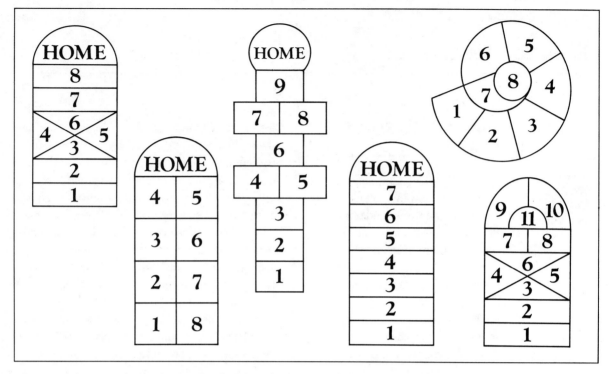

In some places, a player who has finished his turn can write his initials in a square to indicate it is his, and everyone else has to jump over it. By about five-and-a-half, your child may be adroit enough to start capturing his own squares.

Father Abraham

"Father Abraham" is a great action song. Rick and Judy do a fun version on their *Family Album*, J & R Records. March around together as you sing, and each time you sing a verse add different parts of the of the body at the end.

Father Abraham, had seven sons, sir
(Salute
Seven sons sir, had Father Abraham
And they never laughed
Mimic laughing
And they never cried
Wipe eyes
All they did was go like this:

With a left
Circle left arm and start song again
... With a left and a right
Circle both arms, sing again adding indicated actions for each new verse)
... With a left and a right and a foot
... With a left and a right and two feet
... With a left and a right and two feet and a head
... With a left and a right and two feet and a head, and a hip
... With a left and a right and two feet and a head and two hips
... With a left and a right and two feet and a head, and two hips and a MARCH!
(Traditional, North American Summer Camp)

Knees Up, Mother Brown
(There Came A Girl From France)
Dance the actions. This is also a great skipping or clapping game. You can hear this song on the *Stay Tuned* album, Sharon, Lois & Bram, Elephant Records, or *The Corner Grocery Store* album, Raffi, Troubadour Records. It originated from a British Music Hall ditty.

Chorus and First Verse:
Knees up, Mother Brown! Knees up, Mother Brown!
Knees up, knees up, never let the breeze up!
Knees up, Mother Brown!
Verses:
There came a girl from France:
Who didn't know how to dance.
The only thing that she could do
Was "Knees Up, Mother Brown!"

Oh, hopping on one foot,
Hopping on one foot,
Hopping, hopping, never stopping,
Hopping on one foot.

Hopping on the other,
Hopping on the other,
Hopping, hopping, never stopping,
Hopping on the other.

Twirling round and round,
Twirling round and round,
Twirling, twirling, never whirling,
Twirling round and round.
(Traditional, North America)

Step Dance
Step, step, and turn yourself around,
Step, step, and turn yourself around
Reach up high, bend down low.
Clap your hands, and sit just so.
(Traditional, North America)

SHIP TO SHORE

You need one adult or older child to be Captain, and any number of other players. In a large open area, designate one end as the "ship" and the other end as the "shore." The Captain calls out random commands. Start with slow simple calls and add more complex, faster commands as the players become familiar with the game.

Ship — run to one end
Shore — run to the other end
Scrub the decks — down on knees, scrubbing
Captain's daughter — hootchie kootchie dance
Climb the rigging — pretend to climb
Torpedo — lie face down on the floor or ground, arms extended
Captain's coming — Stand at attention and salute
Whales ahoy! — pretend to spout water and swim
Up scope — lie on back, one leg extended
All hands on deck — run to the center of the playing area
Night watch — pretend to fall asleep.

Call "ship" or "shore" every four or five commands so there is plenty of running.

Using Fingers

Your child's fingers are getting stronger and more manipulative. More and more detail is emerging in his drawings. He has enough control to be able to throw and catch a ball quite effectively. Provide opportunities for him to weave, lace cards, and manipulate large buttons and buttonholes.

TAPESTRY SEWING

Cut a piece of burlap into a manageable size, about 6" x 9" or 8" x 10." Thread some brightly colored wool, about fifteen to eighteen inches long, through a blunt tapestry needle or bodkin. Knot one end of the wool and show your child the basic mechanics of pushing and pulling a needle through the cloth. Let him create his own design. Your child may want to come back to his sewing project several times to add to it. Have a variety of yarns and threads available.

TIC-TAC-TOE (XS AND OS)

You need two players, a piece of paper and two pencils. Draw two vertical parallel lines and cross them with two horizontal parallel lines to create nine spaces in three rows. One players is X and one is O. The first player to get a row of his marks in any direction is the winner.

DOMINO TIPPING

Using your entire set of dominos, ask your child to place each domino on its edge close together. Push the first one and watch the others tumble down in a ripple effect.

JEWEL BOX

Provide a box of lacing materials for your child. It could include gimp, dental floss, a tapestry needle, buttons, beads, hollow pasta, and anything else around the house that is stringable. Show him how to lace his beads.

Fee, Fie, Foe, Fum

Fee, fie, foe, fum,
(Extend each finger in turn,
See my fingers?
Wiggle fingers
See my thumb?
Wiggle thumb
Fee, fie, foe, fum,
Remove one finger at a time
Fingers gone
Form fist
So is thumb.
Hide fist.)
(Traditional, North America)

Do Your Ears Hang Low?

Do your ears hang low?
(Pull on earlobes
Do they wobble to and fro?
Wiggle hands
Can you tie them in a knot?
Tying motions with fists
Can you tie them in a bow?
Outline bow
Can you throw them over your shoulder
Cross hands over shoulders
Like a regimental* soldier
Stand at attention, saluting
Do your ears hang low?
Pull on earlobes again.)
(Traditional, Great Britain, North America)

* In the U.S. a "Continental" soldier

Repeat the song faster and faster. Bob McGrath sings this on *If You're Happy and You Know it Sing Along With Bob*, Kids' Records; Sharon, Lois & Bram on *Stay Tuned*, Elephant Records; and Mike and Michelle Jackson on their *Playmates* album, Larrikin/Elephant Records.

I Eat My Peas With Honey
Try a simple rhythmic clapping game.
I eat my peas with honey
I've done it all my life, life, life.
I know it may seem funny
It keeps them on my knife, knife, knife.

I — clap your own hands
eat — clap your partner's right hand
my — clap your own hands
peas — clap partner's left hand
with — clap your own hands
honey — clap your partner's hands twice
I've — clap your own hands
done — clap partner's right hand
it — clap your own hands
all — clap your partner's left hand
my — clap your own hands
life, life, life — clap partner's hands three times.
Repeat pattern for next two lines.
(Anonymous)

Indoor Games

Card games are great for counting, introducing mathematical concepts, and helping your child develop his dexterity. It takes skill to hold a handful of cards! Your child continues to want to help you with everything you do. He'd love a recipe box with his favorite recipes or his own cookbook. An excellent starting cookbook for children is *Kitchen Fun, A Cookbook for Children*, by Louise Price Bell (Derrydale Books). Ask your child to start inventing his own recipes, using his favorite ingredients.

WAR

You need two, three, or four players to play War. If three play, discard one card from a deck of fifty-two. Deal all the cards out evenly, face down, into piles. Each player turns over a card from his pile; the highest one wins the other players' cards. In the event of two or more players turning over a card of identical value, "war" is declared. The tied players place four cards face down. They turn their fourth cards over together, and the high card is the winner of the "war" and his opponents four cards. The object of the game is to collect all the cards.

SLAP JACKS

Slap Jacks is a great game for two or more players. The object is to collect all fifty-two cards in the deck. The cards are dealt out one at a time to all the players, and kept face down. Each player, in turn, turns up one card on a common pile in the middle. Whenever a Jack is turned up, the first player to slap the Jack takes all the cards in the pile. Cards must be turned up away from the player, so he doesn't see it first, and turning up and slapping must be done with the same hand. If there is a pile of hands, the hand closest to the Jack wins. If somebody slaps a card by mistake, he takes a card from the bottom of his pile and slides it under the bottom of the player's pile. You can, of course, play Slap Threes or Slap Sevens too.

TEA PARTY SCONES

No doubt, your child loves tea parties. Why not have a "cream tea?" The cream is traditionally clotted Devon cream, but if this extra-thick cream is not available, serve a dollop of lightly sweetened whipped cream with your strawberry jam and scones. Send out fancy invitations, and serve lemonade. If you want to get elaborate, you could also serve tiny decorative sandwiches, fruit loaf, cake, crumpets, English muffins, or a fancy cake.

We have regular tea parties all year round, but the summertime ones outdoors are the best.

Scones
Sift together:
   2 cups sifted flour
   2 – 3 tbsps sugar
   4 tsps baking powder
   1/2 tsp salt
Cut or rub 4 tbsps of butter into the flour mixture, add 2/3 cup of milk. Knead lightly, just until the dough is smooth. Add 1/2 cup of raisins or currants, if desired. Roll out about 1" thick, cut with a favorite cookie cutter, and bake in a 425°F oven 10 to 12 minutes. Serve piping hot.
(To make baking powder biscuits, omit fruit and sugar)

LEMONADE

Ask your child to select 4 lemons. You cut them in half and show him how to squeeze them with a juicer. Pour the lemon juice into a pitcher. Dissolve 1/2 cup of sugar or honey with 1/2 cup of hot water. Add 4 cups of cold water to the juice and stir in the sugar solution. Add one tray of ice cubes and serve.
(Your child can use the juicer to squeeze orange and grapefruit juice, too.)

DOGGIE, DOGGIE, WHO STOLE YOUR BONE?

Doggie, Doggie is fun when you have a number of children playing quietly inside. Once player is IT, or the Doggie. He scrunches down in the center of the circle and covers his eyes, while the rest of the players sit in a circle with their hands hidden behind their backs. You place a "bone," a small object like a ball or stick, in one of the player's hands. The players chant:

Doggie, oh Doggie, who stole your bone?
Somebody stole it from your home.
Guess who, it may be you,
It may be the monkey from the zoo.
Three guesses, just for you.
Wake up, Doggie, find your bone!
(Traditional, North America)

The Doggie wakes up and tries to guess who has the bone. The players can offer hints such as warm, hot, cool, cold, coldest, HOORAY! The child with the bone becomes the next Doggie.

GOOD MORNING DAISY MAY

IT is Daisy May, who scrunches down and hides his eyes. Another player touches Daisy May on the back and says, "Good Morning Daisy May," and sits down. Daisy May must guess who spoke. If he guesses, that player becomes IT; if he doesn't guess, another player says the greeting.

DRAW A MAGIC CIRCLE

IT scrunches down and hides his eyes. One person draws a circle on IT's back and says:

*"Draw a magic circle, draw a magic circle,
Draw a magic circle, and place it with a DOT."*
(Put a dot in the middle)

Another version of the rhyme goes:

*"Circle circle, dot DOT,
Now I've got my cootie shot!"*
(Traditional, North America)

IT has to guess who drew the circle. (It's especially fun when the players disguise their voices.) If IT guesses, everyone sings: *Forever, and ever, Hallelujah, forever.* If the guess is correct, the drawer is the next IT; if not, another person draws on IT's back.

TELEPHONE

When you have a group of people together, try Telephone or Pass the Message. One person whispers a message to the person next to him. That person in turn whispers it to the next person, who whispers to the next, and so on until it has been passed all around the room. The message can be a rhyme, a silly saying, a question, or simply a statement of fact. The last person says the message out loud. Jan Pienkowski's book *Gossip*, Price/Stearn/Sloan, is fun to read when you introduce this game.

Poor Mary Sits A Weepin'

IT is Poor Mary and she sits in the center of a circle of children, pretending to be crying. The other children circle around her, singing:

Poor Mary sits a weepin', a weepin', a weepin'
(Substitute IT's name for Mary, if you wish)
Poor Mary sits a weepin', on a bright sunny day.

Oh Mary, whatcha weepin' for, weepin' for, weepin' for
Oh Mary whatcha weepin' for, on a bright sunny day?

Mary sings: (Slow tempo)

I haven't any playmate, any playmate, any playmate
I haven't any playmate on this bright sunny day.

Group Sings: (Slow tempo)

Stand up and choose your playmate, your playmate, your playmate
(Mary selects a partner — faster tempo)
Stand up and choose your playmate on this bright sunny day.

Everyone Sings: (Lively tempo, Mary and IT dance together)

And now she's got a playmate, a playmate, a playmate
And now she's got a playmate on this bright sunny day.
(Traditional, Great Britain)

The selected playmate becomes the new Mary.

Outdoor Play _____

Your child may be able to go hand-over-hand along the monkey bars at the playground by now. His balance and agility are improving daily. He loves to climb and jump. Make sure he has a place to practice.

Obstacle Jump — Jump Across the River

Establish a "river," perhaps a garbage bag filled with leaves, to jump over. Encourage him to jump far as well as high. Congratulate him when he makes it across the "river" without falling in. Play "Old Mother Witch" (p 158), too.

Hoop Along

Place two hoops side by side. Have your child travel along by stepping into one hoop, reaching over for the other, placing it in front of the first, and stepping into that one. If you have enough hoops, have a race.

Beanbag Balance

If you have a low wall or beam or curb on which to balance, have your child carry a beanbag on his head while walking along.

Bowling

Save old plastic detergent bottles and line them up as skittles or bowls, in groups of three, six, or ten. Ask your child to roll a large ball towards them and knock over as many as possible. Keep score and award a marble or sticker for every hundred points.

    Hint: You might want to weight the skittle with water or sand.

Bulls-eye (Marbles)

Draw a series of concentric circles on the pavement with sidewalk chalk. Your child can practice "shooting" marbles at the target by flicking or pushing them with his fingers, (Fingies) or placing the side of one foot against the marble and tapping it with the other foot (Footsies).

Sand Play

Let your child spend as much time as possible in the sandbox, pouring, digging, and building with sand. Provide an old sifter or strainer, a funnel, cups, spoons, shovels, toy trucks, a magnet and ferrous washers, a sand pail, squirt and spray bottles containing water, and a nesting toy. If you have your own outdoor sandbox, be sure to cover it when it's not in use. If you use a public one, check the sand for animal feces before letting your child play.

Water Play

Your child can enjoy water at a swimming pool, in a wading pool, under a lawn sprinkler, at a beach, or in the bath. When he is playing, give him items that can change his perceptions of water:

- ice or snow that melts
- sponges
- food coloring or nontoxic colors
- cloths
- shaving cream
- funnels
- soap or bubble bath
- squirt or spray bottles
- sieves
- wine corks, marbles, other floating and sinking objects
- cups, spoons
- a plastic doll

- straws, plastic tubes
- boats
- nesting toys
- hoses
- rubber duckies

Let him help you mop up the floor and give him a chance to help wash unbreakable dishes. Don't forget to show him how to whoosh a hand-held eggbeater in a sink full of soapsuds!

SPONGE TOSS

On a hot summer's day, when everyone is wearing bathing suits, play cool catch with a couple of buckets of water and sponges.

THE BLOB

The Blob is a great tag game when you have four or more players. IT is counted out, and everyone else scatters. When IT touches another player, they join hands and go after the others. The game continues until all the players are part of the Blob. The last person caught is the next IT.

SHADOW TAG

Shadow tag is played on a sunny day or a bright moonlit night. IT tries to step on the shadow of another player, who then becomes IT. Shadow tag is great for showing your child how his shadow changes at different times of the day; in early morning and late afternoon it is hard for his shadow to escape.

FLASHLIGHT TAG

Flashlight Tag is a cross between Hide 'n' Seek and Tag. It is played at night, and you need a clear signal, like *Olly, Olly, Oxen Free* to return "home" without penalty, so children won't get lost in the dark. IT carries a flashlight and tags other players with the beam of light. They rush back to base to shout either *Home Free*, or *1, 2, 3, on* ____. The new IT then takes the flashlight to find the other players. As the children are tagged, they stay at base. Play this game inside, in a back yard, or at the school yard, so nobody gets lost.

Music _____

Your four-year-old demands happy experiences with music. He plays his favorite tapes and records constantly, and memorizes his favorite songs. Songs that tell stories encourage your child to listen carefully. Sing together often, even if you are off-key. If you sing together as you drive along, the miles just roll away.

SHAKERS

Have your child make some musical shakers out of small tin cans or cardboard tubes. Place some beans, dry macaroni, pebbles, or popcorn inside and seal both ends. If desired, decorate with streamers, ribbons and stickers.

THREE BLIND MICE

Improvise your own actions. If you have a group of friends over, divide up into a three-part or six-part catch.

Three blind mice, three blind mice
See how they run, see how they run.
They all ran after the farmer's wife,
She cut off their tails with a carving knife;
Did you ever see such a sight in your life
As three blind mice?
(Traditional, Great Britain, North America)

Cindy

Eric Nagler does a wonderful version of "Cindy" on his *Fiddle Up a Tune* album, Elephant Records.

Chorus:
Git along home, Cindy, Cindy
Git along home, Cindy, Cindy
Git along home, Cindy, Cindy
I'll marry you some day.

Verses:
You ought to see my Cindy, she lives away down
*   South,*
And she's so sweet the honey bees, swarm around
*   her mouth.*

I wish I had a nickle, I wish I had a dime,
I wish I had a Cindy gal, to love me all the time.

I went to see my Cindy, she met me at the door,
With her shoes and stockings in her hand, and her
*   feet all over the floor.*

I wish I was an apple, a hanging on a tree
And every time that Cindy passed, she'd take a bite
*   of me.*

I wish I was a handful of Cindy's cookie dough,
She'd fold me gently in her hands and say "I knead
*   you so."*

I wish I was a banjo, on Cindy's dimpled knee,
And every time she played a tune, she'd always
*   pick on me.*

It's Cindy in the springtime, it's Cindy in the fall,
If I can't have my Cindy gal, I'll have no gal at all.
(Traditional, Southern United States)

Clementine

Chorus:

Oh my darlin', oh my darlin', oh my darlin'
Clementine
You were lost and gone forever, dreadful sorry,
Clementine.

Verses:

In a cavern, in a canyon, excavating for a mine
Dwelt a miner, '49er, and his daughter,
Clementine.

Light she was and like a fairy, and her shoes were
number nine
Herring boxes, without topses, sandals were for
Clementine.

Drove she ducklings to the water, ev'ry morning
just at nine,
Hit her foot against a splinter, fell into the foaming
brine.

Ruby lips above the water, blowing bubbles soft and
fine.
But alas, I was no swimmer, so I lost my
Clementine.

In my dreams she still doth haunt me, robed in gar-
ments soaked in brine,
Though in life I used to hug her, now she's dead I
draw the line.

(Traditional, United States, 1860s)

The Blue-Tail Fly

Chorus:

Jimmie crack corn, and I don't care, Jimmie crack
corn, and I don't care
Jimmie crack corn, and I don't care, my master's
gone away.

Verses:

When I was young I used to wait
On master and hand him his plate
And pass the bottle when he got dry
And brush away the blue-tail fly.

One day he rode around the farm,
The flies so numerous they did swarm,
One chanced to bite him on the thigh
The devil take the blue-tail fly.

The pony run, he jump, he pitch,
He threw my master in the ditch;
He died and the jury wondered why
The verdict was the blue-tail fly.

They lay him under a persimmon tree,
His epitaph is there to see
"Beneath this stone I'm forced to lie
Victim of the blue-tail fly."

(Traditional, North America)

Nickety Nackety

I married my wife in the month of June,
Nickety, nackety, now, now, now,
And carried her off by the light of the moon.
Nickety nackety, hey jock ackety,
Willicky wallicky, rescue the collicky,
Nickety, nackety, now, now, now.

She baked a pie and called it mince,
Nickety, nackety, now, now, now.
I've never known such happiness since,
Nickety nackety, hey jock ackety,
Willicky wallicky, rescue the collicky,
Nickety, nackety, now, now, now.

She rides to town on the old grey mule,
Nickety, nackety, now, now, now.
And when she does I look like a fool,
Nickety nackety, hey jock ackety,
Willicky wallicky, rescue the collicky,
Nickety, nackety, now, now, now.

The halter and bridle they lie on the shelf,
Nickety, nackety, now, now, now.
If you want any more you can sing it yourself,
Nickety, nackety, hey jock ackety,
Willicky wallicky, rescue the collicky,
Nickety, nackety, now, now, now.
(Traditional, Southern United States)

Art

Cleanup is not only an essential part of any project, it is a great source of inspiration for developing the next project! Develop a cleanup patter with your child: "Where do you think we can use these extra sequins?" "This paper scrap looks like a triceratops." Jot down any bright ideas that you both have and come back to them at your next art session.

PENCIL HOLDER

Give your child a clean, empty tin can with smooth edges and white glue. Have him cover the outside with art "stuff"; fabric bits, trims, felt, braid, beads, seeds, sequins, google eyes. Have him use his completed can as a holder for his paintbrushes, crayons, pencils, pencil crayons, felt-tipped pens, scissors, and other art materials.

GLOWING PAINTS

Ordinary tempera powders sometimes dry to rather blah shades and hues. They will dazzle if you mix one part of the paint powder with two parts of powdered laundry detergent (not soap) and two parts water.

GOOP PAINT

This paint makes big blobs on heavy paper or cardboard, so don't apply it too thickly, as it takes a long time to dry. At first, your child will just want to squirt it on, but soon he will begin to make three-dimensional drawings with it. Try the uncolored paint on black poster paper and add some glowing stars to create a wonderful outer space effect. Decorate baker's clay ornaments with goop paint and try it on sandpaper.

Into 1 3/4 cups cold water, slowly sift and stir:
  2 cups presifted all purpose flour
  1/2 cup table salt
  1/4 cup white sugar
Pour the paint into squeeze bottles and add tempera paint for color.

WONDER PLAYDOUGH

This dough is good for creating small ornaments, jewelry, and fine sculptures. Make any holes you need before the piece dries.

Remove the crusts from three or four slices of store-bought white bread, and tear the bread into tiny bits. Add 1 tbsp of white glue and a drop or two of lemon juice per slice of white bread. Mix thoroughly. Model as desired and place on a piece of waxed paper to dry. Allow at least two full days for the objects to dry, and turn them frequently. The pieces can be painted with either tempera or acrylic paints.

Hint: The dough can be separated and colored with a drop or two of food coloring when it is being mixed. It will keep in a tightly sealed bag in the refrigerator for a day or two.

OATMEAL DOUGH

This dough is a different texture than baker's clay and is good for ornaments.

　　1 part flour
　　2 parts oatmeal or cornmeal
　　1 part water

Mix well, and knead or process for at least ten minutes to break up the gluten in the flour.

DIORAMA

Use a shoe box, with one end removed, or a large piece of styrofoam insulation as the base or "stage" for your diorama. Decorate the scene and make popsicle-stick puppets. Salt dough or plasticine make a solid base for the popsicle sticks. Dioramas are especially effective for displaying dinosaurs, zoos, nature scenes, or a favorite story.

Word Play

At about four, your child is going to start asking some of the greatest questions of all time: "Where do babies come from?" "Why doesn't the rain fall up?" "When is it tomorrow?" "Is there a war tonight?" He hears stories from other children or on the daily news or from adults around him, and his questions are his way of finding out about his world. Try to provide him with the knowledge he is seeking. He also loves playing with language, so read lots of poetry and nonsense verse, and tell jokes.

MAGNETIC LETTERS

Keep a bin of magnetic letters handy for writing words on the refrigerator. Your child may be recognizing specific letters, so ask him: "Bring me the C," or "Can you find all the Xs?" Ask him to make the sounds of the letters. Use the magnets to display his artwork on the fridge, too.

LETTER AND NUMBER SEARCH

As your child learns to recognize letters and numbers, make a Search for the "___" game. Cover a piece of paper with random letters or numbers (from 0 to 9). Ask: "Can you circle the 7s?" or "Cross out the Qs." When he is comfortable recognizing the letters or numbers, ask him to draw a line to the letter or number that comes next in the proper sequence. Use separate sheets for numbers and letters.

TONY CHESTNUT

Ask him: *Do you know Tony Chestnut?*
(Touch his toe, his knee, his chest, and his head.)

JOKES AND RIDDLES FROM OUR PLAYGROUND

The Diplodocus is the dumbest dinosaur, and he gets himself into all sorts of silly situations.

Why did the Diplodocus take his aunt on a picnic?
He heard there were going to be anteaters there.

Why did the Diplodocus take a ruler to bed?
To see how long he slept.

Why did the Diplodocus carry a watch when he crossed the desert?
Because it had a spring.

Why did the Diplodocus take hay to bed?
To feed his nightmare.

The sillier the jokes are, the more children love them.

What is gray, has four legs, and a trunk?
An elephant?
No, silly, a mouse going on vacation!

(This one is for city kids)
What's worse than when it's raining cats and dogs?
When it's hailing taxis.

Did you know that it's raining cats and dogs outside?
Yes, I just stepped on a poodle.

Why is a rhinoceros's skin wrinkled?
Did you ever try to iron one?
(You may want to read "How the Rhinoceros Got His Skin," one of Rudyard Kipling's *Just So Stories*.)

What's white on the outside, green on the inside, and hops?
A frog sandwich!

Knock knock.
Who's there?
Kerch
Kerch who?
Bless you!

Knock knock
Who's there?
Canoe
Canoe who?
Canoe come out and play with me?

What month has 28 days?
I dunno, February?
No, silly, they all do!

What's full of holes, but holds water?
A sponge.

RIDDLES FROM THE "OLD" DAYS

Riddle me riddle, I suppose
A hundred eyes and never a nose.
Answer: A sieve

What goes around a house, but never goes in?
Answer: A fence

What is it that is too much for one,
Enough for two, and nothing for three?
Answer: A secret

My mother gives birth to me.
I give birth to my mother. What am I?
Answer: an egg.

What has two lookers, two crookers, and a wig
*   wag? (eyes, horns, tail)*
Answer: A cow

No hands and feet, but he opened the door.
Who is he?
Answer: The wind

Two brothers are we, great burdens we bear,
On which we are bitterly pressed.
The truth is to say, we are full all the day.
And are empty when we go to rest. What are we?
Answer: A pair of shoes

Quiet Times

Be sure to establish a go-to-bed routine that is consistent for every evening of your child's life, no matter where you are. Generally, a short transition time after bath or shower, with a story, reading, poetry, or a "magic" verse, and a cuddle makes a good routine. Talk about the day's happenings, resolve the sad events, and emphasize the happy times. Wish your child "Sweet dreams" and have a Dream Penny tucked under his pillow.

DREAM PENNY

Every child knows that money is magical. Tape a penny onto a piece of card, ask your child to print his name and decorate his card. You write "Dream Penny" on the card and tuck it under his pillow to bring him happy, rich dreams every night.

Cock-a-Doodle Doodle Doo

Cock-a-doodle doodle doo,
Cock-a-doodle dandy!
I have got a pretty maid,
And she is very handy.
She washes all her knives and forks,
And platters in the sea, Sir;
She scrubs the floor with cabbage stalks,
As clean as clean can be, Sir.

Cock-a-doodle doodle doo
Cock-a-doodle didy!
I have got a pretty maid,
And she is very tidy.
She sweeps the cobwebs off the sky,
And rubs with all her might, Sir,
The sun and moon, and stars so high,
Or how could they look bright, Sir?
(Anonymous)

John Had Some Cake

John had some cake; John had some jelly.
John went to bed with a pain in his…

Now don't get excited, don't be misled.
All John had was a pain in his head.
(Anonymous)

Monday's Child

Monday's child is fair of face
Tuesday's child is full of grace
Wednesday's child knows no woe
Thursday's child has far to go
Friday's child is loving and giving
Saturday's child works hard for a living
But the child that's born on the Sabbath day
Is bonny, and blythe, and good, and gay.
(Traditional, Great Britain, North America)

Billy Boy

Sing the chorus together; you sing the verses.

Chorus and First Verse:
Oh where have you been, Billy Boy, Billy Boy
Oh where have you been, charming Billy?
Verses:
I have been to seek a wife for the pleasures of my
*   life,*
She's a young thing, and cannot leave her mother.

She asked me to come in, she had dimples on her
*   chin*
She's a young thing, and cannot leave her mother.

She set me in a chair, she had wrinkles in her hair
She's a young thing, and cannot leave her mother.

She can brew and she can bake, she can make our
*   wedding cake*
She's a young thing, and cannot leave her mother.

She's twice six, and twice seven, twenty eight, and
*   eleven*
She's a young thing, and cannot leave her mother.
(Traditional, Appalachia)

Girls and Boys Come Out to Play

Chorus:
Come with a whoop, and come with a call,
Come with a good will or not at all.
Verses:
Girls and boys come out to play,
The moon doth shine as bright as day.
Leave your supper and leave your sleep,
And join your playfellows in the street.

Up the ladder and down the wall,
A half-penny loaf will serve us all.
You find milk, and I'll find flour,
And we'll have pudding in half an hour.
(Traditional, Great Britain)

Vera Lynn and Kenneth McKellar sing this song
on *The Wonderful World of Nursery Rhymes*,
London Records.

There She Stands

In addition to being a beautiful song, this is a
great rhyme for Single Dutch skipping (p 77). It
was a popular song in North America during the
1850s.

There she stands a lovely creature
Who she is I do not know.
I have caught her for her beauty
Let her answer, yes or no.

Madame, I have gold and silver,
Lady, I have house and lands
Lady, I have ships on the ocean,
All I have is at thy command.

What care I for your gold and silver?
What care I for your house and lands?
What care I for your ships on the ocean?
All I want is a fine young man.
(Traditional, North America)

Growing Interests _____

Elements of drama carry into every aspect of your child's life, from doll and housekeeping play, to construction with blocks, to playing with puppets. Your child may begin to show signs of gender identification; he is not only a small boy, but a knight in shining armor, a cowboy, a rough, tough freedom fighter, or a handsome prince. She is not a little girl, but a fashion plate, a fairy princess, or a space queen. Despite your personal beliefs about bringing up children to be nonsexist, you may find your child disconcertingly "little boy" or "little girl" no matter how you've raised them.

What Are Little Girls Made Of?
What are little girls made of, made of
What are little girls made of?
Sugar and spice and all things nice,
That's what little girls are made of, made of.

What are little boys made of, made of?
What are little boys made of?
Thunder and lightnin', all things frightnin'
That's what little boys are made of, made of.
(Traditional, Great Britain, North America)

COPS AND ROBBERS

One of the great rituals of childhood is joining your friends for a game of Cops and Robbers. In our neighborhood we have "Sherwood Forest," a ravine about two city building lots in size. Here, the children play Robin Hood, which is just one version of Cops and Robbers. Other children play Cowboys and Indians, or Aliens and Earthlings.

This type of action game is great for developing a sense of drama and strategy. Make sure a grownup is nearby to supervise.

THE PRINCESS

Before you introduce this game, be sure to read the story of *Sleeping Beauty*. The Princess (one IT) preens herself in the center of a ring of circling children. The evil fairy (another IT) enters and scowls at the princess, who droops into a swoon. A handsome prince detaches himself from the ring and gallops around the outside. Members of the circle raise their hands high to become a forest. The handsome prince "chops" down the trees to make an entrance into the center of the circle, gives the princess a shake to wake her up, and dances with her. Everyone picks a partner and twirls around for the last verse.

Tune: "Aikendrum"
The princess was a lovely child, lovely child, lovely child,
The princess was a lovely child, long, long ago.

An ancient castle was her home, was her home, was her home
An ancient castle was her home, long, long, ago.

A wicked fairy cast a spell, cast a spell, cast a spell
A wicked fairy cast a spell, long, long ago.

The princess slept a hundred years, a hundred years, a hundred years
The princess slept a hundred years, long, long ago.

The palace trees grew tall and straight, tall and straight, tall and straight
The palace trees grew tall and straight, long, long ago.

A handsome prince came galloping by, galloping by, galloping by,
A handsome prince came galloping by, long, long ago.

He cut the trees down one by one, one by one, one by one,
He cut the trees down one by one, long, long ago.

The princess she did sleep no more, sleep no more, sleep no more
The princess she did sleep no more, long, long ago.

And everybody's happy now, happy now, happy now
And everybody's happy now, long, long, ago.
(Traditional, Great Britain, North America)

Whoopee Ti Yi Yo

As I was a walkin' one mornin' for pleasure
I met a cowpuncher a ridin' along.
His hat was thrown back and his spurs were a-
*   jinglin'*
And as he approached he was singin' this song:

Whoopee Ti Yi Yo, git along little dogies,
It's your misfortune and none of my own.
Whoopee Ti Yi Yo, git along little dogies,
You know that Wyoming will be your new home.

It's early in spring that we round up the dogies.
We mark them and brand them and bob off their tails,
We round up our horses, load up the chuck wagon,
And then throw the dogies out on to the trail.

It's whooping and yelling and driving the dogies,
And oh, how I wish you would only go on;
It's whoopin' and punchin' go on, little dogies,
You know that Wyoming will be your new home.

(Traditional, North American Cowboy)

CONESTOGA WAGON

Cut out four circles from strong cardboard. Attach these wheels to a shoe box with brass fasteners. Tape two sheets of white paper together, arching them and taping them to the inside of the box. If you're feeling ambitious, you can make ribs from bent clothes hangers and cover them with white cloth.

PUPPETS

Create a puppet show to enact favorite stories. Turn a small table on edge, and the puppeteer can scrunch down in back and hold the puppets over the side. Or use a large appliance box, with a window cut out, as a stage.

For simple hand puppets, have your child glue or sew yarn hair, eyes, nose, and mouth on old socks, gloves, or mittens.

Draw and cut out favorite characters and paste them onto heavy paper or light-weight card.

Pieces of greeting cards can be cut up and pasted onto sticks for scenery, or for characters. Glue the characters to wooden tongue depressors, popsicle sticks, or straws. To make jointed paper puppets, simply hinge them with brass fasteners, and attach straws at the back of the figure.

Create puppets from paper bags. Glue on yarn or string for hair, google eyes or buttons for eyes, and paint costumes and other features. Glitter, sequins, and fancy bits of paper or cloth can be added to create wonderful special effects.

Use makeup or nontoxic paint to draw figures on your child's fingers or hands. With a thumb on the outside fist, the area formed when the thumb moves makes a perfect mouth.

Don't forget to add sound effects to your puppet show. Rub pieces of sandpaper together to make a train. Rattle dry peas or beans in a shallow metal pan for the sound of rain. Flex a cookie sheet to make the sound of thunder, crumple some cellophane for the sound of fire. Make clicking and siren sounds, and anything else you can think of, with your voice. Use rhythm sticks to make a galloping horse. Let your imaginations soar. Practice your show a few times, dress up in costumes, then perform for friends.

CHAPTER FOUR

FOUR-AND-A-HALF TO FIVE

"Look Daddy, I'm a Monkey"_____

OUR FOUR-AND-A-HALF-YEAR-OLD is becoming an independent being. She does things to please herself, rather than you. She may be able to hang upside down and go hand-over-hand on monkey bars. She is learning to listen and to follow complex directions. Her sentences are becoming intricate, and her understanding of the world and her place in it is growing daily. She questions everything. She is in love with language, nonsense verse, playground slang, and the effects she is able to create using language. She loves playing long, complicated, dramatic action games, where players take turns being IT.

Her concentration is improving, and she tolerates more frustration. She is starting to distinguish between what is fact and what is her imagination. She loves to sort, compare sizes, do puzzles, and search for infinitesimal differences in detail of what she investigates.

Movement _____

Your child's coordination keeps improving. She can jump down from a height and land on both feet. She is maneuvering on stairs like an old pro. She rides her tricycle competently and can make sharp turns without thinking. She loves to tumble and do somersaults. She is trying hard to bounce balls and swing bats and rackets. She takes great pleasure in all her physical abilities. Introduce her to ice or roller skates.

HIDE 'N' SEEK

IT counts out a rhyme as the other players hide. IT can count by fives, perhaps as high as fifty, by tens to a hundred, or by twos to twenty. Then IT shouts: *Ready or not, here I come!* and tries to find the other players. When she finds a hider, they both race back to the ghoul's nest. If the hider is first back, she shouts: *1, 2, 3, Home free!* If the seeker is back first, she shouts: *1, 2, 3, on (child's name).* If the seeker wins the race, the hider is the next IT; if the hider is the winner, the seeker must find another player. Here are a few old Hide 'n' Seek rhymes that are still in use.

Bushel of Wheat
The seeker chants at home base:
> *Bushel of wheat, bushel of rye*
> *All not hid, holler "I!"*

Anyone not hidden can call out "I" or "not hid." This helps the seeker know where to start looking.
The seeker continues:

> *Bushel of wheat, bushel of clover*
> *All not hid, can't hide over!*
> *Ready or not, you must be caught,*
> *Hiding around the ghoul or not.*
> *First caught's IT! Coming!*
(Traditional, North America)

Five, Ten, Fifteen, Twenty
The seeker chants at home base:
> *Five, ten, fifteen, twenty,*
> *Twenty-five, thirty, thirty-five, forty,*
> *Anyone 'round my base is IT*
> *Here I come, ready or not.*
(Traditional, North America)

Two, Four, Six, Eight

The seeker chants at home base:

Two, four, six, eight,
Meet me at the garden gate.
If I'm late, don't wait,
Two, four, six, eight.
COMING!

(Traditional, Great Britain, North America)

Come Out, Come Out

When Hide 'n' Seek isn't working for the players, when it's lunch time, or when the game is over, be sure to shout:

Come out, come out
Wherever you are!

or:

Olly, Olly, Oxen Free!

(Traditional, North America)

Pawpaw Patch

Pawpaw Patch is a Hide 'n' Seek game where IT goes to hide. Explain that pawpaws are also called papayas, and they grow in the tropics. The players sing:

Where, oh where is sweet little (the hider's name)
Where, oh where is sweet little _____
Where, oh where is sweet little _____
Way down yonder in the pawpaw patch.

Come on (boys) (girls) *let's go find her* (or him)
Come on ____ *let's go find her*
Come on ____ *let's go find her*
Way down yonder in the pawpaw patch.

Picking up the pawpaws, put 'em in your pocket
Picking up the pawpaws, put 'em in your pocket
Picking up the pawpaws, put 'em in your pocket
Way down yonder in the pawpaw patch.

(Traditional, North America)

Sharon, Lois & Bram sing this song on their *One Elephant, deux éléphants* record, Elephant Records.

GOING TO KENTUCKY
(or Chicago, or Toronto, or…)

Going to Kentucky is a circle game. IT is in the middle, and the rest of the group circles around the "pretty lady." When the songs gets to "Oh, shake it," IT hootchie-kootchies and sinks or stretches as indicated. When the song gets to "round and round," IT closes her eyes, points a finger, and spins until "HEY," when the next "pretty lady" is selected. This version of the game came from Nova Scotia, where the "pretty lady" wears purple underwear. In other versions she wears flowers in her hair or dirty underwear.

I'm going to Kentucky, going to the fair
To find a pretty lady wearing purple underwear.
Oh, shake it baby, shake it, shake it if you can.
Shake it like a milkshake, and pour it in the can.
Oh, shake it to the bottom, and shake it to the top,
And shake it round and round and round
Until it's time to stop. HEY!

(Traditional, North America)

Kim and Jerry Brodey sing "Going to Toronto" on their *Simple Magic* album, Kids' Records; Sharon, Lois & Bram on their *One Elephant, deux éléphants* album, Elephant Records.

Using Fingers _____

Your child is probably able to cut along a line now with scissors. She may be starting to print letters and numbers. Show her how to print her name. She loves to paint, and to have you write down her story as she paints her pictures. Give her plasticine as a change from playdough, as her fingers are now getting strong enough to model it. Her drawings of people are becoming more complex. She is ready to start learning some more complicated ball bouncing games.

One Finger, One Thumb Keep Moving

One finger, one thumb, keep moving,
One finger, one thumb, keep moving,
One finger, one thumb, keep moving,
We'll all be happy and gay.

One finger, one thumb, one hand, keep moving,
One finger, one thumb, one hand, keep moving,
One finger, one thumb, one hand, keep moving,
We'll all be happy and gay.

Keep on adding body parts. The last verse would be:

One finger, one thumb, one hand, two hands, one leg, two legs, stand up, turn around, sit down, keep moving…

Bob McGrath sings "One Finger, One Thumb" on his *If You're Happy And You Know It Sing Along With Bob* album, Kids' Records.

ONESIES, TWOSIES, THREESIES…

This game can go on for days. It involves bouncing a rubber ball or tennis ball against a wall and catching it. Once your child starts, it may be her favorite game until she goes to high school.

Introduce this game by showing the routine for the numbers one to twelve, doing each action only once, catching the ball with both hands. If she misses, just continue.

When she is ready for more, ask her to do the entire Onesies routine for the number of times specified.

Later on she can do it with her right hand, her left hand, and add the Twosies, Threesies, Foursies. It's a great game to play with a friend, taking turns on misses.

Onesies:
One: Throw the ball against the wall and catch it.
Two: Throw the ball against the wall, let it bounce and catch it. Do it twice.
Three: Throw the ball against the wall, clap, catch it. Do it three times.
Four: Throw ball, roll hands, catch the ball. Four times.
Five: Throw ball under leg, and catch. Five times.
Six: Bounce the ball six times on the ground, catch it. Do it once.
Seven: Throw ball to wall, clap front, back, front, catch the ball. Seven times.
Eight: Throw ball, clap over, under, and over leg, catch ball. Eight times.
Nine: Throw ball, clap, touch heel (leg flexed up), clap, catch ball. Nine times.
Ten: Throw ball, clap, touch ground, clap, catch. Ten times.
Eleven: Throw ball to ground so it bounces up to wall, catch it. Eleven times.
Twelve: Throw ball, clap, touch alternate heels, clap, catch. Twelve times.

Twosies:
Go through entire routine, letting ball bounce once.
Threesies:
Go through entire routine, clapping on each move.
Foursies:
Entire routine, rolling hands on each move.
Fivesies:
Throw ball under leg for each move.
Sixies:
Bounce on ground before doing the routine.

Sevensies:
Clap front and back while going through the entire routine.
Eightsies:
Clap over and under leg while going through entire routine.
Ninesies:
Clap, touch heel, clap, while going through entire routine.
Tensies:
Touch the ground while going through the entire routine.
Elevensies:
Throw ball to ground so it bounces to wall while doing routine.
Twelvsies:
Touch alternate heels while doing the entire routine.
(Traditional, United States)

ONE, TWO, THREE O'LEARY

Using a large playground ball, have your child bounce it on the pavement, lifting her leg over the ball on "O'Leary."

> *One, two, three, O'Leary*
> *Four, five, six, O'Leary*
> *Seven, eight, nine, O'Leary*
> *Ten O'Leary, postman.*
> (Traditional, United States)

WEAVING

Get a small piece of chicken wire at the hardware store or find a plastic berry box to use as the warp (the fixed threads). Show your child how to weave yarn, strips of fabric, old shoelaces, strips of paper, or any other linear material, in and out of the holes. Dip ends of the weft materials in melted wax (old crayons or candles) or liquid starch, if necessary, to make them stiff.

Indoor Games _____

STRING-CAN TELEPHONE

To make a "telephone," you need two empty tin cans, the same size, and one piece of string. Poke a hole (using a nail and hammer) in the middle of the lids of both cans. Put the string through each hole and tie a knot so it won't pull out. Stretch the string taut, and use the cans alternately as speaking tubes and listening horns as you carry on conversations. If you can't hear clearly, try waxing the string using an old candle or piece of crayon.

Bracelets or Napkin Rings

Soak tongue depressors or popsicle sticks in water until they are pliable. Form them into circles inside a drinking glass. Allow them to dry, and decorate.

Sock Hockey (two or more players)

Move the breakables! Roll an old pair of socks into a tight ball to make the puck. Set up a goal and appoint one player "goalie." The object is to get the puck past the goalie to score a goal. Use hands to hit the puck, shoot at the goal, or stop the puck. Use regular hockey rules, but if you allow tackling in your game, do it gently.

Get the Grownup Out of the Chair (two or more players)

Find an unsuspecting couch-potato grownup snoozing in a chair. The idea is to get the grownup off the chair and onto his feet by pulling, pushing, prodding, or dropping onto the grownup quickly. Warning: Make sure the grownup knows what is about to happen and isn't subject to cardiac arrest.

Steamroller (two or more players)

It pretends to be a steamroller. She rolls around on the floor or outside on the ground, and everyone else tries to stay out of her way by jumping up and down.

Jacks

Jacks is an ancient, almost global, game of skill, originally played with six small stones or animal bones. These have been replaced by six-pointed metal jackstones. Jacks is played with a small, semihard rubber ball about one inch in diameter.

It can be a solitary game or can be played with a friend. If friends play, parallel lines are drawn about ten feet apart. Each player stands on one line and throws one jack at the other line. The player coming closest to the line plays first.

Scatters: Scatters are thrown to begin any game of jackstones. Gather all the jacks into one hand, then throw them onto the floor. If they are entangled, you must pick up one without moving the other, while the ball is in the air.

Baby Jacks: Toss the ball into the air and let it bounce as you pick up one jack, then catch the ball. (Catch the ball and pick up the jack with your dominant hand, and transfer the jack to your nondominant hand to continue playing.) Keep going until you pick up all the jacks, one at a time, without missing. Scatter the jacks again and continue the game by picking up two jacks at a time, then three, then four and two, and five and one, and finally, all six at once.

Upsies: Upsies is like Baby, but the ball mustn't bounce. Throw the ball up, pick up the jack(s), catch the ball, throw the ball up again, transfer the jack to the other hand, and catch the ball.

Downsies: This is like Upsies, but you drop the ball rather than throw it in the air.

Sweepsies: You move the jacks back and forth before picking them up.

Stone Soup

Boil three clean smooth stones for fifteen or twenty minutes, to make sure they are sterilized. Put them into your soup pot. Add some stock, either tinned, instant, or fresh. Add some flavoring: garlic, herbs, pepper, salt. Add lots of vegetables: onions, peas, beans, carrots, celery, tomatoes, cauliflower, cabbage, turnip, whatever you have on hand. Throw in a couple of handfuls of barley, rice, or noodles. Cook the soup for a couple of hours, adding extra water if necessary. While you are waiting, read the book *Stone Soup* by Marcia Brown (Aladdin Books, Collier McMillan).

Outdoors _____

Your child's jackstones, marbles, skipping ropes, and balls are all perfect outside. Be sure to stash them where she has easy access to them on her way outdoors.

OBSTACLE COURSE

Children of all ages love obstacle courses. You can arrange for your child to slither through a box tunnel, roll across a specified area, hop a specific distance, climb into each space in a ladder laid flat on the ground, do a number of somersaults, climb into an empty box, and jump to ring a bell. The obstacle course should vary slow and fast and high and low events.

STANDING BROADJUMP

Ask your child to stand on a stick or behind a line you've drawn in sand. Have her jump as far as she can, beginning with both feet together, and landing with both feet together.

WALKING RACE

Practice speed-walking around four pylons, old tires, or hoops set out on a course. No running is allowed and one foot must be on the ground at all times.

MOTHER, MAY I?

It is a very fickle Mother. The game works best with three or more players, who line up fifteen or twenty feet away from Mother, along a wall or fence. Mother gives a command to each of the players in turn: "Zoe, you may take ten giant steps forward." Zoe *must* ask "Mother, may I?" before she takes her steps. If Zoe doesn't ask properly, she goes back to the wall. Mother can reply, "Yes, you may," and Zoe would then take her steps. Mother can also say, "No, you may not, you may take three baby steps." Zoe *must* say again, "Mother, may I?" Usually Mother is quite generous with her first command, but after the first "Mother, may I?" is less so. While Mother is giving her attention to one player, the others sneak forward with tiny steps to try and touch Mother. If she catches them, they must go back to the fence.

Some steps can include: giant steps, baby steps, twirl steps, frog steps, side steps, jump steps, snake slithers. Of course, Mother may command giant steps backwards, too. The first player to touch Mother is the next IT.

QUEENIE, O QUEENIE (three or more players)

It is Queenie, who hides her face against a wall and throws a ball back over her shoulder, without looking. The other players scramble for the ball. Whoever catches it hides it behind her back. All the players put their hands behind their backs and chant:

> *Queenie, O Queenie, O who's got the ball?*
> *I haven't got it, it isn't in my pocket.*
> *Queenie, O Queenie, O who's got the ball?*
> *Is she big or is she small?*
> *Is she fat or is she thin?*
> *Is she like a rolling pin?*
> (Traditional, Great Britain)

Queenie tries to guess who has the ball. If she's right, she remains IT; if she's wrong, the player hiding the ball becomes the new Queenie.

Music

All of your songs and chants should have simple, rhythmic actions. March, stomp, hop, slide, glide, twirl and skip to the music you hear or sing.

COMB KAZOO

A comb and a piece of folded tissue or waxed paper creates sounds that can drive parents wild. Place the folded paper around the teeth of the comb, place the fold next to your lips, and hum your favorite songs. Leave a slight distance between your mouth and the paper so the vibration from your lips can reverberate. Try to keep the paper dry; it won't work if the paper gets soggy.

I've Been Workin' on the Railroad

I've been workin' on the railroad,
All the live-long day.
  (Swing an imaginary hammer with both arms
I've been workin' on the railroad,
Just to pass the time of day.
Can't you hear the whistle blowing,
  Pull an imaginary whistle cord
Rise up so early in the morn?
Can't you hear the captain shouting
  Cup your mouth)
Dinah, blow your horn?

Dinah, won't you blow, Dinah, won't you blow
  (Create your own motions for
Dinah, won't you blow your horn, horn, horn?
  the rest of this song.)
Dinah, won't you blow, Dinah, won't you blow
Dinah, won't you blow your horn?

Someone's in the kitchen with Dinah
Someone's in the kitchen I know-ow-ow-ow
Someone's in the kitchen with Dinah
Strummin' on the old banjo.

Singing fee-fie-fiddly-I-oh
Fee-fie-fiddly-I-oh-oh-oh-oh
Fee-fie-fiddly-I-OOOOHHH
Strummin' on the old banjo.

Someone's kissing Dinah,
Someone's kissing Dinah I know-ow-ow-ow
Someone's kissing Dinah
'Cause I can't hear the old banjo!
(Traditional, Southern United States)

Miss Polly Had a Dolly

Miss Polly had a dolly who was sick, sick, sick.
She called for the doctor to come quick, quick,
quick.
The doctor came with his bag and his hat,
And he rapped on the door with a rat, tat, tat.

He looked at the dolly and he shook his head,
And he said, "Miss Polly, put her straight to bed."
He wrote on some paper for a pill, pill, pill.
"I'll be back in the morning with the bill, bill, bill."
(Traditional, Canada)

Pick A Bale of Cotton

(Make picking motions as you do the actions suggested by the words)
Chorus:
Oh lawdy, pick a bale of cotton,
Oh lawdy, pick a bale of hay.
Verses:
Gonna jump down, turn around, pick a bale of
cotton.
Gonna jump down, turn around, pick a bale of hay.

Me and my partner can pick a bale of cotton.
Me and my partner can pick a bale of hay.

Me and my wife can…
Me and my brother can…
Me and my papa can…
Me and my woman can…
Went to Corsicana to…
(Traditional, United States Work Song)

One More River

(Hold up the number of fingers called for as you dance to this song)
Chorus:
One more river, and that wide river is Jordan.
One more river, there's one more river to cross.

Verses:
Old Noah built himself an ark, one more river to cross.
He built it out of hick'ry bark, one more river to cross.

The animals came in two by two, one more river to
cross.
The elephant and the kangaroo, one more river to
cross.
The animals came in three by three, one more river to
cross.
The baboon and the chimpanzee, one more river to
cross.
The animals came in four by four, one more river to
cross.
The hippopotamus got stuck in the door, one more
river to cross.
The animals came in five by five, one more river to
cross.
The bees came swarming from the hive, one more
river to cross.
The animals came in six by six, one more river to cross.
The monkey up to his monkey tricks, one more river
to cross.
The animals came in seven by seven, one more river
to cross.
Some went to oops, the others to heaven, one more
river to cross.
The animals came in eight by eight, one more river to
cross.
The giraffe was early, the unicorn late, one more
river to cross.
The animals came in nine by nine, one more river to
cross.
Some drank water, the rest drank wine, one more
river to cross.
The animals came in ten by ten, one more river to
cross.
If you want any more, you can sing it again, one
more river to cross.
(Traditional, United States, Spiritual)

Lazy Mary
Tune: "Nuts in May" or "Lilibullero"
(Substitute your child's name)

*Lazy Mary, will you get up, will you get up, will
you get up?*
*Lazy Mary, will you get up, will you get up this
morning?*

Oh no, mother, I won't get up, I won't get up, I
won't get up.
Oh no, mother, I won't get up, I won't get up
this morning.

*What if I make you bacon and eggs, bacon and
eggs, bacon and eggs?*
*What if I make you bacon and eggs, will you get up
this morning?*

Oh no, mother, I won't get up, I won't get up, I
won't get up.
Oh no, mother, I won't get up, I won't get up
this morning.

*What if I make you porridge and milk, porridge
and milk, porridge and milk?*
*What if I make you porridge and milk, will you get
up this morning?*

Oh no, mother, I won't get up, I won't get up, I
won't get up.
Oh no, mother, I won't get up, I won't get up
this morning.

*What if I give you a thump on the bum, a thump
on the bum, a thump on the bum?*
*What if I give you a thump on the bum, will you
get up this morning?*

Oh yes, mother, I will get up, I will get up, I will
get up.
Oh yes, mother, I will get up, I will get up this
morning.
(Traditional, Great Britain)

Mike and Michelle Jackson sing a great version of
"Lazy Mary" on their *Playmates* album, Elephant/
Larrikin Records. When you sing this song with
your child, sing alternate verses. Perhaps your
child would like to sing: *Lazy Mommy, will you get
up. . .?*

I'm a Nut (Acorn Brown)
Chorus:
I'm a nut, tch, tch, I'm a nut tch, tch,
(Touch temple for "tch")
I'm a nut, I'm a nut, I'm a nut.
Verses:
I'm a little acorn brown
(Make a circle with thumb and forefinger)
Lying on the cold, cold ground
Everybody steps on me
That is why I'm cracked you see.

I called myself on the telephone
(Dialing motions)
Just to see if I was home
I asked myself out for a date
Better be ready 'bout half-past-eight.

I take myself to the movie show
Sit myself in the second row
Put my arm around my waist
When I get fresh, I slap my face.
(Traditional, North American Summer Camp)

Sharon, Lois & Bram sing this on their *Stay
Tuned* album, Elephant Records.

Art

Your child needs a space to do messy work. She also needs to learn how to clean up after herself, so show her a simple, consistent routine. A table or large flat desk and a role of paper or unlimited newsprint are the basics. Open shelves provide space for materials and special collections. A styrofoam or cork bulletin board provides display space, as does the refrigerator door. A standing blackboard or a piece of wall painted with blackboard paint can become a family message center and stimulate brilliant ideas. If you have the space, a stand-up easel is a bonus.

COLORED SAND PAINTINGS

Mix small amounts of tempera paint powder with fine white sand. The sand must be clean, of good quality and even texture. Make several colors and place them in shaker bottles; salt shakers or spice jars, for instance. Mix liquid glue and liquid starch in equal parts and paint a design with it on a piece of paper. For fun, try black paper. Shake the sand onto the design and allow it to dry. Shake off the excess when it is dry.

PORCUPINES/HEDGEHOGS

Have your child choose several squat pine cones from her outdoor collection. Glue toothpicks or wooden matchsticks (without the illuminating tip) into the pinecone, using white glue. Stick on google eyes and use sunflower seeds for mouths. You can make a whole family and glue the figures onto a piece of wood or bark.

STAINED GLASS PICTURES

Place a piece of double-coated waxed paper over newspaper on your ironing board. Have your child make a design on the waxed paper using flat materials like crayon shavings, pieces of tissue paper, a cut-and-paste drawing, leaves, bits of confetti, mylar dots, and so on. Cover this with another piece of waxed paper, cover that with newsprint, and iron the two pieces of waxed paper together. Make a dark-colored frame or mat of light cardboard or construction paper, and hang her picture where the light will shine through.

COLORED POROUS MATERIAL

Shake about 1 tbsp of crushed egg shells, small pasta shapes, or rock salt with a drop or two of food color (diluted with a drop or two of alcohol if less intense color is desired). Use this type of colored material with goop paint (page 56), bread playdough (page 57), or as collage material for any art project.

STENCILS

Make some stencils for your child to use on her own. You can cut them out of styrofoam meat containers, cardboard or Bristol board. An Exacto knife or mat knife does a terrific job of cutting, but *must* be used by an adult. Use your imagination and your child's suggestions to create stars, outer space forms, dinosaurs, zoo animals, pets, foods, or random shapes.

Your child can use her stencils to create larger designs or to practice using chalk, paint, crayons, markers, or pencils. Save the cutouts from the stencils for her to use in collages.

PAPIER MACHÉ

My favorite way of making papier maché is to use strips of newspaper, paper towel or dryer lint dipped in the cheapest wallpaper paste available, and formed over a balloon. Create papier maché in slow stages; it should be given an opportunity to dry between every application of two or three layers, so it won't mildew.

Hint: To get long, even strips of paper, take a section of newspaper and tear it from the fold down. For large objects, tear strips 1" to 1 1/2" wide; for small objects, rip narrower strips. Store leftover paste in a cool spot.

WOODWORKING — BLOCKS

Create wooden blocks out of scrap pieces of soft wood, available at your local hardware store or lumber yard. Ask your child to sand the edges of her blocks until they are smooth. Then she can paint them with tempera paints, and after they are dry, YOU coat the colored blocks with clear shellac or urethane.

Make a crayon block by drilling crayon-thickness holes into a large block, about 2" x 4" x 6". Have your child sand and paint the block, and, *voila,* she has a crayon-holder for her desk.

STONE ANIMALS

On one of your beach walks, collect some smooth, flat stones. Glue small and large stones to create animal shapes, and have your child paint the stones with nontoxic paints. She can also paint faces on some of the stones.

Word Play

Much of your child's attention-getting is done through language, and as a result she is sometimes rude. She discovers that some words have more than one meaning and she loves word "tricks."

SIMILIES

Similies (sayings using "like" or "as") enrich your conversations with your child and give words new meaning. You and your child can make up your own, but here are some old ones to get you started:

As playful as a puppy.
As scarce as dinosaur eggs.
As rare as hen's teeth.
As nice as sugar candy.
As happy as a June bug.
As merry as a cricket.
As ugly as a mud puddle.
Cagey like a bear.
Green as grass.
Strong as an ox.
Brave as a lion.
Clear as crystal.
Neat as a pin.
Hard as a rock.
Light as a feather.

THE MAIL

Your child loves to send and receive mail. One sure way to make sure there is something in the mailbox for her is to send mail to someone else. Often there are free offers for kids; the book *Free Stuff for Kids* (Meadowlark Press) will get you started. Write fan letters to your child's favorite singers, performers, and authors; their addresses are on records and tapes, or can be obtained from publishers. Write to friends, relatives, and children who have moved away. It is never too early for your child to make and send her own "thank yous" for gifts or favors, even if it is nothing more than her handprint and a note from you. Order a subscription to a magazine designed for preschoolers: *Chickadee, Your Big Back Yard, The Sesame Street Magazine, Highlights for Children, Humpty Dumpty.*

Adam and Eve

Adam and Eve and Pinch Me went to the sea to bathe.
Adam and Eve were drowned. Who was saved?

It Was Midnight On the Ocean

It was midnight on the ocean
Not a streetcar was in sight,
The sun was shining brightly,
And it rained all day that night.
One day a boy went walking
And he walked into a store
He bought a pound of sausage meat,
And laid it on the floor.
The boy began to whistle,
He whistled up a tune,
And all the little hotdogs
Danced around the room.
(Anonymous)

Quiet Times _____

Quiet singing and favorite nursery rhymes provide a wonderful break from the day's strenuous activities. Never forget the power and magic of singing old-time favorites together.

Home on the Range

Oh, give me a home, where the buffalo roam,
Where the deer and the antelope play,
And seldom is heard, a discouraging word
And the skies are not cloudy all day.

Home, home on the range,
Where the deer and the antelope play,
And seldom is heard, a discouraging word,
And the skies are not cloudy all day.
(Traditional, North American Cowboy)

Day-O (The Banana Boat Song)

At the end of each line, chant: *Daylight come and me wanna go home.*

Day-o, me say day-o,
Day-o, me say day-o,
Work all night 'till the mornin' come,
A beautiful bunch of ripe bananas,
Stack bananas 'till the mornin' come,
Lift six hand, seven hand, eight hand, bunch,
Come Mister Tallyman*, tally me banana,
(Traditional, British Caribbean Work Song)

* The Tallyman was the worker who counted the bunches of bananas and paid the workers. The bananas were loaded onto the boats during the evening, when it was cooler than during the day. Raffi sings this song on his *Baby Beluga* album, Troubadour Records.

Old Folks At Home

Chorus:
All the world is sad and dreary,
Everywhere I roam
Oh, brother, how my heart grows weary
Far from the old folks at home.

Verses:
Way, down upon the Swannee River, far, far
away,
There's where my heart is turning ever, there's
where the old folks stay.
All up and down the whole creation, sadly I roam,
Still longing for the old plantation, and for the old
folks at home.

All round the little farm I wandered, when I was
young
Then, many happy days I squandered, many the
songs that I sung;
When I was playing with my brother, happy was I,
Oh, take me to my kind old mother, there let me
live and die.

One little hut among the bushes, one that I love,
Still sadly to my memory rushes, no matter where I
rove;
When will I see the bees a-humming, all round the
comb;
When will I hear the banjo tumming, down in my
good old home?

(Stephen C. Foster)

Red River Valley

From this valley they say you are going,
We will miss your bright eyes and sweet smile
For they say you are taking the sunshine,
That has brightened our pathways a while.

Come and sit by my side if you love me,
Do not hasten to bid me adieu,
Just remember the Red River Valley,
And the cowboy that has loved you so true.

(Traditional, North American Cowboy)

Riddle Song

I gave my love a cherry that has no stone,
I gave my love a chicken that has no bone,
I gave my love a ring that has no end,
I gave my love a baby, with no cryin'.

How can there be a cherry that has no stone?
How can there be a chicken that has no bone?
How can there be a ring that has no end?
How can there be a baby, with no cryin'?

A cherry, when it's blooming, it has no stone,
A chicken when it's pipping, it has no bone,
A ring when it's rolling, it has no end,
A baby when it's sleeping, has no cryin'.

(Traditional, Appalachia)

Growing Interests

Now is the time to try to get true rope-skipping and hand-clapping games started. The best way to learn is with a "coach," so get out there and work on your own coordination. If there are older children skipping at your playground, your child will soon be an expert!

SKIPPING ROPES

There are two standard sizes of jumpropes; one for the single jumper, and one approximately double the length used for Double Dutch jumping and for a large crowd of jumpers all skipping together. Some glow in the dark, some have ball-bearing handles, but plain old-fashioned woven cotton clothesline or sashcord is just fine. The important thing is that the rope fits your child. It should extend from the top of one armpit, down under her feet (stand on the rope with both feet), and back up to the other armpit. If her rope is too short, your child will miss too often for skipping to be fun; if it's too long she'll trip. Generally, a single rope is about seven feet long, a Double Dutch about fourteen feet. Tie a single knot at each end of the skipping rope to prevent it from fraying.

Skipping Terms

Salt: The slowest the rope can be turned, and still be jumped with rhythm.

Peppers: The fastest the rope can be turned.

Vinegar: More or less normal speed.

Mustard: Slightly faster than normal speed, the rope slaps the pavement.

Double Dutch: This works with one or two ropes. With one, the rope is folded so half of it is over the skipper's head and half is under her feet; with two ropes, the enders twirl them simultaneously. Either way requires very fast skipping.

Enders: The two people who turn a rope for the skippers.

Keep the Kettle Boiling: One skipper runs out of the rope, and another jumps in without missing a beat. Usually, the same rhyme is repeated for each skipper.

Skin, or Skinning the Cat: Skipping as fast as possible until a miss.

Turning the Corner, or Cor-ner: The skipper runs out, goes around the enders, and jumps back in as part of the rhyme.

Figure Eight: The skipper swings the rope in front of her with both hands together to form a figure eight before jumping.

Doubles: The skipper passes the rope under her feet twice for each jump.

Skipping Luck It's bad luck to jump to 100. The jumper *must* miss before 100.

EEVY, IVEY, OVER

Eevy, Ivey, Over has probably taught more children to skip than any other rhyme. The learner is in the middle, and two enders swing the rope gently back and forth just off the ground, chanting: *Eevy, Ivey, Eevy, Ivey, Eevy, Ivey. . .* Once your child is jumping comfortably over the rope, the rhyme goes:

> *Blue bells, cockle shells,*
> *Eevy, Ivey, Over head.*
>> (On "Over", the rope is rotated completely over the learner's head.)

Skilled jumpers do it this way:

> *Blue bells, cockle shells,*
> *Eevy, Ivey, Over head.*
> *My mother sent me to the store,*
> *This is what she sent me for:*
> *Salt, vinegar, mustard, PEPPER!*
>> (The jumper skips Peppers, Skinning the Cat, as long as she can.)

SINGLE DUTCH

Single Dutch, basic jumprope skipping, is very popular because it can be done alone or with friends. Here are some traditional Single Dutch skipping rhymes to get you and your child started.

Rosy Apple (Captain's Daughter)

Jenny and I love this skipping song so much, we often sing it together as we walk back and forth to school.

Rosy apple, a lemon and a pear.
A bunch of roses she shall wear
A golden pistol by her side,
Soon she'll be a bride.

Take her by the lily white hand,
Lead her across the water,
Throw her a kiss and say goodbye
She's the Captain's daughter.
(Traditional, Great Britain)

Never Laugh

Never Laugh is usually done to a salt tempo, although Josh and Danny both do it Double Dutch. Michael Cooney includes it in a medley of songs on his *Pure Unsweetened Live Family Album*, Alliance Records.

Never laugh when a hearse goes by,
Or you may be the next to die,
They wrap you up in a big white sheet,
And bury you down six feet deep.
The worms crawl in, the worms crawl out,
They come in thin, they go out stout,
And the ants play pinochle on your snout.
So never laugh when a hearse goes by
Or you may be the next to die.
(Traditional, North America)

Not Last Night

This jingle requires two enders and lots of practice.

Not last night but the night before
Twenty-four robbers came knocking at my door
And this is what they said to me:
            (Do the actions of the rhyme
"Lady, turn around, turn around, turn around.
Lady, touch the ground, touch the ground, touch
     the ground.
Lady, show your shoes, show your shoes, show
     your shoes.
Lady, that will do, that will do, that will DO."
            Run out of rope)
(Traditional, Canada)

CLAPPING MOTIONS

You and your child began clapping together when she was an infant. You probably played Pat-a-Cake and then moved on to Pease, Porridge, Hot. It's time now to start clapping more intricate rhythm patterns. The actual pattern for each rhyme isn't important, as long as you work out your motions together. Here are some possible clapping moves:

- Clapping your own hands
- Clapping your partner's hands
- Clapping your partner's right hand
- Clapping your partner's left hand
- Slapping your thighs
- Clapping one hand to the right, the other to the left
- Clapping one hand to the left, the other to the right
- Rolling your hands for a beat
- Passing your right hand over your left
- Passing your left hand over your right
- Crossing your hands and touching your shoulders
- Crossing your hands and touching your back
- Clapping your hands and crisscrossing them
- Doing a double clap
- Clapping back and front

- Clapping front and back
- Clapping together, clap right, clap together, clap left
- Passing the rhythm around a circle of people

You and your child should make up your own patterns to your favorite rhymes and songs. Then practice them to get it right. When a word repeats, do the same action for the number of repeats. Here are some traditional hand-clapping rhythms, with some basic moves. As you get familiar with the routines, vary them.

MISS MARY MACK

Start by clapping your own hands together once for *Miss*. Then clap both of your partner's hands on *Ma*, clap your own again on *ry*, and finally your partner's three times on *Mack, Mack, Mack*. Repeat the pattern for every line.

Miss Mary Mack, Mack, Mack
All dressed in black, black, black
With silver buttons, buttons, buttons
All down her back, back, back.

She asked her mother, mother, mother
For fifty cents, cents, cents
To see the elephant, elephant, elephant
Jump over the fence, fence, fence.

It jumped so high, high, high
It reached the sky, sky, sky
And didn't come down, down, down
'Til the fourth of July, ly, ly.

I asked my mother, mother, mother
For fifty more, more, more
To see the elephant, elephant, elephant
Mop up the floor, floor, floor.

He scrubbed so slow, slow, slow
He stubbed his toe, toe, toe
And that's the end, end, end
Of the elephant show, show, SHOW!
(Traditional, United States)

A SAILOR WENT TO SEA, SEA, SEA

Clap your own hands together, A, clap your partner's right hand, *sail*, clap your own, *or*, clap your partner's left hand, *went*, clap your own again, *to*, then do the action called for three times. Repeat the pattern for each line.

A sailor went to sea, sea, sea
(Touch eye for "sea" and "see")
To see what he could see, see, see
But all that he could see, see, see
Was the bottom of the deep blue sea, sea, sea.

A sailor went to diz, diz, diz
(Twirl finger around ear for "diz")
To see what he could diz, diz, diz
But all that he could diz, diz, diz
Was the bottom of the deep blue diz, diz diz.

A sailor went to knee, knee, knee
(Tap knees for "knee")
To see what he could knee, knee, knee
But all that he could knee, knee, knee
Was the bottom of the deep blue knee, knee, knee.

A sailor went to land, land, land
(Touch ground or table)
To see what he could land, land, land
But all that he could land, land, land
Was the bottom of the deep blue land, land, land.

*A sailor went to diz-knee-land**
(Twirl finger, touch knee, touch ground)
To see what he could diz-knee-land
But all that he could diz-knee-land
Was the bottom of the deep blue diz-knee-land.
(Traditional, Toronto Schoolyard)

*Disneyland, of course

IN THE LAND OF OZ

I can almost guarantee your child will bring this home from the playground, probably in a ruder version. Girls in Spain wash their knickers in champagne; girls in Oz wear no bras, and men don't care 'cause they don't wear underwear; ladies in France dance naked, and the men see it all through a hole in the wall. The clapping pattern is: partners each clap their own hands together, *In*, partners clap each others' right hands, *the*, partners clap their own, *land*, partners clap each others' left hands, *of* partners clap their own again, *Oz*. Repeat the pattern twice for each line.

> *In the land of Oz where the ladies smoke cigars*
> *Every puff they take is enough to kill a snake*
> *When the snake is dead they put roses on his head*
> *When the roses die they put diamonds in his eyes*
> *When the diamonds break, it is 1988.*
>
> (or '89, or whatever year it is)
> (Traditional, Toronto School Yard)

STELLA-ELLA-OLLA

Stella-Ella-Olla is my favorite way of finding IT when nobody wants the job. Five or more players sit or stand in a circle, hands touching. Each player places her left hand, palm up, on top of the next player's right hand, which is also palm up. The object is to pass on a single clapping rhythm around the circle.

One person starts by clapping the next person's right hand with her left hand. The rhythm continues around and around the circle in time to the song, each person receiving it on her right hand and passing it on with her left.

Every time the numbers are counted, one player is eliminated. The person who is 4 must try to get the rhythm to 5 in three tries, while the person who is to be 5 tries to snatch her hand away. If 4 succeeds, 5 is eliminated; otherwise 4 is eliminated.

Hands MUST touch before each of the three tries, and 5 has to be quick in snatching her hand away. The song is repeated until four players are eliminated.

The first two players eliminated scrunch down facing in opposite directions. Backs are up, heads are tucked, and their sides are parallel, knees flexed, to make a human table. The last two players eliminated arm-wrestle across the table. Each of the wrestlers places an elbow on a different side, so only one elbow is on one person. When one arm is forced down to the table, the loser becomes IT. Often, one side of the table will collapse in giggles!

> *Stella-Ella-Olla, clack, clack, clack.*
> *Singing eska chiggo, chiggo,*
> *Chiggo, chiggo, chack, chack*
> *Eska chiggo, chiggo*
> *Velo, velo, velo, velo, velo*
> *So: 1, 2, 3, 4, FIVE!*

Eric Nagler performs "Stella-Ella-Olla" in concert. Charlotte Diamond has recorded it on her *10 Carrot Diamond* record, Hug Bug Records, and so has Deborah Dunleavy on her *Jibbery Jive* album, Kids' Records. My version of the song comes from a Toronto schoolyard, but I would like to hear from anyone who can tell me its origin. Is "eska" perhaps a corruption of *est-ce*?

CHAPTER FIVE

FIVE TO FIVE-AND-A-HALF

"Mommy, Come See What I Found Under the Rock!!!"

OUR FIVE-YEAR-OLD readily gives and receives affection. He is bursting with enthusiasm, joy, and creativity. Growing by leaps and bounds, he is eager to experience life to the fullest and has a keen sense of adventure. Often he has a special friend who shares his interests.

While he may still experience fears and frustration, he is far better able to deal with his anxieties on his own, and may even be able to verbalize them to you.

You child is busy sorting out the world around him. He may be counting, matching shapes, or figuring out weights and measures. He may be fascinated by stars, or extinct animals, or nature, or the types of birds that come to his feeder. He may develop great powers of observation.

Movement

Your five-year-old has new speed and agility. His sense of balance is quite well developed, and he can jump over an obstacle or across a brook; he can hop long distances quickly. He loves to play action and movement games with lots of friends.

STATUES

IT is the sculptor, who twirls all the other players around, one at a time. When he lets them go, they fly into position and "freeze" as a statue. Another IT is a buyer, who touches each statue on the shoulder. The statue has to act out his frozen position. After all the statues are acting, the buyer touches them again to freeze them. If the buyer doesn't manage to freeze all the players quickly, the game turns to Tag, with the unfrozen statues able to tag the frozen ones to free them.

FLY

IT calls out out a number of animals or objects. If the object flies, players stand up and flap their arms. If it doesn't fly, they sit down. For instance: cats fly, bats* fly, rats fly, hats* fly, ducks* fly, flies* fly, hornets* fly, bonnets fly (they're tied on), pigs fly, wigs* fly, mice fly, ice flies, elephants fly, mules fly, fools* fly, robins* fly, turkeys* fly, beagles fly, dogs fly, hogs fly, … Say them fast. If a player makes a mistake, he is "out." The last person out is the next IT.

Old Betty Larkin
Tune: "Skip to My Lou"

Form a circle of partners, facing in, with one extra being IT. While everyone sings the song, IT skips around the circle and "steals" one of the players. Together they skip around to the empty space. The player whose partner was stolen then becomes IT.

Hop around, skip around, old Betty Larkin
Hop around, skip around, old Betty Larkin
Hop around, skip around, old Betty Larkin
Also my dear darling.

Needles in a haystack, old Betty Larkin
Needles in a haystack, old Betty Larkin
Needles in a haystack, old Betty Larkin
Also my dear darling.

Steal, steal, old Betty Larkin
Steal, steal, old Betty Larkin
Steal, steal, old Betty Larkin
Also my dear darling.

You take mine and I'll take another
You take mine and I'll take another
You take mine and I'll take another
Also my dear darling.
(Traditional, Appalachian)

OH, THE GOOD SHIP SAILS

The Good Ship Sails is played as an arch game. The players form a line that threads through an arch made by the two end players. The group winds around and around the arch until everyone is tied up in a large human ball. The two forming the arch try to snake their way out of the ball, with the rest of the line following.

Oh, the good ship sails on the alley alley oh
The alley alley oh, the alley alley oh
Oh, the good ship sails on the alley alley oh
On the fifth day of November*.

The big ship sank to the bottom of the sea
(Squat down for every "sank" and "bottom")
The bottom of the sea, the bottom of the sea
The big ship sank to the bottom of the sea
On the fifth day of November.

We all dip our heads in the deep blue sea
(Dip heads to one side)
The deep blue sea, the deep blue sea
We all dip our heads in the deep blue sea
On the fifth day of November.

The captain said, "This will never do,
This will never do, this will never do."
The captain said, "This will never do,
On the fifth day of November.
(Traditional, Great Britain)

* This is Guy Fawkes Day. You can substitute any other.

Using Fingers _____

Your child has probably developed a good grasp of drawing materials and is able to copy letters, trace drawings, and thread a large-holed needle. Puppets, pinwheels, jacks, hand-clapping, and lots and lots of fingerplays help develop his fingers even more.

Junior Birdsmen

Chant:

Oh my goodness, oh my soul, here comes the junior
bird patrol!

Sing:

Up in the air, junior birdsmen,

(Make thumb and forefinger goggles over eyes,

Up in the air, upside down

bend head low)

· *Up in the air, junior birdsmen,*
With your noses to the ground.

When you hear the grand announcement,

(Hands cupped over ears,

That your wings are made of tin,

Flap wings

Then you'll know you're a junior birdsman,

Goggle eyes)

So send your boxtops in.

You need five boxtops,

(Five fingers up

Four bottle bottoms,

Four fingers up

Three labels,

Three fingers up

Two wrappers,

Two fingers up

One thin dime.

One finger up

Zooooommmm!

Fly away)

(Traditional, North America Summer Camp)

ORDINARY MOVINGS

Ordinary Movings is a catch game, played alone. Say the commands and do the actions as you throw a ball against a wall.

Ordinary: Throw ball to wall and catch it.

Movings: Throw ball to wall, slap thighs but don't move feet, catch it.

Laughings: Throw ball, speak but don't laugh, catch it.

Talkings: Throw ball, Shhh sign to mouth, and catch it.

Right hand: Throw and catch the ball with the right hand.

Left hand: Throw and catch the ball with the left hand.

One foot: Throw and catch the ball while standing on one foot.

The other foot: Throw and catch while standing on the other foot.

Clap at the front: Throw ball, clap hands at front of body, catch ball.

Clap at the back: Throw ball, clap hands at back of body, catch ball.

Front and back: Throw ball, clap at front, clap at back, catch ball.

Back and front: Throw ball, clap at back, clap at front, catch ball.

Tweedles: Throw ball, roll hands forwards, catch ball.

Twiddles: Throw ball, roll hands backwards, catch ball.

It's a curtsy: Throw ball, curtsy, catch ball.

It's a bow: Throw ball, make a bow, catch ball.

It's a right salute: Throw ball, salute with right hand, catch ball.

It's a left salute: Throw ball, salute with left hand, catch ball.

It's a double salute: Throw ball, salute with right, salute with left, catch ball.

It's a double double salute: Throw ball, salute with right twice, salute with left twice, catch ball.

It's a jumpsies: Throw ball, jump in air, land, catch ball.

Away he goes: Throw ball, twirl in a circle or cross hands over chest, slap thighs, clap hands, catch ball.

(Traditional, Canada)

Once the routine is finished, start over again at the beginning, but let the ball bounce before you catch it each time.

GOD'S EYES

You need two sticks and some brilliantly colored yarn. Tie the two sticks together firmly to form an X. Starting at the center of the X, wrap the wool around one stick, turn the X, wrap the wool around the next stick, and so on around until the sticks are covered. Be sure to keep turning the X in one direction. Vary the colors for interesting effects. You might want to make one branch of the X longer, to serve as a handle.

PAPER BEADS

Using bright paper or a page torn from a colored magazine, measure and mark off dots one inch apart across the top of the paper. Turn the paper upside down, measure the first dot 1/2 inch in, and then space the rest of the dots 1 inch apart across the new top. Connect the lines using a ruler, so the paper looks like a backgammon game. Cut along the lines. Starting at the widest end of the triangular pieces, roll the paper up around a toothpick, matchstick, straw, or knitting needle, and glue the point down. When the bead is dry, remove the toothpick and use it again. String the beads together to make a necklace or bracelet, or to use as art materials. You can add sequins or glitter, and dip the beads into watered-down white glue to make them shine.

Indoor Games

You child is getting more and more interested in playing simple board games, cards, and dominoes. You might want to introduce games like Snakes and Ladders, Chinese Checkers, Checkers, or Bingo. He likes to record his thoughts on paper. Write down his stories for him, and perhaps start a daily journal of his activities.

DOMINOES/BONES (two players)

Dominoes, or Bones, are small, rectangular tiles that usually come in a set of twenty-eight. The best sets for kids have the tiles divided in half in such a way that any possible combination of dots from zero to six is shown on each side of the tile. They run from 0/0 to 6/6.

The tiles are placed face down, each player draws seven and stands them on edge so the other player can't see them. The highest double plays first by laying down his tile, face up. If there is no double, the tiles are reshuffled and redrawn. The other player must match the number of spots shown on the tile. If the player doesn't have a tile with the number shown, he draws from the bone-yard until he can match the number of dots or until he has all the pieces. If he can't play, the play passes to the other player. There are always two open ends on which to play. For instance, if a double five (5/5) is the first domino played, the next player can play any domino that has a 5; for instance, 5/6, 5/4, 5/3, 5/2, 5/1, or 5/0. If the second player plays 5/6, then the first player can play any bone that has either a 5 or a 6.

When one player is out of bones he is "domi-no," and the number of spots on the opponent's bones are counted. The first person to reach 100 points loses. By the time Jenny turned six, I gave up playing dominoes, because *I* hate to lose all the time.

CONCENTRATION

Lay out a complete deck of cards, face down. The floor is the easiest place to play because you need lots of room. The cards can be placed randomly or in rows. Each player, in turn, turns over two cards. If the cards match, the player captures those cards. If they don't match, he turns them face down. Each card should be left face up for five seconds. The object is to remember the position of the cards and so collect the most pairs.

DAILY JOURNAL

Put together a journal of your child's stories. The journal might be a record of the day's events or a progressive accumulation of his artwork. You might want to put in a few photos and words of your own. You might want to make a special book for a limited period of time, like a family holiday, a school year, or a first season of Tee Ball. Any parent of grown children who has not kept a book or box of remembrances regrets it.

PROGRESSIVE STORY

One person starts a story, and each player adds a line, in turn. You may want to tape record the adventure or write it down, because it's certain to be eventful! For instance, you might start:

"One night I heard footsteps outside my tent. "Thump, Thump, THUMP-THUMP…"

CRACKERS

Do you seem to be always running out of crackers? They're our favorite snack food and we often make our own.

Cheese Crackers

Shred and measure 2 cups of hard cheese (like cheddar).

Using a food processor, pastry blender, or your hands, blend the cheese with 1/2 cup of butter or margarine, 1 cup of sifted flour and 1/4 tsp of salt. Have your child roll the pastry into balls or worms and flatten them on a cookie sheet, approximately 1" apart. Bake at 375°F for about ten minutes, depending on the size and thickness of the crackers.

Graham Crackers

Cream together 1/2 cup of butter or margarine and 2/3 cup of brown sugar.

Mix together:
2 3/4 cup graham flour
1/2 tsp salt
1/2 tsp baking powder
1/4 tsp ground cinnamon

Add this mixture and 1/2 cup of cold water to the butter and sugar mixture. Mix well and let stand for 30 minutes. Roll out the dough, approximately 1/8" thick, onto a floured board. Cut into 2" squares, place on a greased cookie sheet, and bake 20 minutes in a 350°F oven. Makes approximately three dozen.

Outdoors

RINGER/MARBLES

Draw a circle, between three and ten feet in diameter, with sidewalk chalk on flat pavement. Every player puts a specified number of marbles to use as a target in the middle of the circle. There must be between two and three inches between each marble. Draw another line about ten feet from the outside of the circle. Each player shoots a marble (the shooter) at the circle from behind this line. The player with the closest marble goes first. He tries to hit the target marbles and knock them out of the ring. If he is successful, he gets to keep whatever marbles are outside the circle and takes another turn. If the shooter remains inside the circle, it becomes a target marble for the other players, or it can be ransomed for a specified number (usually five) of target marbles. A player can shoot with either knuckles (Fingies) or by placing the outside of one foot against the marble and kicking his instep with the other foot (Footsies). All players have to agree to either Fingies or Footsies before starting the game and must remain outside the circle at all times. The winner is the person who captures the most marbles. Play for Funsies, not Keepsies.

HIT THE PENNY

You need a sidewalk with a crack (a concrete casting crack will do), two players, a coin, and a ball. Place the coin, on edge, in the sidewalk crack. The players stand one concrete casting block back on opposite sides of the coin, and take turns throwing the ball at the coin, so it bounces and the other player catches it. The first player to hit the coin twenty-one times wins the game, and *maybe* the coin. It counts for two hits when the coin flips.

STONE CATCH

Find six small, flat stones; the skipping stones found at a beach are perfect. Throw one stone in the air and try to catch it on the back of your hand. Then throw two stones and catch them on the back of your hand. Keep on adding a stone until you can catch them all. If you are playing this game with a friend, take turns after you miss one.

ROCKET LAUNCH

Borrow a running shoe from the biggest dad you know. Draw a line on the ground to stand on, put on the shoe, and kick it off as far as you can. Measure the distance and record the best of three tries. Let your friends try, too.

FOX AND GEESE

Draw or stamp out a huge wheel, divided pie-like into spokes, on snow, on sand at the beach or park, or on a paved area. The hub of the wheel is the Fox's den. He tries to catch the other players, the Geese, who are spread out along the rim of the wheel, and put them in his den. Captured Geese can be freed by being tagged by other players. The last Goose caught is the next Fox.

DODGE BALL

You need a large ball, like a beach ball, and lots of people. The players are divided into two equal teams, the Dodgers and the Throwers. The Dodgers are inside a large circle and the Throwers are spread around the outside. The Throwers try to hit a Dodger with the ball. They may throw directly or pass the ball to other members of the Throwers team who are in a better position. If a Dodger is hit, he leaves the center of the ring and becomes a Thrower. Once everyone is out, the original teams trade places. Try to keep the ball low so no one gets hurt.

THE MILLER'S GROUND

The Miller, IT, establishes a Miller's Ground, or jail, at one end of a playground. Another marked space is set up at the other end of the playground to be home base or den. The players sing and dance up to the edge of the Miller's Ground. The boldest may trespass, but should not go too near the Miller. The Miller must not move until the word "Come" is sung. Then all the players scatter and run back to their den, while the Miller tries to capture one, who will be Miller for the next game. The tune of the song is "Aikendrum."

I'm on the miller's ground, the miller's ground, the miller's ground
I'm on the miller's ground, and the miller, he's at home.

He dare not catch me, catch me, catch me,
He dare not catch me, until I do say "Come."
(Traditional, Great Britain)

Music _____

PLINKER

Make your own musical instrument. Cut a large round hole out of the lid of a shoebox. Stretch a half dozen rubber bands lengthwise around the bottom of the shoebox, about an inch or so apart. Put the lid back on. Pluck and release the rubber bands through the hole at the top of the box.

Down By The Bay

Down by the bay, where the watermelons grow,
Back to my home, I dare not go.
For if I do, my mother will say:
"Did you ever see a fish, eating from a dish?"
Down by the bay.

Subsequent verses have different silly fourth lines. Try these or make up your own.

... a frog, dancing on a log?
... a star, driving a car?
... Donald Duck, driving a truck?
... a snail, going for a sail?
... a moose, with a loose tooth?
... a cow, with a green eyebrow?
... a bee, with a sunburned knee?
(Traditional, North America)

Animal Fair

I went to the Animal Fair, the birds and the beasts were there
The big baboon by the light of the moon, was combing his auburn hair.
The monkey he got drunk, and sat on the elephant's trunk
The elephant sneezed, and fell on his knees, and that was the end of the monk, the monk, the monk.
(Repeat until bored or tired.)
(Traditional, North America, Great Britain)

Boom Boom, Ain't It Great To Be Crazy?
Chorus and First Verse:
Boom boom, ain't it great to be crazy?
Boom boom, ain't it great to be crazy?
Silly and foolish all day long.
Boom boom, ain't it great to be crazy?

A horse and a flea and three blind mice.
Sat on a curbstone shooting dice.
The horse he slipped and fell on the flea!
Whoops! said the flea, there a horse on me.
(Traditional, United States)

New River Train

Chorus:

I'm ridin' that new river train
I'm ridin' that new river train
Same old train that brought me here
Gonna take me back home again.

Verses:

Oh darlin' you can't love one
Darlin' you can't love one
You can't love one and still have any fun
Oh darlin' you can't love one.

Oh darlin' you can't love two,
Oh darlin' you can't love two
You can't love two, and hope that I'll be true
Oh darlin' you can't love two.

… three, and keep your love of me.
… four, and love me any more.
… five, and keep our love alive
… six, 'cause six and love don't mix
… seven, and still go up to heaven
… eight, and get through that pearly gate
… nine, and expect the sun to shine
… ten, or I'll sing this song again.

Oh darlin' remember what you said
Oh darlin' remember what you said
Remember that you said you would rather see me
*   dead*
Than ridin' on that new river train.

I'm leavin' on that new river train
I'm leavin' on that new river train
Same old train that brought me here,
Goin' to carry me back home again.

(Traditional, United States)

One Man Went To Mow

One man went to mow, went to mow a meadow
One man and his dog (woof) went to mow a
*   meadow.*

Two men went to mow, went to mow a meadow.
Two men, one man and his dog (woof) went to
*   mow a meadow.*

Three men went to mow, went to mow a meadow.
Three men, two men, one man and his dog (woof)
*   went to mow a meadow.*

This is another of those songs that can be cumulative until infinity. One more man joins the mowers for each new verse. You can end it with:

The village went to mow, went to mow a meadow
The village, 99, 98, 97, 96 men … and his dog
*   (woof) went to mow a meadow.*

(Traditional, North America)

You can hear a fantastic version of "One Man Went to Mow" on the *Banana Split (More Mariposa in the Schools)* album, CBC Records.

The Old Grey Mare

Chorus:

Many long years ago
Many long years ago
The old grey mare she ain't what she used to be
Many long years ago.

Verses:

The old grey mare she ain't what she used to be,
Ain't what she used to be, ain't what she used to be,
The old grey mare she ain't what she used to be,
Many long years ago.

The old grey mare, she sat on an 'lectric chair
Burnt off her underwear, guess what was under
*   there?*
The old grey mare she sat on an 'lectric chair
Many long years ago.

(Traditional, United States)

Oh Susannah!

Chorus:

Oh Susannah, oh, don't you cry for me;
I come from Alabama with my banjo on my knee.

Verses:

I come from Alabama with my banjo on my knee,
I'm going to Louisiana now, my true love for to see.
It rained all night the day I left, the weather it was
*   dry.*
The sun so hot, I froze to death, Susannah, don't
*   you cry.*

I had a dream the other night, when everything was
*   still,*
I thought I saw Susannah dear, a comin' down the
*   hill.*
The buckwheat cake was in her mouth, the tear
*   was in her eye,*
Says I, "I'm comin' from the south, Susannah,
*   don't you cry.*

I soon will be in New Orleans, and then I'll look
*   around,*
And when I find Susannah, I'll fall upon the
*   ground.*
And if I do not find her, then surely I will die,
And when I'm dead and buried, Susannah, don't
*   you cry.*

(Traditional, Southern United States)

Jonathan Edwards sings "Oh Susannah" on the
Grandma's Patchwork Quilt album, American
Melody Records.

There's A Hole In the Bucket

This is a response song. You sing one verse, and
your child responds with the next.

There's a hole in the bucket, dear Liza, dear Liza
There's a hole in the bucket, dear Liza, a hole.

Well fix it, dear Henry, dear Henry, dear Henry
Well fix it, dear Henry, dear Henry, FIX IT!

… *With what shall I fix it, dear Liza…?*
… With straw, dear Henry…

… *The straw is too long, dear Liza…*
… Well, cut it, dear Henry…

… *With what shall I cut it, dear Liza…?*
… With an axe, dear Henry…

… *The axe is too blunt, dear Liza…*
… Well, sharpen it, dear Henry…

… *With what shall I sharpen it, dear Liza…?*
… With a stone, dear Henry…

… *The stone is too dry, dear Liza…*
… Well, wet it, dear Henry…

… *With what shall I wet it, dear Liza…?*
… With water, dear Henry…

… *Where shall I get it, dear Liza…?*
… At the well, dear Henry…?

… *With what shall I fetch it, dear Liza…?*
… With a bucket, dear Henry…

But there's a HOLE in the bucket, dear Liza, dear
*   Liza,*
There's a hole in the bucket, dear Liza, a HOLE!

(Traditional, North America)

Art

With his ever-increasing dexterity, your child can handle more complicated art materials. Generally, he knows what he needs to put together his projects.

PLAITING/BRAIDING

Tie together three equal lengths of gimp, heavy wool, or strands of an interesting fabric. Different colored strands will make the braiding easier when he is learning. Tie the knot onto a doorknob or chair and separate the strands so one is on the left, one is in the center, and one is on the right. Pick up the left-hand thread and bring it over the center one. Pick up the right-hand thread and bring it over what was the left thread, but is now the center. (What was the left thread is now the right, what was the right thread is now the center, what was the center thread is now the left.) Pick up the left thread and make it the new center one. Continue alternating: left to center, right to center. Tie off when your length is complete.

SPOOL KNITTING/CORKING

Corking or spool knitting can provide hours of entertainment once your child has the ability to control the spool. Usually, this occurs when he can print some of his letters recognizably. You can buy a spool or make your own by nailing four small finishing nails equidistant around the top of a wooden spool.

Drop a tail of wool down through the spool, then loop the yarn around each of the nails. Working clockwise, loop the yarn around each nail, giving the tail a tug after each round. When the "rope" of corking gets long enough, you can show your child how to sew it together to make a hot mat for the table or a rug for a dollhouse. For the last round, slip the stitch off each post in succession, pull the tail of the wool through them tightly, and weave in the end. This is a great way to use up old scraps of yarn.

TRACING

Give your child a felt marker and a pad of tracing paper to trace favorite pictures and textures. Give him a piece of chalk, conté, or charcoal, and show him how to make rubbings of tree bark, concrete surfaces, coins, patterned floors, anything flat that has texture. Ask him to cut out his tracings and rubbings to use in collages.

PINWHEELS

Fold a square piece of paper or thin plastic, diagonally. Fold it the other way, diagonally. Unfold the paper. Cut the diagonals at least half way towards the center of the square. Fold the left side of each diagonal into the center, so that all four edges overlap. Pin through all four cuts and the center of the square, and attach it onto a stick or wine cork. Alternatively, you can put a spot of glue onto the center flaps, poke a hole in the middle and put a string through it, so it will rotate when the string is suspended. You can also use a brass fastener to stick through the four flaps and the center. Decorate the pinwheel with markers, glitter, mylar, tinsel, or whatever is at hand.

Words and Ideas _____

You child loves nonsense verse, poetry, riddles, and proverbs. By using the ancient maxims we offer our children the wisdom of the ages. Proverbs introduce your child to the richness of his language and offer complex information subtly. Here are some of the most common ones:

Hold your horses.
Keep your shirt on.
Don't get your knickers in a knot.
You swallowed that, hook, line and sinker.
You might as well eat soup with a fork.
He has brass enough to make a door knocker.
A barking dog never bites.
Never look a gift horse in the mouth.
Make hay while the sun shines.
All that glitters is not gold.
A stitch in time saves nine.
Better late than never.
A watched pot never boils.
Birds of a feather flock together.
Never put off 'til tomorrow what can be done today.
Every cloud has a silver lining.
A fool and his money are soon parted.
It's a long lane that has no turning.
If you want to travel fast, go the old road.
Words cannot be taken back.
Cheerful company shortens the miles.
The road is never long to a friend's house.
Happiness is meant to be shared.
A drop of honey catches more flies than vinegar.
A joy that is shared is a joy made double.
The day is lost in which one has not laughed.

Praise loudly, blame softly.
Sing, and cares disperse.
A bird in the hand is worth hundreds flying.
Frogs in the well are ignorant of the ocean.
Don't leave a thief in charge of the money.
One already wet doesn't feel the rain.
You never get what you want by lying on the ground.
Better the cottage where one is happy than the palace where one weeps.

You probably remember lots more that your grandparents told you — pass them along to your child.

There Was a Young Lady
There was a young lady of Riga
Who went for a ride on a Tiger
They came back from the ride
With the lady inside
And a smile on the face of the Tiger.

A Sailor, Who Sailed From Quebec
A sailor, who sailed from Quebec,
In a storm ventured out upon deck;
But the waves of the sea
Were as strong as could be,
And he tumbled in, up to his neck.

Ladies and Jellybeans
Ladies and jellybeans,
I come before you, not behind you
To tell you something I know nothing about.
I went to the show tomorrow
And took a front seat at the back.
I fell from the floor to the gallery,
And hurt the front of my back.
The man at the door was shouting:
"Admission is free, pay at the door,
Pull up a chair, and sit on the floor."
(Anonymous)

One Fine October Morning

One fine October morning
In September, last July,
The moon lay thick upon the ground,
The snow shone in the sky.
The flowers were singing gaily,
And the birds were in full bloom.
I went down to the cellar
To sweep an upstairs room.
(Anonymous)

Quiet Times _____

Be sure to include singing, cuddling, and reading favorite stories together in your go-to-bed routine. Naps are probably a thing of the past by now, but you can still have a cuddle together in the afternoon.

Cockles and Mussels

Chorus:
Alive, alive oh! Alive, alive oh!
Crying "Cockles and Mussels, alive, alive oh!"
Verses:
In Dublin's fair city, where girls are so pretty,
I first set my eyes on sweet Molly Malone,
She drove her wheelbarrow through streets old and
*   narrow,*
Crying "Cockles and Mussels, alive, alive oh!"

She was a fishmonger, but sure 'twas no wonder,
For so were her father and mother before;
And they each wheel'd their barrow through streets
*   old and narrow,*
Crying "Cockles and Mussels, alive, alive oh!"

She died of a fever, and no one could save her,
And that was the end of Sweet Molly Malone;
Her ghost wheels her barrow through streets old
*   and narrow,*
Crying "Cockles and Mussels, alive, alive oh!"
(Traditional, Ireland)

Deep River (Croon)

Deep river
My home is over Jordan, Lord.
Deep river
I want to cross over into camp ground.
(Traditional, American Spiritual)

On Top of Old Smokey

On top of Old Smokey, all covered with snow
I lost my true lover by courtin' too slow.

A courting is pleasure, and parting is grief,
But a false-hearted lover is worse than a thief.

A thief will but rob you, of all that you save,
But a false-hearted lover, will send you to the
*   grave.*

They'll tell you they love you, to give your heart
*   ease,*
But when you turn from them, they court whom
*   they please.*

Way up on Old Smokey, all covered with snow
I lost my true lover, by sparking too slow.
(Traditional, Southern United States)

Green Grow the Lilacs

Green grow the lilacs, all sparkling with dew,
I'm lonely my darlin' since partin' with you.
But by our next meetin' I'll hope to prove true,
And change the green lilacs to the red, white and
*   blue.*

I once had a sweetheart, but now I have none,
Since she's gone and left me, I care not for one.
Since she's gone and left me, contented I'll be,
For she loves another one better than me.
(Traditional, United States Cowboy)

Oh Shenandoah

Oh Shenandoah, I long to hear you,
Away, you rolling river.
Oh Shenandoah, I long to hear you
Away, I'm bound to go, cross the wide Missouri.

Oh Shenandoah, I love your daughter,
Away, you rolling river!
Oh Shenandoah, I love your daughter,
Away, I'm bound to go, cross the wide Missouri.

Oh Shenandoah, I took a notion,
Away, you rolling river!
To sail across the stormy ocean
Away, I'm bound to go, cross the wide Missouri.

Oh Shenandoah, I'm bound to leave you,
Away, you rolling river!
Oh Shenandoah, I'll not deceive you,
Away, I'm bound to go, cross the wide Missouri.
(Traditional, North America)

Growing Interests

Your child loves investigating, trying out, watching, observing, and exploring the world around him. Help him plant some seeds, be interested when he turns over rocks, watches insects (give him a magnifying glass) and tries different experiments. A trip to a science center, observatory, planetarium, museum, or zoo will all encourage him. If you have a broken clock or small appliance you are about to throw away, give him a screwdriver and let him take it apart.

GROWING "CORAL" CRYSTALS

On a glass plate, place pieces of damp broken brick, charcoal, porous rock, bits of synthetic sponge or foam rubber. Mix together, in a glass jar, 6 tbsps water, 3 tbsps household salt, 6 tbsps laundry blueing, and 3 tbsps nonsudsing household ammonia. Pour this mixture over the materials on the plate. Sprinkle a drop or two of food coloring and 3 tbsps of table salt over everything.

Watch and wait for several days. After the growth stops, squirt on a drop or two more of ammonia, and it will start again. Use ammonia only in a well-ventilated area. An adult must mix and handle the chemicals.

SHINY PENNIES

Have your child get a handful of pennies from his piggy bank. Pick out some that are dull and tarnished. Have him put 1/4 cup of vinegar and 1/4 cup of water in a glass. Add 3 tbsps of salt. Drop in the pennies and leave them for a few minutes. What happens? You can create a similar effect by placing a piece of aluminum foil in an enamel saucepan, adding about 3 tbsps of baking soda, and filling the pot with water. Add the pennies (or any silver that needs cleaning), put the pot on the stove, and bring it to a simmer. Turn off the burner and allow it to cool. Rinse the pennies well and dry. Where did the tarnish go?

BECAUSE

You make a statement and ask your child to tell you "why." For instance, you might say: "The sand castle broke. Why?" Your child might respond: "Because the waves knocked it over," or "Because the tide came in."

GROWING PLANTS

You don't need a lot of space to grow plants; a few small pots on a window sill will do. You can grow plants from dry vegetables like peas, beans, popcorn, lentils, and mung beans. What happens when we plant potato eyes, carrot tops, a garlic clove, orange seeds, an avocado pit or a sprouting onion?

MAGNETS

Give your child several magnets. Ask him, "What can you do with them?" Put a magnet on a string, throw some washers or metal nuts and bolts into a bucket of water or sandbox, and go fishing. Show him that polarity both attracts and repels when you have two magnets together. Crumple some steel wool (not the kind with soap) onto some paper. Put a magnet under the paper and see what happens. Go on a hunt in your house to find out what metals the magnets will stick to and what metals they won't.

SOAP BOAT

Cut two corners off one end of a rectangular bar of "floatable" soap, to form a point. Drill a hole in the middle of the opposite end. Insert a straight magnet, North Pole end to the center, into the hole. The magnet should be between an inch and an inch-and-a-half long. Seal the hole with a few drops of melted soap, candle wax, or crayon. The magnet should be pointing toward the point formed at the other end of the soap bar.

When your child puts the soap in his bath or in a dish of water, the arrow will move around until it points to the magnetic North Pole. Give him a larger magnet and have him place it near his boat. What happens when the North Poles are put near each other? What happens when the South Pole is put near the North Pole?

You can use a block of wood to make a permanent boat, too.

ELECTRIC BALLOONS

Electricity is magic for your child. Explain that electricity is all around us; we use it to start the car, it is lightning in the sky, it runs our appliances and lights our flashlights. When we walk across the carpet and touch the cat, or another person, we sometimes get a shock. When we take off our clothes in a dark room we sometimes see sparks of static electricity. Ask you child to rub a balloon on his hair. Why is his hair flying all around? It's the electricity. Stick the balloon to the wall; that's electricity, too. Try the balloon trick at night, in a dark, dark room. Do you see or hear anything when you rub the balloon on your hair? (This works best on a cold, dry day.)

MAGNIFYING GLASS

Your child needs his own, unbreakable magnifying glass to enable him to look closely at his favorite specimens. Rocks, insects, leaves, flowers, feathers or any of his other "finds" contain minute detail that he would otherwise miss.

CHAPTER SIX

FIVE-AND-A-HALF TO SIX

"Long Ago There Was A Dinosaur Named Dinah Dimetredon Who Was a Downhill Skier."

YOUR FIVE-AND-A-HALF-YEAR-OLD is becoming more interesting, challenging, charming, creative, and original. She loves her friends and usually works well in a group, although there may be some tempestuous moments.

Her teeth may be starting to loosen. She can easily become a member of the group of kids playing around the neighborhood, so you only see her at snack times. Often, she has enough dexterity to print letters, numbers, and words, and do intricate handwork.

Her creativity is blossoming. Her projects are detailed, and require concentration. Her insatiable curiosity is apparent in all aspects of her life. She is probably strong, steady, graceful, and nimble in her movements. Her self-esteem is growing. She is learning the rewards of generosity and how to wait for turns. Sometimes she is even able to delay her own desires.

Her increased vocabulary enhances her ability to use words effectively and to tell her experiences at length. The stories she listens to can increase in complexity, as she listens for longer and longer periods of time.

Movement _____

Full of the joy of life, your child's physical activity seems nonstop. Dancing, swimming, gym, and sports activities all contribute to your child's growing body skills. She jumps high as the sky, climbs higher than the tallest mountain, is as noisy as can be, and runs as fast as the wind. Just ask her, and she'll tell you all about it; her activity games are full of drama.

DOWN, DOWN, BABY

Down, Down, Baby is a great action game. It's a wonderful skipping rhyme that also works for hand-clapping rhythms. Do the body motions, too.

Down, down, baby, down by the rollercoaster
(Hand movements like a rollercoaster
Sweet, sweet baby, I'd never let you go
Hug self, blow kisses
Shimmy shimmy cocoa pop
Shimmy dance, arms up for "pop"
Shimmy shimmy pow!
Shimmy dance, arms out for "pow")
Shimmy shimmy cocoa pop
Shimmy shimmy pow!

Doctor Knickerbocker number nine
(Continue shimmying, nine fingers up
He sure got drunk on a bottle of wine
He called for the doctor and the doctor said:
Dial imaginary telephone
Now let's get the rhythm of the head, ding dong
Now let's get the rhythm of the head, ding dong
Flip head back and forth
Now let's get the rhythm of the hands, clap clap
Now let's get the rhythm of the hands, clap clap
Clap hands
Now let's get the rhythm of the feet, stomp stomp
Now let's get the rhythm of the feet, stomp stomp
Stomp feet
Now let's get the rhythm of the hot dog, hot dog
Now let's get the rhythm of the hot dog, hot dog
Wiggle and swivel hips
Now put them all together, and what do you get?
Ding dong, clap clap, stomp stomp, hot dog!
Do all the actions
Now put them all backwards, and what do you get?
Hot dog, stomp stomp, clap clap, ding dong.
Do all the actions in reverse)
(Traditional, North America)

FIRE

Fire is a great game of strategy, a cross between tag and keep away. IT is the arsonist who tries to keep the other players, the firefighters, away from a fire. If IT grabs or tags another player, that player becomes IT, and the first IT becomes a firefighter. A line, about ten feet long, is scratched or drawn on the ground. The fire station is behind the line (out of reach of IT), and four spots, called "F," "I," "R," or "E" can burn down unless the firefighters reach the fire. These spots are on the other side of the line. IT can roam any place on the line, but one foot must always be on the line. IT calls out letters, and the firefighters have to race to the spot that's burning, without being tagged. When fires are not burning, firefighters return to the fire station, again without being caught.

RED LIGHT

You need at least two players. One is IT; the others form a line about thirty feet away. IT turns her back, covers her eyes, and counts *1, 2, 3, RED LIGHT* and turns around. Anyone caught moving goes back to the starting line. IT turns back again, counts *1, 2, 3, RED LIGHT*, and again sends back those caught moving. IT can turn and then swivel back suddenly without starting to count to try and catch a moving player. However, once IT starts counting she must go all the way to *RED LIGHT* before she turns. The first person to touch IT while her back is turned becomes the next IT.

BROWN GIRL IN THE RING

Brown Girl in the Ring is a popular circle game played thoughout the Caribbean. Brown Girl, IT, skips around inside the circle of players, who are also dancing and singing:

There's a Brown Girl in the ring, la la la la la,
There's a Brown Girl in the ring, la la la la la la,
There's a Brown Girl in the ring, la la la la la,
She likes sugar, I like plum, plum, plum.

Show me your motion, la la la la la,
(The Brown Girl twists, hops,
Show me your motion, la la la la la la
hootchie-kootchies, or does any
Show me your motion, la la la la la,
other motion, as the rest circle)
She likes sugar, I like plum, plum, plum.

Very pretty motion, la la la la la
(The circle of players drops hands
Very pretty motion, la la la la la la,
and imitates the Brown Girl's
Very pretty motion, la la la la la
motion, she skips around again.)
She likes sugar, I like plum, plum, plum.

Spin and find a partner, la la la la la,
(Brown Girl spins, eyes closed,
Spin and find a partner, la la la la la la,
arm pointed to select the next
Spin and find a partner, la la la la la,
Brown Girl.)
She likes sugar, I like plum, plum, plum.
(Traditional, British Caribbean)

THE ENGLISH SOLDIERS

Two teams advance and retreat in time to the music, singing alternate verses. The players on each team have their arms linked. When they get to "fight," they have a mock battle, while hopping on one foot and trying to push a member of the opposite team over. If the other foot touches the ground, that person is deemed "killed in action" and is out of the game.

Have you any bread or wine for we are the Romans?
Have you any bread or wine for we are the Roman soldiers?

Yes, we have some bread and wine for we are the English.
Yes, we have some bread and wine for we are the English soldiers.

Will you give us some of it for we are the Romans?
Will you give us some of it for we are the Roman soldiers?

No, we'll give you none of it for we are the English.
No, we'll give you none of it for we are the English soldiers.

Then we'll tell our King on you for we are the Romans.
Then we'll tell our King on you for we are the Roman soldiers.

What care I for King or you for we are the English?
What care I for King or you for we are the English soldiers?

Are you ready for a fight, for we are the Romans?
Are you ready for a fight, for we are the Roman soldiers?

Yes, we're ready for a fight for we are the English.
Yes, we're ready for a fight for we are the English soldiers.

(Traditional, Great Britain)

JENNY JONES

Jenny Jones is a group drama game with two ITS; one plays Jenny and one plays Mother. Something dreadful has happened to Jenny, who plays dead in a corner. The friends call on Mother and want Jenny to come out and play. When Mother says that Jenny is dead and carried to the grave, the entire group carries Jenny off by her wrists, ankles, under her back, however they can carry her. When her ghost screams, all the players scamper, and Jenny is IT for a game of tag. The first one tagged is the next Jenny Jones.

The group sings the first verse and alternate verses; Mother sings the rest of the song.

Group:
We've come to see Miss Jenny Jones, Miss Jenny Jones, Miss Jenny Jones.
We've come to see Miss Jenny Jones, and how is she today?

Mother:
Miss Jenny Jones is washing, washing, washing,
Miss Jenny Jones is washing, you cannot see her now.

Group:
We've come to see Miss Jenny Jones, Miss Jenny Jones, Miss Jenny Jones.
We've come to see Miss Jenny Jones, and how is she today?

Mother:
Miss Jenny Jones is ironing, ironing, ironing,
Miss Jenny Jones is ironing, you cannot see her now.

Mother's Responses:
Miss Jenny Jones is scrubbing...
Miss Jenny Jones is sick in bed...
Miss Jenny Jones is dying...
Miss Jenny Jones lies stiff and dead...

Group:

Well, when can we see her, see her, see her,
Well, when can we see her, and how is she today?

Mother:

You can see her at the funeral, the funeral, the funeral,
You can see her at the funeral, you cannot see her now.

Mother:

Miss Jenny Jones is dead, dead, dead,
(Mother joins the group to
Miss Jenny Jones is dead, and carried to the grave.
carry off Jenny)

All:

I dreamt I saw her ghost last night, her ghost last night, her ghost last night
I dreamt I saw her ghost last night, under the apple tree.

The ghost rose up and said to me, said to me, said to me,
The ghost rose up and said to me...... SCREAM!
(Jenny shrieks)
(Traditional, Great Britain, North America)

Using Fingers

Your child is able to distinguish left from right most of the time, for both mittens and shoes. She can thread a large tapestry needle or bodkin to use in her art projects, and sew and lace quite effectively. She is probably able to copy most, if not all, capital letters of the alphabet, draw a triangle, and write her own name from memory.

POTSIES (MARBLES)

At this age, play marbles for "funsies," not "keepsies." Two or more players can play Potsies. One player twirls on her heel on soft ground to make a hole about five inches in diameter and three inches deep. This is the Pot. Decide whether you will play Fingies or Footsies. Fingies means the marbles are aimed with a flexed index finger; Footsies is done by tapping one foot with the other to roll the marble that is propped against the outside edge of one foot.

A line is drawn about ten feet away from the Pot, and each player throws one marble. The closest to the Pot (or the last in the Pot) starts rolling the rest of the marbles in, starting with the closest. If this person misses, the player with the second closest marble plays next, and so on. Whoever gets the last marble in takes the Pot.

BOUNCE (MARBLES)

Draw a circle about a foot in diameter. Each player places two or more marbles in the circle and takes turns standing over the top of the circle and dropping her marble straight down, from eye-level, trying to knock the most marbles out of the circle. The player captures any marbles she's knocked out of the circle and takes back her shooter. If the shooter misses, it remains to become another target marble. The game is over when no marbles are left as targets.

STRADDLES (MARBLES)

Two players sit opposite each other, about six feet apart, legs in a straddle position. Each player places four or five marbles inside her straddle. The first player flicks a marble to try and hit one of the marbles of the other player. If she is successful, she takes the marble; if not, it stays on the other player's side. Take turns. If shooters are used, the player can reclaim her marble by ransoming it for five dibs.

SEED MOSAIC

Collect a number of different-colored dried beans, peas, pasta, and seeds. You can use watermelon seeds, dried kidney beans, popcorn kernels, lima beans, pea beans, lentils, black beans, sunflower seeds, or anything similar you have in your cupboard. Glue the seeds to Bristol board, sturdy cardboard, or a piece of wood paneling in a mosaic design.

DOTS AND LINES

You need two players, a piece of paper, and two pencils. Draw a square of three, four, five, or six dots. Each player, in turn, joins two dots with a straight line. The object is to complete as many boxes as possible. When you finish a box, you write your initial in it and take another turn.

Indoor Games

Your child is probably getting more and more interested in playing board games. Depending on your own interests, you may want to play Scrabble (try the children's edition first), Monopoly, Cootie, Parcheesi, Snakes and Ladders, Checkers, Chinese Checkers, Dominoes, Backgammon, or simple card games. Cards develop skill in counting, separating, and organizing.

GO FISH (two to five players)

Deal six cards to each player and place the remaining cards face down in the center of the table. Each player picks up her cards and holds them in a fan. The players check their hands to see if they have any pairs. If they do, they place them face down on the table, each new pair overlapping the one beneath it so they can be counted at the end of the game. The object of the game is to get the most pairs.

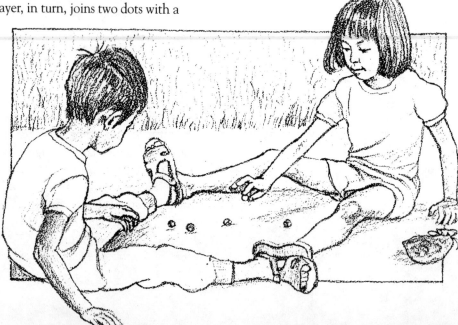

The player to the left of the dealer asks the player to her left "Do you have any (jacks)? The asker must have at least one of the card in her hand. If the player asked has the card, he must hand it over. If not, he tells the asker to "Go Fish." The asker then selects a card from the pile. She continues to ask for matches to her cards as long as she is successful in making pairs. When she misses, it's the next player's turn.

The game is over when all the cards are paired, and the winner is the player with the most pairs. If your child doesn't know numbers, she can ask "Do you have any of these (nines)?" and show the card.

CHEAT

You need between two and seven players. The object is to get rid of all your cards. All the cards are dealt to the players, one at a time, face down. The last card is turned face up in the middle of the table. Each player sorts her cards into the four suits.

The players lay down one card at a time, face down, on top of the card on the table. The cards *should* be the same suit as the one on the table, but any card *can* be laid down. If a player suspects another player has cheated, she says "Cheat," and the player must turn over the card she has just played. If she cheated, she must pick up all the cards on the table; if she didn't, the caller must pick up all the cards. The player who picks up the cards places a new card of a different suit face up on the table, and play continues. The first player to get rid of all her cards is the winner.

PICKUP STICKS

Pickup Sticks come in a package of about 24 very slender wooden or plastic sticks, about 7 inches long. The player gathers the sticks into one hand and drops them. When they land, some are on top of others, and the object is to pick up as many sticks as possible without moving any of the others. The first stick can be used as a lever to move another stick without touching it.

BASKETBALL PICKUP STICKS

Native people in British Columbia play a type of pickup sticks that is a little more interesting and a little more complicated. Attach a ring about 2 1/2" in diameter to one of the pick-up sticks, so it looks like a miniature basketball hoop. (A twisted pipe cleaner will work.) Stick it into the ground, and drop the sticks, one by one, from one hand. The player with the highest number in the ring wins. Once your aim gets really good, try it blindfolded! And once you're all good at that, spin the blindfolded person around before she plays.

SHOPPING

Take the time to show your child how to select the freshest and healthiest ingredients, and how to comparison shop. Talk about why you select certain brands, why certain-sized packages are a better buy than others, why you read the list of ingredients on some packages. Take the time to make some of your foods from "scratch," so she will learn that not all food appears from a carton, can, or package. What better way is there to learn about money, math, and being a smart consumer?

FRUIT SALAD

When you go to the market, select an assortment of fresh, seasonal fruit. When you get home, prepare a large bowl of fresh fruit salad that you can cover and keep in the refrigerator for several meals. You can mix apples, oranges, bananas, pears, peaches, plums, grapes, mangoes, pineapples, or whatever else looks good. Have your child wash and dry the fruit well, and show her how to peel, cut, and chop with a cutting board and a sharp paring knife. Show her how to keep her fingers well back from the knife blade. When her fruit salad is ready, throw in a handful of sunflower seeds, walnuts, or raisins.

Outdoors _____

Do join in the fun your child is having with her friends in their outdoor play. Remember, though, that you are grown up and larger than the other players. Have a good time, but don't stampede the kids.

SHOT PUT

Put one sock inside another. Fill the toe with sand, leaving enough room to tie a knot. The players stand on the edge of a large circle on the ground. The thrower throws the sock horizontally from her chest, not overhand, or up in the air. Measure the furthest distances.

SCOOP BALL

Make Scoops out of old plastic bleach bottles, fabric softener jugs, or vinegar jugs. Cut off the bottom, leaving the handle as a holder. Use your Scoops to catch India rubber balls, mush balls or tennis balls. No hands allowed.

KEEP AWAY

IT tries to keep other players away from a specific object, while they, in turn, try to avoid being tagged. Often, this game is played on steps, with the object being to reach a door. If IT touches someone, she becomes "poison" and is out of the game until another player becomes IT. The object of the game is to be the first person to touch the object and become IT.

STOOP BALL

You need a set of steps, two players, and a tennis ball. Stand five or six feet in front of the steps. Throw the ball, either overhand or side arm, so it will rebound. The other player catches the ball. The number of bounces the ball makes before it's caught indicates the number of bases awarded to the first player.
Hint: Try for the edge of the steps to get the most elevation and distance.

RELEVIO

A group of players divides into two equal teams, the hiders and the seekers. The hiders disappear. The seekers designate an area as jail, and some members of the seekers team are told to guard it. The rest of the team tries to find the hiders. If a hider is found, she is put into jail. Prisoners can only escape when a member of their team enters the jail and yells, *RELEVIO*, whereupon all the jailbirds scatter and hide again. The game ends when all the hiders are caught and put in jail. The hiders become the seekers for the next game.

MONKEY IN THE MIDDLE

The Monkey stands inside a circle of players and tries to catch the ball being thrown to other players in the circle. If the Monkey catches the ball, the thrower becomes the next Monkey.

RED ROVER

Red Rover, Red Rover
Send (child's name) right over.

Two lines of players face each other, hands firmly clasped, approximately twenty feet apart. One team captain calls a runner on the opposing team, who then tries to break through the linked hands of a pair of her opponents. She runs as fast as she can and hurls herself at what she judges to be the weakest link.

If she succeeds, she captures one member of the opposing team, and they return to her team. If she is caught, she must stay there. The game continues until only one player remains on a side.

Red Rover is a game of strategy, as the players try to select someone who is weak enough to capture, but strong enough to forge a link on their own team.

Warning: Adult supervision is **MANDATORY**. Children need to be warned not to hold on too long when somebody is trying to break through; Red Rover has caused some arm and collarbone fractures.

Music

You child is attracted to melodic and rhythmic music of all types, especially traditional folk music. Her singing is getting stronger, and her pitch is improving. She loves to skip, dance, clap, and play simple percussion instruments to the music she hears. She may be able to sing a simple round, or catch.

Sweetly Sings the Donkey
(Three part catch)
Sweetly sings the donkey, at the break of day.
If you do not feed him, this is what he'll say.
Hee haw, hee haw, hee haw, hee haw, hee haw!
(Traditional, North America)

White Coral Bells
(Four part catch)
White coral bells upon a slender stalk
Lilies of the Valley deck my garden walk.
Oh, don't you wish that you could hear them ring?
That will happen only when the fairies sing.
(Traditional, North America, Great Britain)

Buffalo Gals
Chorus:
Buffalo gals, can't you come out tonight,
Come out tonight, come out tonight.
Buffalo gals, can't you come out tonight
And dance by the light of the moon?
Verses:
As I was walking down the street,
Down the street, down the street,
A pretty girl I chanced to meet
Oh, she was fair to view.

I asked her would she have some talk,
Have some talk, have some talk,
Her feet covered up the whole sidewalk,
As she stood close by me.

I asked her would she have a dance,
Have a dance, have a dance,
I thought that I might get a chance,
To shake a foot with her.

I'd like to make that gal my wife,
That gal my wife, that gal my wife,
Then I'd be happy all my life,
If I had her by me.
(Traditional, North America)

Cathy Fink sings "Buffalo Gals" on the *Grandma's Patchwork Quilt* album, American Melody Records.

Sweet Betsy From Pike

Chorus:
Sing too-ral-i-oo-ral-i-oo-rali-ay,
Sing too-ral-i-oo-ral-i-oo-rali-ay.

Verses:
Did you ever hear tell of sweet Betsy from Pike,
Who crossed the wide prairies with her lover Ike,
With two yoke of oxen and one spotted hog,
A tall Shanghai rooster, and old yaller dog?

One evening quite early they camped on the Platt,
'Twas near by the road on a green shady flat;
Where Betsy, quite tired, lay down to repose,
While with wonder Ike gazed on his Pike County
rose.

They swam the wide rivers and crossed the tall
peaks,
And camped on the prairies for weeks upon weeks.
Starvation and cholera and hard work and slaughter,
They reached California spite of hell and high
water.

Out on the prairie one bright starry night
They broke out the whiskey and Betsy got tight,
She sang and she shouted and danced o'er the plain,
And kicked up her heels for the whole wagon train.

The Injuns came down in a wild yelling horde,
And Betsy was skeered they would scalp her
adored;
Behind the front wagon wheel Betsy did crawl,
And there she fought Injuns with musket and ball.

The alkali desert was burning and bare,
And Isaac's soul shrank from the death that lurked
there:
"Dear Old Pike County, I'll go back to you."
Says Betsy, "You'll go by yourself if you do!"
(Traditional, American West)

Jack Was Ev'ry Inch a Sailor

Chorus:
Jack was ev'ry inch a sailor,
Five and twenty years a whaler,
Jack was ev'ry inch a sailor
He was born upon the bright blue sea.

Verses:
Now 'twas twenty-five or thirty years since Jack
first saw the light,
He came into this world of woe one dark and
stormy night.
He was born on board his father's ship as she was
lying to,
'Bout twenty-five or thirty miles southeast of
Baccalieu.

When Jack grew up to be a man he went to
Labrador,
He fished in Indian Harbour, where his father
fished before.
On his returning in the fog, he met a heavy gale,
And Jack was swept into the sea and swallowed by
a whale.

The whale went straight for Baffin's Bay, 'bout
ninety knots an hour,
And ev'ry time he'd blow a spray he'd send it in a
show'r.
"Oh, now," says Jack unto himself, "I must see
what he's about."
He caught the whale all by the tail and turned him
inside out.
(Traditional, Newfoundland Shanty)

Fred Penner has recorded "Jack" on his *A House For Me* album, Troubadour Records, and Sharon, Lois & Bram sing it on their *Elephant Show* album, Elephant Records.

Pat on the Railway

Chorus:

Fil-i-me-oo-re-oo-re-oo,
Fil-i-me-oo-re-oo-re-ay,
Fil-i-me-oo-re-oo-re-oo,
To work upon the railway.

Verses:

In eighteen hundred and forty-one
I put me cord'roy breeches on,
I put me cord'roy breeches on
To work upon the railway.

In eighteen hundred and forty-two
I left the old world for the new.
Bad luck to the mess that brought me through
To work upon the railway.

It's "Pat, do this," and it's "Pat, do that,"
Without a stocking or cravat,
And nothing but an old straw hat
To work upon the railway.

In eighteen hundred and forty-three
'Twas then I met sweet Biddy Magee
An elegant wife she's been to me
While workin' on the railway.

In eighteen hundred and forty-four
I found my back was terrible sore.
I found my back was terrible sore
While workin' on the railway.

In eighteen hundred and forty-five
I found myself more dead than alive.
I found myself more dead than alive
While workin' on the railway.

In eighteen hundred and forty-six
I sat on a keg of dynamite sticks.
I sat on a keg of dynamite sticks.
While workin' on the railway.

In eighteen hundred and forty-seven
I found myself on the way to heaven.
I found myself on the way to heaven
While workin' on the railway.

In eighteen hundred and forty-eight
I was pickin' the lock at the pearly gate.
I was pickin' the lock at the pearly gate
While workin' on the railway.

In eighteen hundred and forty-nine
I finally got to the end of the line.
I finally got to the end of the line
While workin' on the railway.

(Traditional, North American Irish Work Ballad)

Boston, Come All Ye

Chorus:

Then blow ye winds westerly, westerly blow,
We're bound to the southward, so steady she goes.

Verses:

Come all ye young sailors and listen to me,
I'll sing you a song of the fish of the sea.

Oh first came the whale, the biggest of all,
He clumb up aloft and let every sail fall.

And next came the mackerel with his striped back;
He hauled aft the sheets and boarded each tack.

Then came the porpoise with his short snout;
He went to the wheel, calling, "Ready, about!"

Then come the smelt, the smallest of all;
He jumped to the poop and sung out, "Topsail,
*   haul!"*

The herring came saying, "I'm king of the seas,
If you want any wind, I'll blow you a breeze."

Next came the cod with his chuckle-head;
He went to the main-chains to heave at the lead.

Last come the flounder as flat as the ground;
Says, "Damn your eyes, chuckle-head, mind how
*   you sound."*

(Traditional, Grand Banks Shanty)

Art

Your child's drawings are getting more and more intricate. Her houses suddenly show individual bricks, windows, doors, chimneys with smoke, and shutters. Her people have faces and features and the correct number of fingers and toes.

WEAVING A POTHOLDER

Now is the time to invest in a simple frame weaving loom and a few bags of stretch loops. Potholder looms, about seven inches square, are simple to use. Stretch individual loops around the pegs from one side of the loom to the opposite side. Cross weave by pushing a loop alternately over and under two strands (one loop) from side to side. Hook the loop before starting to weave it over and under, and then hook it again at the other side. When all the pegs are full of woven loops, interlace one with another by starting at a corner and catching the second loop. Pull it through the corner loop, then take the third loop and pull it through the second. When only one loop is left in the fourth corner, pull it to use as a hanger.

SPRINKLE BOTTLES

Sprinkle bottles contain materials that your child can use for different art activities. You can use old salt shakers you find at a flea market, empty spice bottles, or baby food jars with holes punched in the lids. (Use a nail and hammer and make sure the rough side is inside.) Place glitter, sand, colored sand, colored cornmeal, salt, or powdered paint in the sprinkle shakers. Store the shakers together so they are ready to use at a moment's notice. Sprinkle materials can be added to either glue or paint.

SAND PAINT

Paint takes on a different quality when it is mixed with sand. Have your child add clean, sieved sand to tempera paint and then vary the design with some paint without sand.

SAND GLUE

Sand can be mixed with white glue for a three-dimensional effect in collage. Your budding paleontologist can use it to glue some clean bones onto a styrofoam meat container to create a dinosaur bone site. She can create a seascape using sand glue for the ocean floor, and adding shells and fish cut out of bright paper.

STRING SCULPTURE

Cut several lengths of flexible string or wool. Blow up a balloon and tie it off so it won't leak. Dip the lengths of string into an equal mixture of glue and water, and form the string over the balloon. When it's dry, pierce the balloon and remove it, and you're left with a free-form string sculpture.

SPLATTER CHALK

Moisten a piece of paper with a half and half mixture of liquid laundry starch and water. While it's still damp, ask your child to rub pieces of colored chalk over a wire screen or sieve onto the paper. If you have been doing chalk painting (see p 40), you can clean your chalk by doing splatter chalk.

Word Play _____

Talk, talk, talk, about everything under the sun. Using riddles, tongue twisters, jokes, collective words, affinities, and proverbs will make your child interested in the structure of language and the sounds the letters make.

OPPOSITES

Start off slowly and build up speed when you and your child give each other challenges. Your child will know the opposite of hot, light, up, out, red, stop, inside, and many many more.

AFFINITIES

Some words simply belong together. You say one word, and ask you child to say another one that goes with it. Or, if a word comes up in conversation, you reply with the other word. Once you start this game, you'll be amazed at the suggestions your child has. Of course, there are no wrong answers. Butter can go with bread or popcorn or cookies. Her explanations of why she chose certain words are exciting to hear.

Here are some words that may belong together:

pen and ink	pork and beans
paper and pencil	ham and eggs
pen and paper	coat and hat
salt and pepper	black and blue
cookies and milk	black and white
rain and snow	fair and warmer
knife and fork	dog and cat
day and night	house and mouse
cart and horse	horse and carriage
thunder and lightning	William and Mary
far and near	cat and mouse
rat and cheese	hot and cold

WORD SEARCH

Your child may be recognizing or reading some words. Simple word-search puzzles are lots of fun when she can find and circle words she knows. Make up a few simple puzzles with random letters and words your child is able to recognize. To begin, have all the words reading across in a square grid. As her skills build, add words going down. Gradually, add diagonal, backwards and upside-down words. Hide your child's name somewhere in the puzzle.

HANGMAN

Hangman is a pencil and paper game for two people. One player selects a word, that she knows how to spell, and draws the number of spaces that are in the word. For instance, YES would be _ _ _. The other player tries to guess the letters in the word. For every letter guessed, that space is filled in; for every one missed a stroke is added to a drawing of a hanged person on a gallows.

ANALOGIES

As day is to night, so light is to dark. Analogies help us draw conclusions and explain similarities. Do some with your child. See if she can find the missing words for these, and then make up your own.

> As son is to father, so daughter is to _____. (mother)
> As foot is to shoe, so hand is to _____.
> (glove, or mitten)
> As hat is to head, so coat is to _____. (body)
> As lamb is to sheep, so fawn is to _____. (deer)
> As pack is to wolves, so schools are to _____.
> (fish, children)
> As dog is to puppy, so bear is to _____. (cub)
> As bee is to hive, so pig is to _____. (sty, pen)

Quiet Times _____

You look with wonder at your sleeping child, astounded at her tranquility after an exciting day. Her exuberance often wears you out, and it's really you who needs the quiet times! Continue her go-to-bed ritual, reading and singing together. Don't forget her favorite poems, rhymes, and just talking quietly about the day's events.

NIGHTTIME ENVIRONMENT

Your child may need something special to help her deal with the night. It might be a night light so she can read herself to sleep. It might be a glow-in-the-dark poster or drawing she makes with glow-in-the-dark stickers or stars. It might be a special paint on her ceiling that glows small sparkles once her lights are turned off. There may be a special routine; for instance, first the sheet, then the bear, then the small blanket, then the large blanket, then a hug and a kiss, then the lights go out. She may be comforted by a music box, the sound of the pump on her fish tank, or her cat purring at her feet. Let her know that her room is a protective, special place of her own.

The Man on the Flying Trapeze

Oh, once I was happy, but now I'm forlorn,
Just like an old coat that is tattered and torn;
Left in this wide world to fret and to mourn,
Deceived by a maid in her teens.

The girl that I loved, she was handsome to see;
I tried all I could her to please
But I could not please her one quarter as much
As the man on the flying trapeze. O-o-o-h…

He'd float through the air with the greatest of ease,
That daring young man on the flying trapeze.
His movements were graceful, all the girls he did
  please,
And my love he has stolen away.
(Traditional, United States)

The Man in the Moon

Pray tell me how the man in the moon
Contrives his time to kill, Sir.
For since he lives there quite alone,
It might require some skill, Sir.

Oh, though his pasttimes are but scarce,
He's at no loss for fun, Sir;
He plays at marbles with the stars,
And trap-ball with the sun, Sir.
(Anonymous)

The Children's Hour

Classics of the Victorian age deserve to live forever.

Between the dark and the daylight,
When the night is beginning to lower,
Comes a pause in the day's occupations,
That is known as the Children's Hour.

I hear in the chamber above me
The patter of little feet,
The sound of a door that is opened,
And voices soft and sweet.

From my study I see in the lamplight,
Descending the broad hall stair,
Grave Alice, and laughing Allegra,
And Edith with golden hair.

A whisper, and then a silence:
Yet I know by their merry eyes
They are plotting and planning together
To take me by surprise.

A sudden rush from the stairway,
A sudden raid from the hall!
By three doors left unguarded
They enter my castle wall!

They climb up into my turret
O'er the arms and back of my chair;
If I try to escape, they surround me;
They seem to be everywhere.

They almost devour me with kisses,
Their arms about me entwine,
Till I think of the Bishop of Bingen
In his Mouse-Tower on the Rhine!

Do you think, O blue-eyed banditti,
Because you have scaled the wall,
Such an old mustache as I am
Is not a match for you all!

I have you fast in my fortress,
And will not let you depart,
But put you down into the dungeon
In the round-tower of my heart.

And there will I keep you forever,
Yes, forever and a day,
Till the walls shall crumble to ruin,
And moulder in dust away.
(Henry Wadsworth Longfellow)

Growing Interests

Your child's new abilities with rhythmic patterns, and her more developed fingers encourage complex ball games. Many children who live in neighbourhoods where skipping is popular are able to skip Double Dutch by the time they are six.

A, MY NAME IS ALICE

Your child bounces a ball in front of her. Every time she says a word with the letter of that verse, she lifts her leg over the ball as it hits the pavement. Help her work her way through the alphabet for girl's names, boy's names, places, and products.

*A, my name is **Alice**,*
*My husband's name is **Al**,*
*We come from **Alabama***
*And we sell **Apples**.*

*B, my name is **Brian**.*
*My wife's name is **Barb**,*
*We come from **Boston***
*And we sell **Beans**. ...*

*Z, my name is **Zoe**,*
*My husband's name is **Zack**,*
*We come from **Zambia***
*And we sell **Zippers**.*
(Traditional, North America)

ADVANCED ROPE SKIPPING

My friend Norma, who teaches kindergarten, invited me to watch her kids skip. Wow! There are many quirks to be added to straight skipping. Both feet, alternate feet, covering a distance, crossing and uncrossing arms, super-fast swings (where the rope passes under the feet twice during one high jump), can all be added. Of course, the rope can be swung backwards, so it comes from behind and you can't see it coming! All of these can be done singly, with enders, or Double Dutch.

RUN THROUGH
(two enders, one or more skippers)

Two people swing the rope. If a jumper misses, she takes the end, and one of the swingers takes the jumper's place in line. Each jumper runs through the swinging rope, without jumping. When all are finished, the first jumper runs in, jumps once, runs out, and the rest follow. Next time around, there are two jumps, then three, and so on. Remember, it's bad luck to jump to 100.

Had a Little Sports Car
(two enders, one or more jumpers)

I had a little sports car 9.48
Went around the cor-ner
> (Turn corner, see page 76
And SLAMMED on the brakes.
> Rope slams on pavement
The brakes didn't work so I had a little jerk
Bumped into a lady, bumped into a man
Bumped into a POliceman. Man, oh man.
> Emphasize PO
Policeman caught me, put me in jail
All I had was ginger ale
How many bottles did I have?
> Do peppers)
10, 20, 30, 40...*

* It's bad luck to do 100.
(Traditional, Canada)

Hey Baby

Hey, baby, how about a date?
I'll meet you at the cor-ner
> (Turn corner
'Bout half-past eight
She can do the wibble wobble
> Hootchie-kootchie
She can do the splits
> Jump in air, legs straddle
I'll bet you five bucks you can't do this.
Close your eyes and count to six.
1, 2, 3, 4, 5, 6.
> Skip with eyes closed)
(Traditional, Canada)

Here Comes a Noble Knight of Spain
You need two jumpers, one knight and one mother. The knight starts skipping alone.

Here comes a noble knight of Spain
Come to court your daughter Jane
Be she young or be she old
For a bride she must be sold.

My daughter Jane is much too young
> (Mother jumps in)
To hear your false and flattering tongue
Turn back, turn back, thou scornful knight,
And rub thy spurs, they are not bright.

My spurs are bright and richly wrought
> (Both skip)
In THIS town they were not bought
In this town they'll not be sold
Neither for silver, nor for gold.

So fare thee well, my lady gay,
> (Knight hands mother the rope,
For I must turn and ride away
> knight leaves, mother is the
I'll call again, another day.
> new knight.)
(Traditional, Great Britain)

DOUBLE DUTCH

Double Dutch is advanced skipping, done at double speed, with two ropes passing overhead. A skipper can either swing the rope herself or have two enders swing for her. Double Dutch rhymes contain some of the most remarkable poetry in the English language.

Tiny Tim

I had a little baby, his name was Tiny Tim
I put him in the bathtub, to see if he could swim.
He drank up all the water, he ate up all the soap,
He died last night, with a bubble in his throat.

I called the doctor, I called the nurse,
I called the lady with the alligator purse.
In came the doctor, in came the nurse
In came the lady with the alligator purse.

"Penicillin," said the doctor, "Penicillin," said the
nurse.
"Candy," said the lady with the alligator purse.
Out went the doctor, out went the nurse,
Out went the lady with the alligator purse.
(Traditional, Canada)

Sharon, Lois & Bram sing "Tiny Tim" on their *Stay Tuned* album, Elephant Records. Their version is called "Miss Lucy."

I'm Shirley Temple

I'm Shirley Temple, the girl with the curly hair.
I have two dimples, and wear my skirts to there,
o-o-o-h,
I'm not able, to do the Betty Grable,
I'm Shirley Temple, the girl with the curly hair.
(Traditional, Great Britain, North America)

CHINESE JUMPROPE — YOKI

A Chinese Jumprope is a piece of elastic, about six feet long, in a continuous loop. You need at least three players. Two are inside the loop to stretch it taut. The jumper starts inside the "box" formed by the taut rope. She jumps out (straddle) over the elastic, in again, out straddling one side of the box, in again, out straddling the other side, in again, out straddling both sides, and then on the elastic, pinning it to the ground. Josh's dad told me that when he was a boy, they all did Chinese Jumprope with a rhyme:

Yoki and the kaiser,
Yoki addy ay,
Tam-ba, so-ba,
Sa-du, sa-day.

They start the rope at the ankles, then move it to their knees, their bums, and finally their waists, as the players jump each level.
(Traditional, Toronto Schoolyards)

ADVANCED HAND CLAPPING

While you *can* still keep it simple, it's time to work in some of your own more complex patterns to some longer or faster rhythms. Start clapping a basic pattern, maybe your own hands and your child's hands, alternately. When you get to "be, be, be," clap the fronts, backs, and fronts of your hands together. Once you can do that, vary it any way you like. Just be sure to try to stay together.

I Am a Pretty Little Dutch Girl

*I am a pretty little Dutch girl, as pretty as can be,
be, be.*
*And all the boys in my town, are crazy over me,
me, me.*

*My boyfriend's name is Fatty, he comes from
Cincinatti*
*He has turned-up toes, and a pimple on his nose,
and this is how the story goes:*

*One day as I was walking, I heard my boyfriend
talking*
*To a pretty little girl, with a big fat curl and this is
what he said to her:*

*I love you very dearly, but I love someone else sin-
cerely,*
*So jump in the river and swallow a snake and come
out dry with a belly ache.*

*My boyfriend gave me peaches, my boyfriend gave
me pears.*
*My boyfriend gave me fifty cents and kissed me on
the stairs.*

*He made me wash the windows, he made me scrub
the floor,*
*He made me sew his smelly socks, so I kicked him
out the door, door, door.*

Shave and a haircut, SHAMPOOOOO!

(Traditional, North American Schoolyard)

Three, Six, Nine

Three, six, nine, the goose drank wine
The monkey chewed tobacco on the streetcar line.
The streetcar broke, and the monkey got choked
And they all went to heaven but the old billy goat.

(Traditional, Great Britain)

Kim and Jerry Brodey do "Three Six Nine" on their *Simple Magic* album, Kids' Records, and their *Hats On/Hats Off* video, Golden Book Video.

JUBA

Juba is a very old Black American hand clap, dating back to the days of slavery. The town of Juba is in the southern Sudan. Often, Juba is clapped in a ring of people with one player leading the actions. Eric Nagler does "Juba" on *Making Music With Eric*, Golden Book Video.

Juba this and Juba that
And Juba skinned the yellow cat
And gives us double trouble. Juba.

You sift the meal, you give me the husk.
You bake the bread, you give me the crust.
You cook the meat, you give me the skin
And that's where my mama's trouble begin. Juba.

My old massa promised me,
When he died, he'd set me free.
He lived 'til his head got slick and bald.
He give up the notion of dying at all. Juba.

The big bee flies high
The little bee makes the honey.
The black folks make the cotton,
The white folks get the money. JUBA!

(Traditional, Black American)

CHAPTER SEVEN

READING, BOOKS, VIDEOS, RECORDS, SPORTS, LESSONS, TOYS

Reading Together

Y OUR CHILD NEEDS to see you reading, and he needs to be read to, daily. Establish the habit of reading together for at least fifteen minutes a day, every day of the year. You may want to do your reading just before "lights out," or as you travel together on the bus or subway, or at lunchtime. Read whenever you have a chance; the rewards will be tremendous.

Reading together is an active process. As you read and reread favorites, your child may memorize many of them and be able to read them to you. Share the reading, using your most dramatic voice and performance. Both you and he will fall in love with sharing the adventures in his books together.

WHAT TO READ TOGETHER?

Remember your own childhood favorites and share them with your child. If you have happy memories; for instance, eating cheese sandwiches and reading *Heidi*, share both the books and the memories with your child.

Add new children's selections, fairy tales, folk tales, and fables. While your child is probably too young to read complete novels, read bits of classics like *Alice in Wonderland, Treasure Island, Robin Hood,* or *Little House on the Prairie.* You may want to add C.S. Lewis's tales of Narnia, too.

Don't limit yourself to storybooks. We read bits of Elspeth Huxley's *The Flame Trees of Thika* when Jenny's friend Ricker moved to Tanzania. We read *Anne of Green Gables*, a chapter a night, and then watched it when it was televised.

As your child's attention span grows, you will want to move into easy-to-read books. Dell Yearling puts out a great series that includes *The Secret Garden* by Frances Hodgson Burnett, the *Ramona* stories by Beverly Cleary, *Mary Poppins* by P. L. Travers, and many others. You will enjoy the "Step into Reading" series by Random House; our favorite was *Dinosaur Days.* Avon Camelot has a great series of "Snuggle and Read Story Books," including Peggy Parish's *Amelia Bedelia* stories that cause great giggles of glee. Seal Books, McClelland & Stewart, publish two wonderful adventures by Mordecai Richler, *Jacob Two-Two Meets the Hooded Fang* and *Jacob Two-Two and the Dinosaur.* Don't forget the *Pippi Longstocking* series, Astrid Lindgren; *Rip Roaring Russell,* Joanna Hurwitz; The *Betsy, Tacy, and Tib* stories by Maud Hart Lovelace, and anything by Carolyn Hayward.

Match books with favorite toys: *Paddington Bear*, *Curious George*, or *Raggedy Ann*.

ANTHOLOGIES

Anthologies are a good way to find out what stories your child likes best. My favorite is *The World Treasury of Children's Literature*, two volumes, edited by Clifton Eadiman (Little Brown). Other terrific anthologies are the *Treasury of Literature for Children* (Hamlyn Publishing); and *English Literature for Boys and Girls*, H.E. Marshal (Nelson).

MAGAZINES

Your child loves receiving mail and some children's magazines are absolutely terrific. Pick up some copies at a newsstand or borrow some from the library to test your child's reaction before spending money for a subscription. Some possibilities include: *Chickadee*, *Your Big Back Yard* (both exceptional nature magazines), *Humpty Dumpty*, *Sesame Street Magazine*, *Highlights for Children*.

FAVORITE TOPICS

Most preschoolers are interested in information about the world around them. Look for well-illustrated, well-written books on topics that are of special interest to your child. Books on insects, dinosaurs, trains, machines, birds, swamps, weather, wild animals, space, and nature will fascinate him. Buy field guides on his favorite topics; the Golden Guides, the Audubon Society Guides, and the Peterson series are all great and will last for years.

SONG BOOKS

Sharon, Lois & Bram's Mother Goose (Douglas and McIntyre) and *Elephant Jam* (Crown Publishing) or Raffi's *Baby Beluga* (McClelland & Stewart), will have many of your child's favorite songs.

POETRY

A special edition of poetry is a great investment for your child's bookshelf. There is Robert Louis Stevenson's *A Child's Garden of Verses* (Rand McNally), *The Oxford Book of Children's Verse in America*, Donald Hall (Oxford), *The Oxford Book of Poetry for Children*, compiled by Edward Blishen (Oxford); *Edward Lear's Complete Nonsense Book* (Dodd Mead), and *The Moon is Shining Bright as Day*, Ogden Nash (Lippencott). Don't forget favorite Mother Goose books, such as *Lavender's Blue*, Kathleen Lines (Oxford) or *The Real Mother Goose* (Rand McNally).

FOLK TALES

Four-year-olds love folk tales. Read many versions of the same story and explain the different ways in which stories are passed on. Read your child folklore and folk tales from other cultures. Some favorites:

When the Drum Sang, Anne Rockwell, Parent's Magazine Press
Nomi and the Magic Fish, Phumla, Doubleday & Company Inc.
The Invisible Brer Anansi, David P. Makhanlall, Blackie & Son, Glasgow
Anansi the Spider Man, Philip Sherlock, K.B.E., Oxford University Press
Indian Legends of Canada, Ella Elizabeth Clark, McClelland & Stewart
The Jack Tales (North Carolina) Richard Chase, Houghton Mifflin

Chinese Myths and Fantasies, April Birch, Oxford
Mead Moondaughter and Other Icelandic Folk Tales,
   Alan Boucher, Ropert Hart-Davis

FAIRY TALES AND TALES OF HEROS

Classic fairy tales lend enchantment to your
child's life. Read many versions of the same tales
and explain that these stories have been told to
children in many different countries. For
instance, when you read Cinderella in all its wonderful variations, be sure to read *Yeh-Shen*, retold
by Ai-Lin Louie, Sandcastle. Search out the classic fairy tale collections: *Tales from Grimm*; *The
Arabian Nights*; the *Laing Fairy Books*; *Celtic Fairy
Tales*, Joseph Jacobs; *The Classic Fairy Tales*, Iona
and Peter Opie (Oxford); The Favorite Fairy
Tales Told In series (Little Brown).

You may want to add tales of mythology and
heroes: *King Arthur and His Noble Knights*, Mary
McLeod (Lippincott); *Hero Tales from Many
Lands*, Alice L. Hazeltine (Abington); *Pecos Bill,
New Tall Tales of Pecos Bill*, Harold W. Felton
(Prentice Hall), *Paul Bunyan and His Great Blue
Ox*, Wallace Wadsworth (Doubleday).

SERIES OF BOOKS

Your child loves books that have a familiar
"feel." He might love books by the same author;
for instance, Robert McCloskey's *Make Way for
Ducklings*, *Blueberries for Sal*, and *One Morning in
Maine* (Puffin Books), or *Peter Rabbit* and all the
rest of Beatrix Potter's stories (Warne Books). He
might love to read about familiar friends in different situations; there is Paddington, Amelia
Bedelia, Clifford, Babar, and Curious George.

The Berenstain Bears books (Random House
First Time Books), are great for preschoolers
because they show happy resolutions for problems
that your child might find troublesome. Titles
include: *Visit the Dentist*, *Get Stage Fright*, *Moving

Day*, *In the Dark*, *And the Messy Room*, *The Week
at Grandma's* and *The New Baby*.

Little Golden Books (Western Publishing) are
available at most supermarkets and cost about the
same as a bag of potato chips. Some of them are
practically classics: *Dinosaurs*, *My First Book of
Planets*, *A Day in the Jungle*, *Hiram's Red Shirt*,
Tootle, *The Saggy Baggy Elephant*, *The Train to
Timbuctoo*, *The Tawny Scrawny Lion*, *Scruffy the
Tugboat*, *The Poky Little Puppy*, *Cars and Trucks*,
The Animals of Farmer Jones, *The Shy Little Kitten*,
Cars, *Cats*, *The Little Red Caboose*, etc., etc. Fill
up his bookshelf.

Mercer Meyer's Little Critter stories (Golden
Look Look Books), deal with many of your child's
concerns, and are also great fun. Titles include
Just Me and My Dad, *I Was So Mad*, *Just Go To
Bed*, *The New Baby*, *All by Myself*.

YOUR CHILD'S LIBRARY

Your child needs to have his own books, so he can
read and reread his favorites. Of course, you can
borrow books from your library, but by giving him
his own collection as well, you convey the impor-
tance of reading to him. Ideally, his library contains:
- at least a dozen picture books
- an anthology of bedtime stories
- a nursery rhyme book
- a book of children's poetry
- a book of fairy tales
- a book of folk tales and legends
- four or five fact books about his favorite topics
- a complex ABC book
- an atlas
- a half-dozen easy-to-read stories
- a children's dictionary
- field guides
- a song book

Books are a good investment because your
child will be reading most of them for years to
come. Add to his collection frequently. You don't

have to spend a fortune, paperbacks are fine, although some reference books may be worth getting in hardcover.

Videos

Rent videos before you purchase them. Some children's videos are wonderful, but some are horrendous. With careful selection we can avoid those made with no respect for children or how they think. Some videos come straight from television: Sesame Street, The Muppets, Reading Rainbow, Pee Wee Herman, The Elephant Show, Polka Dot Door. Depending on the availability of quality children's programming in your locality, you may want to consider these.

Jim Henson, creator of the Muppets, has done a great series of "Play Along" videos. These are fun when you and your child try some of the suggested activities.

Golden Book Video has put together a series of videos with quality children's performers such as Bob Schneider, Robert Munsch, Eric Nagler, Kim and Jerry Brodey, But I'm Just a Kid, Sharon, Lois, & Bram, Katharine Smithrim, and Sandra Beech. They have also put out animated videos of some of their children's stories.

When you start reading fairy tales together, there is an amazing selection of quality videos available. My favorite is Cannon Film's *Rumpelstiltskin*, with Amy Irving and wonderful songs and dancing. CBS-Fox Video has released Faerie Tale Theatre, a series of videos with well-known actors and actresses in classic fairy tales. Read three or four versions of your child's favorite fairy tale, THEN rent the video. Both Cannon Home Video and CBS-Fox Video do the classics, and most of these are far more interesting and rich in detail than the animated versions.

View Master Video has done a series of sing-along versions of favorite children's songs you might want to check out if you don't know the tunes. I enjoy "I'd Like to Teach the World to Sing" in this series.

Random House Home Video has put out a series of magnificent *Storybook Classics*, Rabbit Ears Productions. Our favorites are "Pecos Bill," narrated by Robin Williams and with music by Ry Cooder, and "How the Rhinoceros Got His Skin" and "How the Camel Got His Hump," narrated by Jack Nicholson. Other titles to look for are: "The Emperor and the Nightingale" and "The Legend of Sleepy Hollow," both narrated by Glenn Close, and "The Steadfast Tin Soldier," narrated by Jeremy Irons.

As your child gets interested in science and nature, enhance his knowledge with quality videos on the topics that interest him. The "Tell Me Why" series, Prism Entertainment, Penguin Home Video, covers topics like space, water, insects, mammals, fish, reptiles, and many others. National Geographic has a series of Vestron Videos that cover virtually all the Society's topics; Jacques Cousteau's "Odyssey" series explores underwater areas, and Lorne Greene's "New Wilderness" series has some great videos about the wilds.

The major *caveat* is to beware that tape, video, or television does not take over your child's experiences of books but enriches it. Some children do teach themselves to read by watching a video or listening to a tape, but never substitute videos for books; provide the books that go with the videos.

Records

Listen to all kinds of music, from Grand Opera to Rock-a-Billy, from Maori chants to James Bay Cree fiddle music, and listen frequently.

Share your own musical interests with your child. If you love classical music, introduce your child to the great composers. *Mr. Bach Comes to Call*, with the Toronto Boy's Choir and Studio Arts Orchestra, produced by Classical Kids'

Records, has been winning awards. *A Child's Look at Mozart*, Kids' Records is also great. Veronica Tennant's *The Nutcracker* is a wonderful introduction to the fascinating Hofmann tale, Kids' Records. Britten's *Young Person's Guide to the Orchestra*, and Prokofiev's *Peter and the Wolf* are together on a tape by the Philadelphia Orchestra, Eugene Ormandy conducting, CBS Records. Children love parts of Peer Gynt, Night on Bald Mountain, 1812 Overture, William Tell Overture (to the dump, to the dump, to the dump, dump, dump…), Golliwogs Cakewalk, Toy Symphony, Hansel and Gretel, the list goes on and on.

Your child may love jazz. Listen to everything from Ragtime to Fusion. Be sure to include some of the great Louis Armstrong hits that appeal to children. Virtually any early jazz from New Orleans will probably delight him.

Many great performers, from Ladysmith Black Mambazo to Cab Calloway to James Taylor to Itzhak Perlman show up regularly on Sesame Street. Your child may have favorites you don't even know about. Ask him about Placido Flamingo (sic), if he watches Sesame Street.

Don't limit yourself strictly to children's entertainers. Having said that, I have to admit I ADORE children's entertainers. You can't go wrong with Sharon, Lois & Bram, Eric Nagler, Michael Cooney, Fred Penner, Chris and Ken Whiteley, Raffi, Kim and Jerry Brodey, Pete Seeger, Charlotte Diamond, and the French performers, Matt, and Suzanne Pinel.

There is also some terrible stuff out there, what I call "Munchkin Music," so if you aren't familiar with the performer, borrow the record from your library before you buy it.

Some performers have done work in other genres. Kids love Robin Williamson and his *Songs for Children of All Ages*, Pig's Whisker Music, Peter, Paul and Mary's *Peter, Paul and Mommy* on Warner Bros. Records, and Anne Murray's *There's a Hippo in my Tub*, A & M Records.

Rather than list innumerable record albums, here is a list of addresses where you can obtain good children's music.

Distributors

Elephant Records
24 Ryerson Avenue
4th Floor,
Toronto, Ontario,
Canada   M5T 2P3

A & M Records
(*Elephant Records and Troubadour Records*)
1416 N. Labrea Avenue
Los Angeles, California,
U.S.A. 90028

Larrikin Records
(*Larrikin Records, Elephant Records, Troubadour Records*)
282 Oxford Street
Paddington, NSW,
Australia 2021

Kids' Records
(*Distributed in the U.S. by Silo*)
68 Broadview Avenue
Suite 303
Toronto, Ontario,
Canada   M4M 2E6

Classical Kids' Records
134 Howland Avenue
Toronto, Ontario,
Canada   M5R 3B5

Troubadour Records
(*Distributed in the U.S. by A & M, in Australia by Larrikin*)
6043 Yonge Street
Willowdale, Ontario,
Canada   M2M 3W3

Silo Records
(*Distributor of Kids' Records in the U.S.*)
Box 429
South Main Street
Waterbury, Vermont,
U.S.A 05676

Hug Bug Records
(*Distributed By A & M*)
Box 58174, Station "L"
Vancouver, British Columbia
Canada   V6P 6C5

Pig's Whisker Music
P.O. Box 27522,
Los Angeles, California
U.S.A. 90029

Sports

Your child is eager and enthusiastic and this might be a good time to start him in lessons. By finding the best possible instruction available, he will learn quickly and easily, and won't have to unlearn bad habits that he might pick up from an inexperienced instructor. Swimming and gymnastics are probably the best sports for three- to six-year-olds.

ICE SKATING/ROLLER SKATING

Make sure your child has boot-type skates that fit him properly and provide ankle support. Hold his hand and help him roll or glide along. When he is balancing comfortably, put on your own skates and join in the fun. He may want to hold onto the back of a chair for balance if he's just learning to ice skate.

If you have an indoor ice arena in your area, enroll your budding Wayne Gretzky or Brian Boitano in skating lessons.

DOWNHILL/CROSS COUNTRY SKIING

If you are planning to cross-country ski, invest in a children's package with boots and no-wax, fish-scale skis. Make sure he has one or two introductory lessons before heading for the trails, mostly so he will know how to fall without hurting himself. Start going short distances on relatively flat terrain and give him a chance to build up his skills gradually.

If you are a downhill skier, find a downhill ski area that offers nursery ski lessons for your child before you take him out on the slopes yourself.

Whether downhill or cross country, it's easier to learn to ski without ski poles until age seven.

LEAGUE SPORTS

You may want to investigate "Junior Peanut" and "Senior Peanut" sports leagues for games like Soft Lacrosse, where there is no body contact, Tee Ball, a form of baseball without pitching, Nerf Hockey, or Soccer.

If you decide on one of these leagues, ensure that your child will be learning skills; he is NOT ready for competitive team sports. Right now, he is not able to determine with consistency whether he is to run to first base or third base when he hits the ball. He needs to learn how to swing a bat, how to run bases, how to catch or dribble a ball, how to handle a hockey stick. Until he has mastered these basic skills, he shouldn't need to worry about winning or losing.

GYMNASTICS

If your child is interested in gymnastics, make sure you find a program that stresses individual development and growth, and is tailored for your child's level and ability. Make sure you have accredited coaching and a noncompetitive program that focuses on the proper way to mount and dismount equipment, how to fall, roll, enter, and leave moves. Your child's body can sustain permanent damage from both gymnastics and classical dance if his individual needs aren't met.

SWIMMING

Enroll your child in a certified swim program, so he learns the correct strokes as well as water safety. Red Cross levels start when your child can stand up at the shallow end of the pool, usually between three and four years of age. There are parent and tot classes for younger children.

Dance

Make sure that any dance classes you choose for your child will not put undue stress on his developing bones and muscles. He will probably have more fun if he has Eurythmics, folk dancing, or Orff music classes where he can bounce around to the music, rather than ballet where he has to hold difficult positions and postures.

Music Lessons

The best musical training your child can receive is what he gets making happy music with you. You need to sing songs that demand participation, whether by singing, jumping, tapping, clapping, patting, skipping, running, dancing, or inventing your own motions.

Before you enroll your child in any music class, at any age, you need to ask if you and your child are going to enjoy the process. If your desire is to have your child perform, you need to look hard at your child's interest in music, his personality, and YOUR willingness to take the necessary steps for him to become a musician. Even Mozart had major family involvement in his development as a musician. If your child is not going to enjoy learning music, the lessons will be a waste of time and make the whole family miserable.

Make sure you provide many happy experiences with music before you introduce a solo instrument that requires solitary practice. The best beginning for music lessons may be group classes, taken simply for the fun of them.

Here are some of the musical programs available for small children. Some demand more parental participation than others.

PREPARATORY MUSIC

Preparatory Music classes are generally offered for three-, four-, and five-year-olds, although some classes start with singing and bouncing games for babies as young as six months. Children play singing games, move to music, and play simple percussion instruments. The standard text for this style of class is *Move, Sing, Listen, Play* by Donna Wood. Preparatory Music is a springboard for Orff, Kodaly, choirs, the Suzuki method, dance instruction, and private instrumental instruction.

EURYTHMICS/DALCROZE

Developed by Emile Jacques-Dalcroze, Eurythmics is a method where your child's natural sense of rhythm is developed by using his body as an instrument. It emphasizes moving to music, playing musical games and simple musical instruments, which makes a good foundation for both music and dance. Classes are for children between the ages of three and ten.

ORFF MUSIC

Orff music classes generally start when a child is four or five, and continue until about age ten. Developed by composer Carl Orff, the group program combines movement, singing, speech, and the playing of simple rhythmic instruments, including glockenspiels, rhythm sticks and xylophones. Orff is a good basis for gymnastics, dance, and instrumental/music.

KODALY

Zoltan Kodaly, composer, folk music collector, and music educator, developed a program to provide a musical foundation to last a lifetime. The emphasis is on developing rhythmic and melodic skills, and on gaining the ability to read, write, hear, and think music. Classes are usually for children from four to ten, although some teachers will take children as young as two. Kodaly teachers believe that perfect pitch is part of every child's makeup, and will last a lifetime if the voice is trained at a young age.

THE SUZUKI INSTRUMENTAL METHOD

Dr. Shinichi Suzuki believes a musical instrument is learned in the same manner as a language. Each child must have his own instrument, and a parent must attend weekly instruction and practice with the child on a daily basis. Most Suzuki students receive one private lesson a week and a group lesson every other week. Children learn to play violin, cello, flute, or piano. The violins, cellos and flutes are child-sized, and this may necessitate changing instruments as your child grows. Children are accepted into Suzuki classes about age three, and are usually not admitted after age eight.

KELLY KIRBY KEYBOARD

The Kelly Kirby Keyboard method is a simple introduction to piano for children between four and eight. A piano at home is required, and parental supervision of daily practice is recommended. Instruction is usually private. Children are taught ear-training, sight-reading, technique, and musical theory.

Toys

The toys that get used the most are the ones that encourage creativity and can be used in the most imaginative ways. The old-fashioned toys that children have played with over centuries: balls, dolls, stuffed animals, Whizzers (p 16), Jacob's Ladder (p 34), and pinwheels (p 89), will fascinate for hours.

TOY RATINGS

Many toys sit gathering dust on shelves or lie broken at the bottom of toyboxes. The Consumer's Association of Canada each year issues the *Toy Report*, by the Canadian Toy Testing Council. This report evaluates and rates all toys according to age, appeal, price, value and safety, and offers comments. If you avoid even one lemon, this book will pay for itself. If it is unavailable at your bookstore, write to:

The Consumer's Association of Canada
2660 Southvale Crescent, Level 3
Ottawa, Ontario Canada K1B 5C4

While there is no similar guide in the U.S., you may want to refer to the Bank Street Educational Foundation's book *Buy Me, Buy Me*.

BEST TOYSHOPS

Some of the best, and most inexpensive, toys come from gift shops at conservation areas, zoos, science museums, and planetariums. There are packages of small animals for imaginative play, wonderful puzzles, science stencils, stuffed animals, and investigative and observational toys. Do visit the gift shops with a view towards birthdays and holidays, as well as a memento of the day's outing.

You would do well to find a small, independent toy store. The smaller stores are able to research suppliers and pick out top quality merchandise, so you don't have to waste time sorting through everything manufactured in the past year. Dealing with smaller quantities, they are able to find the best, and sometimes small, producers, and obtain more interesting toys than the department stores.

FRUSTRATING TOYS

Most of the frustration that occurs with toys happens when pieces break, pieces are too small for small fingers (for instance, earrings, shoes, and skates on fashion dolls), and when toys have limited play value (they can only be used one way). In our neighborhood we have found that the toys kids reject first are the licensed ones, generally those associated with television shows or cartoon characters.

WHAT WE'VE FOUND THAT WORKS

Most of the preschoolers in our neighborhood loved these toys at some stage between three and six years.

- nesting and stacking toys
- puzzles
- unlimited art materials
- playdough, baker's clay, plasticine
- small animals, small dinosaurs, small figures
- crayons, paper, activity books
- a set of dishes for tea parties
- blackboard and chalk
- magnetic letters and numbers
- bubble solution, wands, joystick
- interlocking blocks (DUPLO, LEGO, etc.)
- kaleidescope
- wooden blocks, all shapes and sizes
- knapsack or lunchbox, with unbreakable thermos or water bottle
- huge blocks with ramps
- dressup materials

- balls, jumpropes, jacks, sidewalk chalk, tops, marbles
- anything on wheels, from matchbox cars to ride-em toys: trucks, trains, airplanes, firetrucks, cars, tricycles, wagons
- sandbox, water, sand toys, water toys, rubber duckie, water squirter
- anything to support dressup and role playing
- stuffed animals
- boxes, all sizes
- play money, cash register, shopping basket, pretend food cartons
- music boxes
- lawn sprinkler, lawn shower, outdoor wading pool
- magic slates
- dolls
- bug bottle
- dip nets
- magnifying glass (unbreakable)
- ant farm
- kites
- lotto games
- playing cards and flash cards
- board games: Dominoes, Chinese Checkers, Scrabble, Snakes and Ladders

CHAPTER EIGHT

THE MAGIC WORLD AROUND US

 OUR CHILD OBSERVES minute differences in her life: how the clouds change as she gazes up in the sky, what a bug does, how the moon changes during the month, what the creepy crawlies do when she turns over a log, the sounds of birds at her feeder. By taking the time to share her observations, you share her wonder at her discoveries. Spend as much time as you can looking at the world through the eyes of your child. Slow down and renew your world.

BUT WE LIVE IN THE CITY!

Smell the flowers that bloom in the parks. Identify the weeds growing out of cracks in the sidewalk. Closely examine a tree. Is the shrubbery along your sidewalk a ground cover for birds? How does ivy grow on buildings? Look up at the sky and talk about the weather, watch how it changes. Identify planets and major constellations on a clear night.

Even cities have a diversity of wildlife. Migratory swans even stop at Central Park, there is a national seashore wildlife refuge in New York city, and migratory waterfowl turn up all along flyways. Songbirds will drop into cities where they spot patches of green. Peregrine Falcons, a highly endangered species, are being reintroduced to office towers in urban environments. Nighthawks, kestrels, and killdeer are visitors on city roofs on warm summer nights. (Listen to a recording of bird calls and then listen for them on a warm summer evening.) Owls, nuthatches and woodpeckers live in trees in city parks. Rabbits, squirrels, chipmunks, raccoons, skunks, and rodents thrive in ravines and fields; foxes and porcupines live in urban greenbelts. Is there any city without its resident population of pigeons, starlings, and sparrows? Be sure you read Robert McCloskey's *Make Way for Ducklings* (Puffin Books), especially if you live in a city.

THE COUNTRY

Visit the country on day trips and vacations. Visit wetlands or the seashore. Look for habitats of interesting critters and unusual plants, and investigate what lives wherever you visit. Take a walk in the woods or through a field and investigate with your binoculars and magnifying glass, gaze up at the stars. Besides getting fresh air, you and your child will relax and have fun together in the great outdoors.

OBSERVATION LISTS

Talk about all the animals, birds, and insects you see together, and make a field list of where you saw them and what they were doing. For instance:

Robin, hopping along the lawn, pulling worms, March 15

Black squirrel, at bird feeder, lives in nest in oak tree, November 3

Toad, in garden, June 1

Raccoon, in garbage can, lives in deserted garage, February 2

Pigeons, live under the eaves at the store, year round

White-tailed Deer, at the old apple tree eating twigs, April 7.

Ask your child to tell you stories about the animals she sees. You write them down.

ANIMAL HOMES

We share the world with animals. Where do they live? Look for animal homes together when you are out walking. What species live in lakes? Oceans? On farms? In swamps? In forests? In trees? Underground? In the lawn? In the garden? At the park?

You might want to mention that all animals live in neighborhoods, called habitats. Sometimes we share our home with animals; for instance, with pets or dust mites. Sometimes animals have special homes. Birds have nests, bees have hives, cows have barns or pastures, pigs have stys, bears have dens, beavers have lodges, snails carry their houses on their backs, and your child has her home, with you.

WHAT DO ANIMALS EAT?

Talk about what different animals eat. What foods do animals eat that we eat? What do we eat that animals don't? For instance, we eat lettuce and carrots, so do rabbits. A squirrel eats nuts, monkeys eat bananas, seals eat fish, birds eat fruit, but also worms and birdseed. You may want to go "Owling" at your conservation area. Read *Owl Moon* by June Yolan, Scholastic books. As you walk in the woods, check under spruce trees to see if you see any hairy pellets dropped by owls. If you find one, pull it apart and show her the undigested bones and hair cast off after the last meal of mouse or rodent.

HOW DO THEY LOOK?

As you watch the animals around you, talk about how they look. Do they have skin? Fur? Feathers? Feet? How many legs? Ask your child to describe the animals you have seen after a trip to a zoo or farm.

HOW CAN YOU MOVE LIKE AN ANIMAL?

You and your child can have fun moving like various animals. Here are a few ideas to get you started.

Dragonfly Flap: To be a dragonfly, your child can wave her arms up and down slowly, then quickly. Use both short and wide strokes. Then ask her to run, so she'll be flying like a dragonfly.

Frog Hop: Have your child crouch down with her hands between her legs, and hop along. Try going both forwards and backwards. Ask her to say "ribbit, ribbit" like a great big bullfrog and take huge hops, then make small hops and "peeper" sounds. Try to get out into the country on a warm spring evening to hear frogs at a swamp.

Snake Slither: Once your child can slither sinuously along the ground with her hands in front of her, ask her to put her hands on her ears and wriggle like a loping lizard.

Snail Snuggle: Ask your child to curl up into a tight ball, with her back up like a snail in its house. Ask her if she can move while she is rolled up in her house.

Crab Walk: Tummies up, walk around on all fours like a crab. Then have a race. Try to walk sideways the way a crab does, too. Now, sit down on the floor and cross your legs. Put your hands beside your bottom and push down hard, so your body lifts up. How long can you stay up? How many times can you do it?

Stork Stretch: How long can you stand balanced on one leg? On the other? Try it again with your eyes closed. What did you notice?

HOW DO THEY MOVE?

Ask your child to do the motions of all the following animals. Say:

> Frogs jump, inchworms hump;
> Bugs jiggle, worms wriggle;
> Rabbits hop, horses clop;
> Eagles glide, snakes slide;
> Kangaroos leap, mice creep;
> Wallabees bounce, kittens pounce;
> Hawks soar, bulls roar,
> Cheetahs run, lions sun;
> Tigers stalk, I walk.
> (Traditional, Canada)

Add your own favorites. You may want to talk about which animals move slowly and which are fast. Read Aesop's wonderful fable, *The Tortoise and the Hare*.

WHERE DO ANIMALS COME FROM?

Investigate how different animals are born. Mammals, like your child, come from a mother. So do all other mammals: gerbils, rabbits, hamsters, mice, rats, kittens, lions, elephants, deer, dogs, bears. Special moms carry babies in pouches. This type of animal, 'possums, kangaroos, koalas, is called a marsupial.

Birds, insects, bees, ducks, turtles, snakes, spiders, and chickens come from eggs. You can talk about incubation, nesting, and hatching.

Some animals transform; for instance, a caterpillar forms a chrysallis and emerges to become a butterfly. A frog lays an egg mass, which transforms from pollywogs to tadpoles to frogs.

Animal babies often have different names from their parents: kids, cubs, chicks, puppies, kittens, fawns. Children are fascinated by baby animals, so try to visit a farm or zoo in the spring.

THE HABITAT GAME —
EARTH, AIR, OR WATER

Two or more players take turns. One player names a habitat; for instance, "Water, the sea bottom." The next player names a species that lives in that habitat; for instance, "lobster." The next player performs the actions or makes the sounds; for instance, crawling along the floor on her tummy, antennae wiggling in front. The next player describes the animal. Remember that plants, birds, and insects live in habitats, as well as animals.

COLLECTIVES

One lion is a lion (just lyin' around); more than one lion is a pride. Your child will be fascinated by the collectives of some animals. You can refer to the classic *An Exultation of Larks* by James Lipton (Grossman Publishers), to keep you going forever. Here are a few to get you started:

A gaggle of geese	A paddling of ducks
A stand of flamingos	A leap of leopards
A school of fish	A string of horses
A parliament of owls	A plague of locusts
A drove of cattle	A swarm of bees
A crash of rhinoceroses	A clutch of eggs
A peep of chicks	A brood of hens

BABY NAMES

Animals have names, but their babies often have different names.

> Ducks have ducklings
> Chickens (or hens and roosters) have chicks
> Wolves have cubs
> Kangaroos have joeys
> Bears have cubs
> Cows have calves
> Horses have foals

Cats have kittens or catlings
Dogs have pups
Goats have kids
Sheep have lambs
Moose have calves
Geese have goslings
Pigs have piglets or shoats
Swans have cygnets
Deer have fawns
Frogs have polliwogs and tadpoles
Owls have owlets
Insects have grubs and maggots
Hares have leverets or bunnies

Other small animals are called nestlings, fledglings, yearlings, or whelps.

Tell your child she has other names, too. You can call her "my little chickadee" or *enfant*, *bambino*, kid, child, youth, tot, brat, mite, urchin, sprig, lassie, damsel, cadet, colleen, chick, tike, whippersnapper, wench, lad, laddie, scion, chip-off-the-old-block, heir, progeny, cherub, imp, babe, and of course "my very own baby," when you give her a hug.

WOLF WALKING

When you and your child are out on a hike, practice Wolf Walking. Wolves look back over their shoulders as they walk along, so they won't get lost! By looking back over her shoulder, your child will see how her route looks from behind as well as in front. She can find her way back by reversing the landmarks she sees on her way.

ANIMAL MAPPING

Using an atlas or globe, show your child where different animals live; for example, tigers in Asia, kangaroos in Australia, giraffes in Africa.

WATER VIEWER

It's hard to see what lies beneath the surface of water. A Water Viewer is simple to make, and lets you see what lies underwater, if you don't have a snorkelling mask or swimming goggles. Find a waterproof plastic or rubber tube, or cut both ends out of a tin can. Pull plastic wrap tautly over one end and seal it with a tight rubber band or rubber cement. Place the sealed end of the tube in water and look through the top.

STONE SKIPPING

When you are at the beach, look for small, flat, round skipping stones. Show your child how to hold the stone flat between your thumb and index finger. Hold your hand low and flat over the water, and spin the stone off your forefinger. Practice makes perfect.

DIP NETTING

Dip netting is great fun at swamps, marshes, bogs, fens, ponds, lakes or brooks. You need a dip net on a solid handle, a shallow basin or dishpan filled with local water, a magnifying glass, and some way to identify what you find. Wetlands field guides are available at bookstores and libraries, and conservation areas often provide species identification lists.

Dip at a transition area, a place where habitats change. For instance, stand on a boardwalk or the edge of a dock, and swish your dip net along hummocks of sedge or cattails, or along the edge of the shoreline. Swish the net through the water gently and try to avoid scooping up huge quantities of mud. What can you find? Depending on your habitat and the season of the year, you might find: baby turtles, frogs, pollywogs, insect larvae, insects, insect cases, water striders, water boatmen, beetles, nymphs, minnows, newts, leeches, snails, egg cases...

Put your finds into the basin so you can examine them closely and identify what you have found. Write down your finds on a checklist and return the mud and plant life to the water. After researching your finds, return them to the habitat where you caught them. Wash your hands thoroughly after dip netting.

This is the Alligator

This is the alligator
(Two arms extend to form an alligator
He sits on a log
One arm extended for log
Down in the pool
Make a circle of both arms
He sees a frog.
Hands like binoculars around eyes
In goes the alligator
Diving motions with hands
Round goes the log
Rotate hands
Splash! goes the water
Splashing motion
Away swims the frog.
Swimming motions)
(North American Nursery School)

Mr. Frog

Mr. Frog jumped out of his pond one day
And found himself in the rain.
Said he, "I'll get wet, and I might catch cold."
So he jumped in the pond again.
(Anonymous)

FISHIN'

"Fishin' is easy, it's the catchin' that's hard."
(Old Yankee Proverb)

Fishing can be fun if you and your child have the patience for it. Make sure you have any necessary licenses before dropping your lines in the water. Keep her fishing tackle simple for now; she isn't ready for fancy casting rods and complicated lures. The best fishing rod will have a simple reel, a line, a bobber, and a single hook lure. If you use live bait, I recommend staying away from frogs and minnows until she is older. Worms are okay. A simple slug-like plastic jig is fine. Are you prepared to clean and cook the fish? If not, cut (or file) the barb from her hook. Make absolutely certain she wears her life jacket or personal flotation device when she is fishing.

One, Two, Three, Four, Five

One, two, three, four, five
> (Extend one finger at a time

Once I caught a fish alive.
> Make fish motions with hands

Six, seven, eight, nine, ten.
> Extend fingers of other hand

Then I let it go again.
> Release imaginary fish

Why did you let it go?
> Open hands

Because it bit my finger so!
> "Ouch!" shake hand

Which finger did it bite?
> Extend hands palms up

This little finger on the right.
> Point to right baby finger)

(Traditional, Great Britain)

Seven Black Friars

Seven black friars, sitting back to back
Fished from the bridge for a pike or a jack.
The first caught a tiddler,
The second caught a crab,
The third caught a winkle,
The fourth caught a dab.
The fifth caught a tadpole
The sixth caught an eel
The seventh one caught an old cart wheel.
(Traditional, Great Britain)

WOODS WALKING

Go for a walk in the woods with your child. Take along a map or follow a marked trail at a conservation or wildlife area. Allow yourselves at least two unhurried hours and go slowly. Take along a water bottle and snacks in a knapsack. Bring field guides, binoculars or field glasses, a magnifying glass, and a bug bottle, so you can see, watch, and identify what is around you. If poison oak, ivy, sumach, stinging nettles, black flies, ticks or mosquitoes are apt to be around, wear long pants and sleeves.

Proceed slowly. Listen for bird calls and see if you can spot the bird. Look for mushrooms on dead logs. Roll over logs or rocks carefully and see what lives there; then replace them after you look, so the critters' homes aren't disturbed. What's under the fallen leaves on the forest floor? Have you found any salamanders? Slugs? Worms? Insects? Grubs? Touch the different tree barks and look up at the different shapes of trees. Compare the different shapes and colors of leaves. Explain that trees breathe through their leaves or needles and that leaves give off the oxygen we breathe.

Smell the flowers and plants. Listen to the insects. Watch for the darting of a chipmunk. Enjoy the great outdoors together, in all the different seasons.

A Tiny Worm

A tiny, tiny worm
> (Wriggle index finger of one hand

Wriggled along the ground
> up opposite arm

It wriggled along like this
Without a sound.
> Finger to lips

It came to a tiny hole
> Make hole with

A tiny hole in the ground
> thumb and index finger

It wriggled right inside
> "Worm" crawls into the hole

Without making a sound.
> Finger to lips)

(North American Nursery School)

There Was a Tree

This song is cumulative, adding a new item to the list with each verse, much like *Alouette*. Have your child echo the first lines, then join in for the list, pretending to be all the different features as they are named.

> *There was a tree*
> > (echo)
>
> *The biggest tree*
> > (echo)
>
> *The biggest tree that you ever did see*
> > (echo)
>
> *And the tree was in the ground*
> *And the green grass grew all around, all around*
> *And the green grass grew all around.*
>
> *And on that tree*
> > (echo)
>
> *There was a limb*
> > (echo)
>
> *The straightest limb*
> > (echo)
>
> *That you ever did see*
> > (echo)
>
> *The limb was on the tree*
> *And the tree was in the ground*
> *And the green grass grew all around, all around*
> *And the green grass grew all around.*

> Subsequent verses:
> *. . . strongest branch . . .*
> *. . . smallest twig . . .*
> *. . . deepest nest . . .*
> *. . . smoothest egg . . .*
> *. . . prettiest bird . . .*
> *. . . strongest wing . . .*
> *. . . softest feather . . .*

(Traditional, United States)

Kookaburra

(Can be sung as a four-part catch)

Explain that this song comes from Australia, and look for Australia on a map or globe. The Kookaburra is like a woodpecker and has a raucous "laugh."

Kookaburra sits in the old gum tree
Merry, merry king of the bush is he.
Laugh, Kookaburra, laugh, Kookaburra,
Gay your life must be, Ha-ha-ha.

Kookaburra sits in the old gum tree,
Eating all the gumdrops he can see.
Stop, Kookaburra, stop, Kookaburra,
Please save some for me, Ha-ha-ha.

Kookaburra sits on the electric wire,
Tears in his eyes and his pants on fire.
Ouch, Kookaburra, ouch, Kookaburra,
Hot your tail must be, Ow-ow-ow.

(Traditional, Australia)

GRASS WHISTLE

Pick a flat blade of tall grass. Hold it firmly stretched between your two thumbs, put it up to your mouth, and blow. Practice until you can make a screeching sound.

GARDENING

If at all possible, grow a garden with your child. Get outside and dig in the early spring. Look for worms. Plan what you are going to plant, whether flowers or vegetables, and buy the seeds. Plant the seeds according to the directions on the package. Weed, water and nurture them tenderly. Think about growing a Hallowe'en pumpkin, too. Plant sunflower seeds and leave the huge flowers for birdseed in the winter. If you don't have access to a garden plot, sprout some seeds in a plant pot or grow some narcissus or crocus in the wintertime from bulbs.

Talk about how seeds grow into trees; for instance, maple keys, hazelnuts, chestnuts, acorns, and apple seeds. When you go on nature walks, collect a sample of the seeds and leaves of different common plants, and press them to make a book. You might want to read *The Tiny Seed* by Eric Carle (Philomel).

HOW DO PLANTS EAT?

You need a piece of celery or a lily-of-the-valley flower. Place it in a glass of water with a few drops of red, green, or blue food color. Wait a few hours and see what happens. Explain that the food goes into the plant through roots and veins. Your child has veins in her body, too, to get the food to her cells, to make her grow. Visit a maple-sugar bush when the sap is running.

NOT ALL PLANTS COME FROM SEEDS

Explain that not all plants grow from seeds. Some plants, like molds, mushrooms, ferns, bracken, and lichens, grow from yeast spores. Leave a piece of bread out of the package overnight. Moisten it slightly and seal it in a plastic bag or glass jar, and put it in the dark for a few days.

Some plants grow from cuttings. Try growing carrot tops, an avocado pit, flower cuttings, or a sweet potato vine in water. After they sprout roots, plant the avocado or flower in a pot.

BACK YARD RESTAURANT

You can establish a back yard restaurant for birds even on a high-rise balcony. Of course, the more natural your habitat, the greater the number of species you can attract to your feeders. You may find that you want to discourage certain animals like squirrels or raccoons, or you may want to avoid ground feeding so you won't attract too many pigeons or starlings.

Different types of birds are attracted to different foods and different shapes of feeders. When you visit your conservation areas, visit the gift shop and talk to the naturalists about the types of birds you want to attract. They will get you started. Contact your local Audubon Society and natural resources agencies for information about the species you are attracting. You may want to get involved in the Audubon Society's Annual Christmas Bird Census, where you report the number and type of birds at your feeder.

CHICKADEE CRUNCH

Chickadees love this! Grind some raw beef suet and place it in the top of a double boiler. Heat it over boiling water until the fat melts, then set it aside to cool and harden. Reheat. Tie strings onto pine cones. Spoon the warm suet over the pine cones until they are well coated, and roll them in millet seed. Have your child press some sunflower seeds up under the scales of the pine cones. Chill until firm and hang outside. You may want to decorate the "feeders" with ribbons and have your child give some as gifts.

Our favorite cross-country skiing area is at a large marsh. We take along pockets full of sunflower seeds and call "chick-a-dee-dee-dee." We've had the birds literally eating out of our hands.

WEAVE A BIRD'S NEST

Collect some sticks, bits of fluff from your dryer, string, yarn, and dried grass to weave a bird's nest. Talk about how birds make their nests, lay eggs, and hatch and feed their babies. Be sure to have your child leave some tiny bits of dryer fluff and short bits of string or wool outside during the nesting season for the birds to use.

OBSERVATION FIELD LISTS

We spend lots of time, year round, outside, and it was natural to want to identify what we were seeing. We are now avid birdwatchers, plant-identifiers, and animal-spotters. We have good binoculars, four or five field guides (I recommend the Audubon series), and several field lists. These lists are available from conservation groups, conservation areas, and the Audubon Society. Some are for day trips, some are for a season, some are for a specific area, and some are lifetime observation lists. By all means, start a lifetime list for your child now, and keep track of what you see. You will be amazed at how soon you start seeing some of the rare, exotic species.

Two Wrens

Two wrens there were upon a tree
(Extend arm and fingers upwards
Whistle and I'll come to thee;
Two fingers of other hand make "wrens"
Another came, and there were three,
Extend another finger
Whistle, and I'll come to thee;
Another came, and there were four,
Extend another finger
You needn't whistle any more,
And there are none to show to you
Shake head "no"
For being frightened, off they flew.
Fly fingers away)
(Anonymous)

Little Robin Redbreast

Little Robin Redbreast
(Make fist and join thumb and index fingers
Sitting on a rail
Rest wrist on edge of other hand
Nibble, nabble, goes his head
Move thumb and index fingers up and down
Wiggle, waggle, goes his tail.
Tilt wrist over other hand)
(Anonymous)

INSECT COLLECTION

Your child is probably mesmerized by watching insects and spiders. Give her The Bug Bottle, which comes with *The Bug Book* (Workman), to help her capture and identify her specimens. If you already have an insect field guide, simply punch holes in the top of a jar lid.

Never touch insects directly with your fingers or disturb their nests; some of them bite, some of them sting, most of them are easily squashed. Use the bug bottle or a clean, dry dip net to capture specimens. Observe, identify, and investigate the insect with a magnifying glass. Your child should always return the insect to the place she caught it. Try to capture fireflies on hot summer evenings in the country.

TRANSFORMATIONS

Talk about transformations in nature: eggs hatch into baby birds, egg masses turn into pollywogs, which turn into tadpoles, which turn into frogs. One of the easiest transformations to observe is the caterpillar into a butterfly. Monitor milkweed that has larvae eating. Watch for the spinning of a cocoon and for the chrysallis opening to become a beautiful Monarch butterfly. Milkweed is noxious to most species, and only the Monarch thrives on it in a symbiotic relationship. Read *The Very Hungry Caterpillar*, by Eric Carle (Philomel Books), as you discuss transformation.

Fuzzy Wuzzy Caterpillar

Fuzzy wuzzy caterpillar
(Index finger creeps up opposite arm
Into a corner will creep
He'll spin himself a blanket
Then he'll fall asleep.
Rest head on hand)

Fuzzy wuzzy caterpillar
Wakes up by and by
(Wake up
To find he has wings of beauty
Flap arms
And now is a butterfly.
Flap hands, thumbs interlocked)
(North American Nursery School)

This Little Caterpillar

This little caterpillar on a cold, stormy day
(Creep fingers up arm
Crept out on the branch of a tree.
to crooked elbow.
And spun a wee house out of spiderweb threads
Spinning motions
Where he slept safe and warm as can be.
Rest head on folded hands)

The snowflakes fell softly down from the cold sky
(Flutter hands down
And the north wind wailed "whooo-eeee"
But the caterpillar cared not, he was fast asleep
Rest head on hands
In his tiny, warm house in the tree.
Close left fist over right hand)
(North American Nursery School)

One, Two, Three

One, two, three
> (Extend fingers, one at a time

There's a bug on me!
Where did it go?
> Open hands

I don't know!
OOPS.
> Wriggle)

(Traditional, Nursery School)

CLOUDS AND CLOUD FORMATIONS

Your child will be fascinated by the shapes made by clouds. Watch for changes in the weather and talk about the different types of cloud formations. Watch the clouds blow, mention that the wind moves the clouds, and that when the wind blows strongly or changes direction, it means a change in the weather.

Watch the weather forecasts on the news. Visit a meteorologist at your local airport and request an old weather map for your child's wall. Ask if you can see the radar screen and see if it's showing any precipitation.

Try making your own weather forecasts, using some of the age-old adages about the weather:

Red sky at night, sailor's delight,
Red sky at morning, sailor's warning.

Evening red and morning gray, send the traveler on his way.
Evening gray and morning red, bring the rain down on our heads.

If March comes in like a lion, it goes out like a lamb.

Plant peas for July 4th on March 17th.

If squirrels run crazily gathering nuts, it will be a long, hard winter. If not, the winter will be mild.

The snow will be as deep in the winter as the weeds are high in the summer.

A windy March and rainy April make a beautiful May.

April showers bring May flowers.

If the horns are up on a crescent moon, the month will be dry. If the horns are down, it will be wet. All the water falls out.

Count the stars inside the moon's halo. It will indicate the number of days of bad weather, or the number of days before the weather changes.

When the stars twinkle more and are brighter than usual the wind is going to blow.

(Traditional, Yankee Proverbs)

THE WEATHER

Enjoy all types of weather, not just the clear and sunny days. Sing songs, recite poetry, go for walks in the rain, roll in the snow, fly a kite, feel the wind in your hair, watch your breath on a cold day, see if you can find identical snowflakes.

The Rain

The rain is falling all around
It falls on field and tree,
It rains on the umbrellas here
And on the ships at sea.

(Robert Louis Stevenson)

It's Raining

It's raining, it's pouring,
The old man is snoring,
He went to bed and bumped his head
And couldn't get up in the morning.

(Traditional, North America)

I Hear Thunder

Tune: Frère Jacques

I hear thunder, I hear thunder
Hear it roar, hear it roar?
Pitter patter raindrops,
Pitter patter raindrops,
I'm all wet, you're wet too.

(Traditional, North America)

If All the Raindrops

If all the raindrops were lemon drops and gumdrops
Oh, what a rain it would be.
I'd stand outside with my mouth open wide
I wouldn't care if I ever went inside.
If all the raindrops were lemon drops and gumdrops
Oh, what a rain it would be.

(Traditional, North America)

MAKING RAINBOWS

Talk about the weather that makes rainbows. Usually, there is a rapidly moving cold front, a squall line and a temperature drop. The sun shines through water droplets in the air, which act like a prism.

Make your own rainbows on a sunny day:

• With your back to the sun, adjust the nozzle of a garden hose to a fine spray. The sun will create a rainbow for you.

• Place a small mirror in a glass of water. Turn the glass so the sun shines on the mirror and reflects a rainbow.

• Hang a cut-glass prism in the sun to create many small rainbows.

WHERE DOES THE WATER GO?

Place some water in a flat dish outside on a sunny morning. Come back in a few hours. What has happened to the water? Talk about how the water evaporates into the air from lakes, oceans, rivers, streams, and washing hung outside. As it evaporates, it rises into the air to eventually form clouds, and turn into rain.

We can make "rain" by boiling a pot of water. Hold the lid over the pot so steam forms. The steam creates drops of water, which eventually fall back into the pan. The same thing happens when evaporated water drops form clouds. The clouds get saturated with water and condense to fall back to earth as rain.

MAPPING

Show your child that maps can help her find her way around. Draw a map of your own neighborhood and draw the route to her best friend's house or to school. Road maps show you how to get further away, perhaps to grandma's house or the zoo. An atlas or globe shows where animals come from, where news happens, or where her banana stickers come from. A map of the solar system shows us where the earth is. A map on the subway shows us where to find our stop. Show your child aerial photos (there may be some of your own neighborhood available from government agencies), use maps when you are on nature trails. If you are boating or flying in light aircraft, let her see the navigation charts that are essential to finding your way home again.

THE HIDDEN LUNCH

My dear friend and swimming instructor, Marie, has drawn maps for her children to follow to find their lunches ever since they were in kindergarten. Her youngest child is now in university and still hunts for her lunch. Marie draws a map of where to find hidden clues that lead to the prepared lunch. Of course, it's usually either in the oven or fridge, but there are numerous stops along the way.

STORYBOOKS

Many of your child's favorite stories are based on the natural world. When you read stories together, include more information. For instance, when you read *The Very Hungry Caterpillar*, by Eric Carle (Philomel), talk about foods that are healthy for us to eat, too. What foods did the caterpillar eat that she eats? Talk about the differences between butterflies and moths. For instance, you will never see a butterfly at night and moths can't fold their wings straight up. Ask her to pretend to be a butterfly, a caterpillar, and a cocoon. Some of our favorite nature books include:

The Little Island, Golden MacDonald, Doubleday (Caldecott Winner, 1946)

The Loon's Necklace, How Summer Came to Canada, The Fire Stealer, William Toye, Elizabeth Cleaver, Oxford University Press

Seasons of Delight, Tasha Tudor, Philomel Books

The Chick and the Duckling, Mira Ginsburg, Aladdin Books

Make Way For Ducklings, Robert McCloskey, Picture Puffins

A Koala Grows Up, Rita Golden Gelman, Scholastic

The Grouchy Ladybug, The Very Hungry Caterpillar, The Tiny Seed, The Very Busy Spider, A House for Hermit Crab, Eric Carle, Philomel

The Quicksand Book, Tomie de Paola, Holiday House

Cloudy, With a Chance of Meatballs, Animals Should Not Wear Clothing, Judi Barrett, Athaneum

Frederic, Swimmy, The Biggest House in the World, Mouse Days, Leo Leonni, Pantheon Books

DISPELLING MYTHS ABOUT NATURE

She eats like a bird. In winter, a grownup would have to eat about forty pounds of food a day to eat like a bird, just to stay alive.

Snakes are harmful. Snakes eat lots of insects, especially mosquitoes. We should leave them alone.

Dragonflies will sew up your lips! Wrong, wrong, wrong.

Wolves attack people. The only recorded instance in North America occurred with a rabid wolf. Wolves leave people alone, unless they are cornered.

We all have some erroneous ideas about nature. Try to present your child with facts, not falsehoods, about the natural world. By all means, tell her the traditional native legends and folk tales, and talk about the old proverbs, but be sure to include scientific information.

THE NATURE CREED

When you are out on your travels in the natural world, remember the nature creed to ensure that those who come after will have the same enjoyment that you and your child share:

Take only memories.
Leave only footprints.
Shoot only photographs.
Kill only time.

CHAPTER NINE

FACTS AROUND A THEME — SPACE

"How Many Stars Are in the Sky?"

Y OUR CHILD MAY ENTHUSE about one particular topic, to the near exclusion of any other interest in his life. When it happens, run with it! It might be dinosaurs, it might be animals, it might be knights of old, it might be trucks, it might be leaves, it might be unicorns. It might be an interest he shares with many other children, with one special friend, or it might be a solitary interest. He is seeking knowledge about his topic, and he won't be sloughed off with superficiality once his curiosity and imagination have been excited.

Go for depth, fact and understanding of the topic yourself. Include his insatiable desire for this knowledge in all aspects of your lives. This is the beginning of true research and experimentation that may well last a lifetime. Find all the support materials possible, at your child's level of understanding and beyond it. You will be amazed at the concepts he can grasp.

Although space is presented as a special interest topic, it could as easily be any other interest. Find materials, think up projects, look for songs, rhymes, and games. Adapt ideas that will support your child's special interests. Constantly ask yourself, "What else can I find out about this topic that will interest my child?"

Often your child's first introduction to space is star wishing, as he stares up at the night sky. Sing "When You Wish Upon a Star," and remind him never to tell his wishes, or they won't come true.

Star Light
Star light, star bright
First star I see tonight
I wish I may, I wish I might
Have this wish I wish tonight.
(Traditional, North America)

SUMMER SKY

T ry to get out into the country sometime during the summer, or better yet, on a warm night in the early fall. Spray yourselves with insect repellant if necessary, lie down on a blanket, and look up at the heavens. Do it on a night of a new moon, if possible, or when the moon is far from full, or late to rise. Talk about the stars. Look for the Big

Dipper, Cassiopeia, and whatever constellations you can recognize. Use his star gazer, opera glasses, binoculars, a telephoto lens on your camera or a telescope to show greater detail of the night sky. See if you can spot the difference between the planets, stars, airplanes, and satellites. If the moon is out, talk about the phases of the moon as it goes from new to full and back again. Talk about the astronauts who have visited the moon and traveled in space. The object isn't to identify everything, but to experience the majesty of the night sky in its glory. Are stars different colors? Can you see any meteors? Can you see any Aurora Borealis?

There is an old riddle: *The greater it is, the less you can see it. What is it?* Answer: *darkness*.

STAR MYTHS

From prehistoric times, the stars have been used to organize the world. Tell your child the stories of how the heavens were formed, such as the Mohawk story about the Pleiades. Some native people believe the Aurora Borealis is the pathway of souls to heaven. Explore the mythology of the constellations: the legends of native peoples and the Greek myths. The stars have also lent themselves to more practical purposes, such as navigation and telling time.

STAR GAZER

Swish around some thin, black, watercolor paint inside a cardboard tube from toilet tissue or paper towel. The coating of paint eliminates extra light when he peers through the tube, and he is able to see more stars at night, even in the city. You can also use binoculars, a telescope, a birdwatching scope, or the telephoto lens on your camera. Say rhymes and sing songs about the sun, moon, stars, and planets, too.

Twinkle, Twinkle, Little Star
Twinkle, twinkle, little star,
How I wonder what you are!
Up above the world so high,
Like a diamond in the sky.

When the blazing sun is gone,
When he nothing shines upon,
Then you show your little light,
Twinkle, twinkle, all the night

Then the traveller in the dark,
Thanks you for your tiny spark.
He could not see which way to go,
If you did not twinkle so.

In the dark blue sky you keep,
And often through my curtains peep,
For you never shut your eye,
Till the sun is in the sky.

As your bright and tiny spark,
Lights the traveller in the dark,
Though I know not what you are,
Twinkle, twinkle little star.
(Jane Taylor, 1806)

FINDING CONSTELLATIONS

Look for the constellations. Cassieopeia, The Big Dipper, the Pleiades, and Orion are the easiest to find in winter in the northern hemisphere. Using a star map, copy your choice of constellation (perhaps your child's astrological sign) on a piece of paper and glue it to the bottom of an empty tin can. Using a hammer and nail, have him punch out a hole for each star in the constellation. Vary the size of the hole in the can, according to the size and brightness of each star. Use different sizes of nails, if necessary. When finished, hold your constellation up to a bright light to see how it looks in the sky. Then, at night, go outside and see if you can locate your constellation. Shine a flashlight through to see the pattern.

CITY WATCHING

The moon and city lights can be your best friends when you are learning about the stars. Constellations can be easiest to spot in the city or on the night of a full, or nearly full moon because they are made up of the brightest stars. It's easy to pick out Orion, the Big Dipper, Polaris, and Cassiopeia from the night sky. Try cupping your hands around your eyes to block our surface light, and avoid looking directly at streetlights or headlights that can interfere with your night vision. You will be amazed at how your night vision improves with time spent in the dark. How many stars can you see? Try to count them.

Find north, as a reference point, and have a flashlight with a red beam to point out what you are seeing. Polaris, the pole star, stands nearly still in the northern sky. It is the very end star in the handle of the Little Dipper, and can be easily found by extending a line from the bottom to the top of the front stars in the Big Dipper.

Depending on the season, the Big Dipper takes different positions around Polaris. In the spring, the Big Dipper looks as though it has just poured Polaris out; in the summer, Polaris is about to be scooped up by a left-handed person; in the fall, Polaris could fall into the Dipper; and in the winter a right-handed person would be able to scoop Polaris quite easily.

SPACE ART MATERIALS

Certain art materials cry out "SPACE."

- Styrofoam or cardboard cone shapes
- Red, yellow, white, and orange crepe paper, ribbon, cloth, foil, shredded paper for streamers.
- Black paper, black Bristol board
- Glow-in-the-dark stars
- Gummed stars, all sizes and colors
- Metallic, fluorescent, white, yellow crayons.
- Orange, yellow, white, fluorescent paper
- Hologram stickers
- Crushed eggshells
- Space stickers
- Metallic foils, all colors
- Aluminum foil
- Aluminum pie plates
- Deep-dish paper plates
- Mylar and mylar dots
- White, grey, yellow, orange, black paints.

SPACE PAINT

Mix equal parts of flour, salt and water in a plastic squeeze bottle. Shake thoroughly to mix and add tempera color, if desired. Squirt the paint on cardboard or construction paper for a lovely glittery effect.

CLOUD DOUGH (for ornaments)

Sift two cups of cornstarch and 4 cups of baking soda together into a pot. Mix well. Mix in 2 1/2 cups of cold water, and place the pot over medium heat. Stir until the mixture becomes the consistency of mashed potatoes. Turn off the heat, remove from stove, cover with a damp cloth, and allow to cool. Knead for five minutes. Roll between two pieces of waxed paper, using a rolling pin. The ideal thickness is about 1/4 inch. Use cookie cutters to made designs or form the dough with your hands.

Allow your creations to dry overnight. (Thicker objects may require a longer drying time.) If holes are desired, make them before the object dries. Paint on a design, if you wish. You can glue magnets or pin-backs onto the ornaments, or use them for Christmas decorations. Try making planets, stars, rocket ships, meteors, comets, or the moon.

SPACE PUPPET SHOW

Make stick-figure puppets using drinking straws attached to the back of jointed paper puppets. Make the puppets from special metallic foils, black paper, and mylar, and join the pieces with brass fasteners. Create your own outer space story and special effects. To make a space puppet theater, cut a square hole out of a box and cover the box with aluminum foil.

U.F.O.s

Make your own space stations by gluing together two aluminum pie plates or two deep paper plates covered with aluminum foil. You may want to glue a few bells or dried beans inside the plates before you seal the edges. Ask your child to decorate the U.F.O. with his art materials.

You can also hold glow-in-the-dark jumpropes or frisbees next to a light bulb to create more U.F.O. effects.

SPACE BOOK

Create a Space Book with all your child's space pictures and stories. Design a word-search puzzle using familiar words: moon, star, rocket, space, planet, light years, solar system, atmosphere, extra terrestrial, shuttle, oxygen, earth. Copy his new words into his book.

THE GALAXY QUIZ

You are both learning about the solar system and outer space. How much is a light year? How far away is the moon? What is the moon made of? Make up a quiz and ask each other questions about everything you learn. You might want to make a question and answer type of game, like Trivial Pursuit.

STAR BOX CONSTELLATIONS

Cut out a square window at one end of a shoebox that has a cover. Paint the inside of the box black. Using your star map, pinprick holes in cards to outline various constellations and write the name of the constellation on the card. Make a series of interchangable cards to put in the window of your Star Box viewer. Take your viewer outside with you, put a flashlight in the box, and try to pick out your constellation in the night sky. Of course, you can use your Star Box inside in the daytime, too.

GLOWING PAINTING

Use glowing stars on a huge piece of black paper to create a picture of the galaxy. If desired, add glitter, bits of metallic paper, metallic stars, space ships, planets and rings. You may want to tape your child's galaxy to his ceiling.

CAMERA

If you have a good camera, set it to the highest F-stop number, usually F-16. Place your camera on a tripod pointed at Polaris and take a time exposure of how the stars travel.

VISIT AN OBSERVATORY

Some scientific observatories are open to the public and welcome children. Some even have telescopes where you can attach your own 35 mm camera. If your museum doesn't have an observatory, try local scientific organizations and universities.

VISIT A PLANETARIUM

Go to the star show for children at the planetarium. Walk through the displays, push all the buttons, ask lots of questions, see all there is to see.

MEASUREMENT OF TIME AND SPACE

Distances in space are measured by the speed of light. A light year is the distance light can travel in a year. At approximately 186,000 miles per second, one light year equals about six trillion miles! Let your child learn something about long distances by finding a point one mile from your home on your daily walk. Discuss the different ways people travel long distances. If a destination is too far to walk, we may take a bus or car; if it's further still we go by train or small plane; if it's very far, we take a jet; in space, we take a rocket ship or space shuttle.

STAR COLORS

Stars have different colors and different intensities of brightness. Red stars are the coolest, yellow stars are moderately hot (like the sun) and blue-white stars are the hottest. Can you see any other colored stars in the night sky? Using colored gummed stars, make a star picture of your own.

PAINT THE MILKY WAY

Explain that earth is in the solar system, and our solar system is in a collection of stars called a galaxy. We live in the Milky Way galaxy. Using diluted white glue, have your child paint a wide streak across a piece of black paper. Then he can sprinkle glitter or crushed eggshells over the glue, allow it to dry, and shake off the excess.

When the Milky Way you Spy

When the Milky Way you spy
Slanting stars across the sky,
The eggplant you may safely eat,
And all your friends to melons treat.
When it's divided toward the west
You'll need your trousers and your vest.
When like a horn you see it float
You'll need warm trousers and a coat!
(Traditional, Chinese)

SPACE TRAVEL

Draw a map of the solar system, starting with the sun at the center. You might want to give your child an idea of the proportion of the solar system by taking a shooter and a dibs marble to a football field. If you place the dibs on one goal line and call it the moon, and place the shooter at the other goal line and call it earth, you'll be able to show him some of the sizes and distances involved.

Make a fleet of rocket ships, using cones, paper tubes, and all your various art supplies. Add streamers. Your child can fly his rocket ship from one end of the football field to the other, from the earth to the moon.

Zoom, Zoom, Zoom

Zoom, zoom, zoom
>(Rocket arms up
We're going to the moon
If you want to take a trip
Climb aboard my rocket ship.
>Climbing motions
Zoom, zoom, zoom
>Rocket arms again
We're going to the moon
>Circle arms for moon
10, 9, 8, 7, 6, 5, 4, 3, 2, 1, BLAST OFF!
>Crouch down, rise slowly, then jump high!)

Float, float, float
>(Make swimming motions
We're floating out in space
See the light from all the stars
>Peer
Look at Saturn, there goes Mars.
Float, float, float,
>Swimming motions
We're floating out in space.
Space shuttle _____
>Use your child's name)
Come in for a landing.

Katharine Smithrim and Bob McGrath sing "Zoom, Zoom, Zoom" on *Songs and Games for Toddlers*, Kids' Records.

THE MOON

Talk about the moon. It's the only place in our solar system, besides earth, that humans have visited! Talk about and show pictures of the *Eagle* landing on the moon. You may want to rent the video *Apollo 9, The Eagle Has Landed* from the science section of your video store.

What is the moon made of? Tell your child that there have been myths about the moon, including one that says it's made of green cheese. Is there an old man who lives there? Can you Moonwalk, like Michael Jackson? Show your child how. Talk about gravity, and what would happen on the moon if we tried to walk there. (Since there is less gravity, there is more bounce.)

We say, "Once in a blue moon," but how often is there a blue moon? It occurs when there are two full moons in the same calendar month. Show your child the moon phases for a full calendar month, as the moon goes from full, to new, to full again. If you live near the ocean, mention that the moon's gravity is what causes the tides here on earth. Sing songs and recite poetry as you look at the moon. Be sure to take your binoculars along to look at the "Old Man." His features are craters, caused by meteors. Decorate your child's wagon or tricycle to create his own lunar buggy.

Mr. Moon

O Mr. Moon, Moon, Mr. Silvery Moon
Won't you please shine down on me?
O Mr. Moon, Moon, bright and silv'ry moon
Hiding behind that tree.
These little children are asking you
To please come out so we can dream with you
O Mr. Moon, Moon, Mr. Silvery Moon
Won't you please shine down on, shine your light on,
Please shine down on me, me, me, me, me.
(Traditional, Southern U.S.)

In the Evening by the Moonlight

In the evening by the moonlight
You could hear those young folks singing;
In the evening by the moonlight
You could hear those banjos ringing.
How the old folks would enjoy it,
They would sit all night and listen
As we sang in the evening
By the moonlight.
(Traditional, Southern United States)

MOBIUS STRIP HIGHWAY

Where does the universe end? Some scientists think if you travel long enough, you come back to where you started. Take a strip of paper, about 1" by 12", and glue it into a ring, with one twist. Just turn one end of the paper over before gluing.

Think of your strip as a highway. Ask your child to draw a straight line down the center of the highway. Have him keep going until he gets back to where he started. What happens if you cut it in the middle instead of drawing the line? What happens if you put in *two* twists before cutting it? Your child can decorate his mobius strips with space stickers and make some mylar or foil mobius strip chains for the Christmas tree.

GOIN' ON A SPACE TRIP

Create your own space version of the childrens' classic "Goin' on a Bear Hunt." Listen to the original, first, if you don't remember it. (Mike and Michelle Jackson do a great version on their *Playmates* album, Elephant/Larrikin Records.) Start with a countdown and a blastoff from mother Earth, go in towards the sun, visiting Venus (phooey, smelly), stopping at Mercury (huff, puff, it's HOT!), heading in towards the sun (Let's get outta here before we burn up!). Stop off at Mars to look for Martians; admire the rings of Jupiter; visit the asteroid belt (plink, plunk, plink, plonk) between Mars and Jupiter; visit the outer planets, Saturn, Uranus, Neptune, and Pluto (woof, woof); and have a drink from the Milky Way. Then reverse actions and come back to earth.

After taking your space trip, you may want to listen to Gustav Holst's beautiful classical music, *The Planets*. Children especially like "Jupiter, Bringer of Joviality" and "Mars, Bringer of War."

CREATE A SPACE STATION

Convert a large appliance box into a space station or rocket ship, complete with decorations. Talk about what it would be like to live in a space station. What do astronauts eat? What kind of food would your child want to take into space with him? Perhaps you can have a space picnic in your space station. How would you sleep in space? Sling a hammock or pump up an air mattress for a "weightless" nap. You might want to listen to David Suzuki's wonderful album *Space Child*, El Mocambo Records, as you discuss what it would be like to live in outer space.

MOONSCAPE OR PLANETSCAPE

Create your own moonscape or planetscape using "found" materials around your house. You can work small, using a piece of Bristol board and small art materials, or you can create an entire space city, using boxes, patio furniture, benches, tables, and draped blankets. What would it be like to live in a space city? What would you do about air and water? How would you grow food?

SPACE GARDEN

Bend and twist some pipe cleaners to form stems, leaves, and petals for space flowers. Cover them with tissue paper, mylar, aluminum foil, glitter, interesting fabric bits, or what have you. Stick the stems in plasticine or baker's clay, or mount them in a piece of styrofoam.

THIS IS ONLY THE BEGINNING

As your child's interests expand, here are support materials you will find useful:

Books

The Astronauts, Random House Picturebacks

All About the Planets, Random House

Finding Out About series, including: *Sun, Moon, and Planets*, Usborne/Hayes Explainers

First Guide to the Universe, which includes: *Our Earth* and *Rockets and Space Flight*, Usborne/Hayes

Discovering the Stars, Kim Jackson, Troll

Stars, Golden Books

Sky Observer's Guide, Golden Books

Exploring the Night Sky The Equinox Astronomy Guide for Beginners, and *Exploring the Sky by Day*, Terrence Dickenson, Camden House

The Glow in the Dark Night Sky Book, Clint Hatchett, Random House

Skyguide, A Field Guide for Amateur Astronomers, Golden Books

The Night Sky, Collins Gem Guide

Periodicals

Odyssey Magazine, 1027 N. 7th Street, Milwaukee, Wisconsin U.S.A. 53233. Although designed for school-age children, your preschooler may find it interesting.

Sky News, Newsletter issued four times a year. National Museum of Science and Technology, P.O. Box 9724, Ottawa Terminal, Ottawa, Ontario Canada K1G 5A7. They don't charge for a subscription, but please send a donation to cover printing and handling costs. Checks should be payable to: The Receiver General for Canada.

Videos

Apollo 9 — The Eagle Has Landed and *N.A.S.A. (25 Years)*, National Aeronautics and Space Administration (available in the science section of your video store)

The Wonders of Earth and Space, National Film Board of Canada

Space, Earth, and Atmosphere, Tell Me Why Series, Prism Video

Movies

Star Wars, Return of the Jedi, The Empire Strikes Back, CBS Fox Video

E.T. — The Extraterrestrial, MCA

Explorers, Paramount

Flight of the Navigator, Disney

Space Camp, Vestron Video (actually filmed at the Children's Space Camp in Georgia)

Television _____

Watch for television specials. "Nova" and "National Geographic" often show items on space. Watch for "space happenings" on the news; what's going on with satellite launches, human travel, the space probes? Watch *Star Hustler* on PBS channels to check on what's happening in the sky on a weekly basis.

Other Support Materials _____

Look for star maps and globes, available at science book stores, and at gift shops at observatories, science centers, and planetariums.

At four, Jenny loved the record *Space Child*, David Suzuki, El Mocambo Records, 464 Spadina Avenue, Toronto, Ontario Canada M5T 2G8.

Watch for newspaper columns in your paper. Large city papers usually have weekly features about sky events. Your planetarium or observatory may have a Star Information Line you can telephone to get a recorded message of what to look for in the week or month ahead.

CHAPTER TEN

HOLIDAYS, THE FESTIVALS OF LIFE

olidays create special magic, whether they are a time of out-and-out revelry or a time of warmth, reflection and peace. Holidays give us a chance to truly appreciate our families and friends. They also give us a great opportunity to sample the festivals of other cultures. Join in and share with your child every holiday you can find or create.

Her Birthday

With the exception of Hallowe'en, and possibly Christmas, your child's birthday is her most important holiday of the year. Cake, candles and gifts on the anniversary of her birth let her know she is special and loved. She's the reason for the celebration, she's the STAR! Her friends' parties are important too; "Will you invite me to your party?" starts months in advance of the actual day.

SPOON HANGING

You need one ordinary human nose and one spoon. Rub the bowl of the spoon until it's warm. Tilt your head back and press the inside of the spoon against your nose, handle down. Tilt your head forward until the spoon balances. Practice makes perfect! You may want to keep this trick to yourself, or you may want to show your child and her guests how to do it.

HER PARTY

Trust your child to be the best judge of what she wants her party to be. Forget about what your friends and neighbors do for their parties; this is your child's celebration, and the two of you together should figure out what will work for you. Childrens' parties that fail are usually overly ambitious and have too much adult direction. To a child, a party is simple; friends, balloons and decorations, cake and ice cream, presents, and perhaps music. Everything else is window dressing.

I brainstormed with friends around the neighborhood to put together what has worked and what hasn't worked for us. Between us, we've given over a hundred children's parties. The consensus was: KEEP IT SIMPLE!

WHAT KIND OF PARTY?

Ask your child "What kind of party do you want?" and then negotiate something YOU can handle. Keep your child's interests in mind as you offer alternatives:

- A video and snacks for a few friends
- A trip to the museum, science center, aquarium, or zoo with two or three special friends with the same interests
- A wading pool party at the park
- A sleepover with a best friend (or two)
- An adventure hike along a nearby nature trail
- A parade of decorated trikes, bikes, and wagons
- A skating party at an outdoor rink
- A theme party, where all the activities, decorations, snacks and favors match the theme: dinosaurs, pirates, favorite toys, snow, puppets, etc.
- The traditional, at-home, blow-out birthday bash, with huge numbers of kids of all ages and party games

Think about the season as you plan your party. A wading-pool party with water squirters, sprayers, bubbles, boom box, popsicles and cupcakes is a natural in July. A fireside wiener roast in January is perfect. Of course, if you hire an indoor pool and a couple of lifeguards (which may be inexpensive from your Parks department), you can turn January into July.

Remember, your preschooler doesn't need restaurant meals, clowns, magicians, or a whipped cream fight.

THE GUEST LIST

Plan your guest list carefully and listen to your child. "I don't want her, she's too bossy!" is a clear message to you. Invite only as many guests as YOU can deal with; it's best to keep the party small. Do all the children know each other? If they don't, will you have to spend all your time trying to include shy children or dealing with a showoff instead of paying attention to the party?

Generally, the greater the similarity of interests of your child's guests, the easier the party. Do you want kids of the same age or of varying ages? Do you want all girls, all boys, or a mixture? How well do the children get along? Never hesitate to eliminate a name you *know* will cause trouble. You can always fulfill social obligations in a more intimate fashion: "Melissa is inviting her Tee Ball team for her party. We thought you and Anastasia would prefer to have a birthday picnic at the beach sometime next week."

CONTINGENCY PLANS

Always make contingency plans for your party. If you plan a party at the park, have backup arrangements in case of rain. Lindsey's mom found out thirty minutes before their first guest arrived that the filters at the swimming pool had broken and the pool was out of service. Fortunately, she was able to rent a video.

FOOD

Check with other parents about special food. You may need to arrange tofu hotdogs for a vegetarian or have vanilla ice cream instead of chocolate.

Keep food as simple as possible. The basics are best: ice cream, cake and juice. If you *must* add more, serve fresh fruit, vegetable sticks with a dip, popcorn, chips, or pretzels. If you need a meal, stick with kid food: hotdogs, hamburgers, simple sandwiches, or make-your-own pizza. Do your food preparation in advance, so you don't have to think about it during the party.

DETAILS, DETAILS

Time your party so guests will be alert and fresh. Generally, morning or early afternoon is best for three-year-olds. Four-and five-year-olds don't usually nap, so the time can be more flexible. Morning parties may be best for going to the zoo or on a hike. Begin slumber parties with a light supper at 7:00 P.M.

Be explicit in your invitations. The only thing worse for a child than waiting a couple of hours for a parent to collect her is showing up for a party all dressed in ruffles, lace, and patent leather shoes to find the other guests in bathing suits under the lawn sprinkler. State: "The party is from 2:00 to 4:30 P.M. Please send Elisa in her bathing suit. Bring dry clothes and a towel," or "Please wear long sleeves, long pants and rubber boots. We are going dip-netting at the Marsh," or "Party Clothes!"

HELP

Get another competent party-giving parent to help you out. This *doesn't* mean your spouse. One of you can deal with food and the other with activities. Your babysitter could probably use a few extra dollars and would be glad to paint faces and organize games. If your spouse is around, that's a bonus; the more the merrier!

WHEN GUESTS ARRIVE

Show your guests where the bathroom is. Designate two or three areas for children; one for food and gifts, one for activities, and a third, if available, for running around and being a kid. Make sure all the areas are childproof. The rest of the house is "off limits" or "out of bounds."

The decorations should all be up, balloons attached to the door, and a tape or record playing (perhaps Sharon, Lois, & Bram's *Happy Birthday*,

Elephant Records.) You might have a cartoon playing on your VCR. You have all the toys you are allowing out available; the rest are hidden in the off-limits area. Start a craft project right away; making a party hat, decorating balloons, putting together a simple puppet, or pinwheels (p 89). Don't force guests immediately into a specific activity, provide several alternatives. Try to have some quiet activities, as well as a place to run around and play party games. Save a big adventure game until the end of the party.

Many of the children already know each other and may just want to gab with friends for a few minutes or play together in a different way than usual. Let them set their own pace.

LOOT BAGS

Every child needs a Loot Bag to take home after the party. Your child can prepare them ahead of time or your guests can decorate them as a craft project. My canny friend Susan showed me the wisdom of giving Loot Bags on arrival. She includes a toy that can be used with other toys at the party or a game that she can teach; for instance, jacks, marbles, or a new ball-bouncing game.

When you think of what to put into Loot Bags, think about what you would want your own child to bring home. Many parents hate war toys, action figures, bubble gum, and lollipops. Some things we've found that work are: beads, stickers, water squirters, activity books, jacks, balls, marbles, markers, small cars, dinosaurs, bubble solution, small animals, pencil cases, pencils, boxes of raisins or animal crackers. You don't have to put much in; a bag of marbles and a package of stickers go a long way.

PARTY GAMES

Try to avoid games where you give prizes, where there are winners and losers, and where kids have to wait for the entire group before they have their turn. If you *must* give prizes, make sure everybody gets one, including the birthday girl. This party is for fun, and you don't need hurt feelings, tears, or boredom.

The best games are adventure games, circle singing games, and action games. Tag (p 37), The Blob (p 53), Hide 'n' Seek (p 63), Goin' to Kentucky (p 64), Brown Girl (p 95), Old Mother Witch (p 158), and Red Light (p 95), are all great party games. Teach a game like marbles, jacks, ball bouncing or skipping, something associated with the loot bags, and a few hand-clapping games.

MAKE YOUR OWN FOOD

At Ethan's last party, Susan put out ice cream, crushed pineapple, banana slices, hot fudge, hot butterscotch, a squirt can of whipped cream, nuts, coconut, and cherries, and each child designed her own sundae. I took the hint, and for Jenny's last party I baked cupcakes and put out bowls of different colored icing, cinnamon red-hots, sprinkles, silver dragées, colored sugars, and candles. Everyone decorated her own birthday cake and had her own candle to blow out. Dan spent forty minutes decorating his masterpiece!

PRESENTS

After cake, it's time for presents. Try to get through it quickly. If you are giving, you seldom go wrong with books, records, craft materials, science projects, or a magazine subscription. Everyone loves a new box of crayons, markers, or pencil crayons and a pad of paper.

MRS. CRANE

You are no longer yourself, but the evil Mrs. Crane, who is always IT for a game of Catch Tag. Mrs. Crane looks just like you, but the children never know when Mrs. Crane is going to take over. She threatens to throw nasty children in the garbage can, or whomp them with her rolling pin. The children call "Mrs. Crane, where are you?" while you slip back and forth between your normal, nurturing self, and the evil, witchy, Mrs. Crane. Imagine Irene's surprise when she first met Susan holding Irene's second-born son over the garbage can! Of course, you never play this game with a timid child; the children will participate when they are ready.

SLEEPOVERS

Some preschoolers love sleepovers, if they are used to being away from home overnight and know their hosts well. Sometimes the children even sleep! Around here, the kids have two rules for sleepovers: "Raid the fridge," and "Don't sleep." Be sure you have plenty of snacking food around.

A little planning makes sleepovers a breeze. Try to invite children that fall asleep at approximately the same time. Find out the visitors' go-to-bed routines. Make sure the children and their parents are comfortable with you and your parenting style. Sometimes, a good-night phone call to her parents will reassure a homesick child. Familiar toys, a favorite blanket or pillow, a favorite book, can all make unfamiliar surroundings seem more comfortable. Make a special breakfast after the sleepover.

Simple Trips

One mom organized a train trip bowling party when her son turned five. Three friends went along on the commuter train to a station about twenty miles away where there was a bowling alley next to the train station. She took along some activity books and pencil crayons for the trip. They bowled a game and had cake and ice cream at the snack bar. Was it fun? "Totally awesome, man!" They opened presents on the way home.

Another mom invited two guests to a children's concert for her son's fourth birthday. Ice cream and cake were served at home after the concert, and the party was deemed to be "The best ever!"

New Year

Every culture celebrates new beginnings, and many traditions abound in different parts of the world.

- Take a bath, or you'll have bad luck all year.
- Start whatever you want to do in the coming year. Take the first step towards what it is you want to accomplish.
- Place a loaf of bread, a bowl of salt, and a silver or gold coin on the table on New Year's Eve. This ensures bread, good luck, and money through the coming year.
- Sleep with a horseshoe under your pillow. At midnight, hold the horseshoe and make a wish.
- Set a tub of water out in the yard. Drop in a penny. You will be lucky in money matters.
- Wish EVERYBODY you see a "Happy New Year."
- Never, ever, sweep before noon of a New Year's Day, or you'll sweep all the good luck away!

Hogmanay

The Scots celebrate the festival of Hogmanay on the last day of the year. They hang mistletoe in a doorway on New Year's Eve to protect their houses against evil spirits. They smooch whoever comes through the door, too.

Children beg for, and get, a piece of cake on Hogmanay. It is a night of wassailing to drive evil spirits away.

First Footing is the most essential part of Hogmanay. The first person to cross your threshhold after midnight brings the luck of the year. The most-desired visitor is a handsome, dark, male stranger carrying a lump of coal, a slice of bread, salt, and a piece of evergreen. You *never* want a red-headed woman to be first.

Chinese New Year

The first day of the Chinese New Year occurs on the second New Moon after the winter solstice, late January to mid-February. Take your child to enjoy the festivities if you have a Chinatown near you. Wish everybody *"Bai-nein,"* Happy New Year. Go into a restaurant for lunch and sample from the Dim Sum carts.

New Year is a season lasting for about six weeks. It is the most important and festive celebration in the Chinese calendar and is very much a children's festival. The last month of the year is spent preparing for the New Year, which lasts for five days. The holiday continues until the final three-day festival on the first full moon after the New Year.

Little New Year

In the month before, every corner of the house is scrubbed, special foods are preserved, all debts are paid, books are cleared, and feuds are settled. No cutting is allowed during the five days of New

Year, so many foods are prepared in advance. One week before, the kitchen god, Tsao Wang, is sent back to heaven to report on the deeds of the family.

NEW YEAR'S EVE

On New Year's Eve the spirits return to earth. Firecrackers drive away the evil spirits and frighten away demons such as the dragon and lion. Incense, fir branches, sesame and cypress wood are burned to encourage good spirits to bring peace, health and prosperity. Tsao Wang's picture is rehung in the kitchen as children hold incense sticks to welcome him back. Ancestral altars are laden with fruit, bowls of rice, and cups of wine. There is a feast for the family where tables are laden with food, candles, lanterns, fruit and wine.

LANTERN

Stuff a clean, empty juice can with wet newspapers. Trace a pattern onto the outside and make holes in the pattern with a hammer and nails. When the pattern is completed, remove the papers. Place a votive candle inside the lantern and light it. If you want to hang the lantern, you can put three holes equidistant at the top of the can and add a hanger.

You might want to use moon phases, a dragon, or a lion as the motif on your lantern. Lanterns come in many shapes: the carp represents success through endeavor, the butterfly and the peach signify long life, and the moon brings good luck.

NEW YEAR

Day one: Family day. Wear new clothes and exchange gifts. Give children packages of money wrapped in red and gold. Po-Po, steamed white dumplings filled with surprises bring good fortune through the new year. There is much snacking of sweets: candy, rice cakes, litchis, longans, lotus seeds.

Day two: Family visits are returned. Branches are placed in a large vase and decorated with paper flowers, old coins, and fruit charms to bring prosperity.

Day three: Everyone takes to the streets! This is the day for parades, the Dragon Dance, and firecrackers. One person is under the head of the dragon, and others form a long snake-like procession under the dragon costume. One person, holding a white ball called the Pearl of Fire, goes ahead of the dragon. The Dragon is joined by a similar figure, the Lion, doing the Lion dance. Magicians, musicians, drummers, dancers, and little boys throwing firecrackers at the feet of the Lion accompany him along his travels. The Dragon appears only on day three. The Lion appears on days three, four, and five.

Day four: It's open house and everyone visits. Anyone can drop in, including strangers and casual acquaintances.

Day five: The day to visit friends who live far away. It is a day of travel, reunion, and joy. As dark settles, life returns to normal, shops are open, and foods can be prepared again.

THE FEAST OF THE FIRST FULL MOON

The first full moon of the year signals the Lantern Festival, which lasts for three days. Women dress in white and wear pearls. Lanterns are everywhere, and houses are decorated with colored lights and shiny beads. Buy moon cakes at a Chinese bakery. They are a sweet fruitcake made with light flour, citron, orange peel, and almonds.

Saint Valentine's Day

Valentine's Day is the special holiday to say, "I Love You," or "You are my special friend." Decorate your house with red hearts and golden arrows, flowers, cupids, pairs of birds, and lots of lace. Recite love poetry, listen to romantic music, dance together. Exchange presents, write love letters, give candy and flowers. Leave a special letter at a best friend's door.

Read the myths of Venus, Cupid and Psyche. Make Valentines for all your friends. Traditional Valentine's Day motifs include: flowers, trees, tulips (two lips), angels, hearts, cupids, love birds, and lover's knots. Traditional Valentines are made of silk, satin, velvet, chiffon, net, lace, mirrors, locks of hair, feathers, jewels, beads, and seeds.

FLOWERS

The Victorians had an entire vocabulary of love based on flowers. Here are a few:

Rose — *I love you*
Bleeding Heart — *Hopeless, but not heartless*
Forget-me-not — *Forget me not*
Gladiolus — *You pierce my heart*
Lily of the Valley — *Let's make up*
Violet — *I return your love*
Gardenia — *I love you in secret*
Sweet William — *You are perfect*
Goldenrod (*wear it*) — *You'll see your sweetheart*

POSTAGE STAMPS

Those clever Victorians had another secret vocabulary hidden in the placement of a stamp on a letter! Have your child send "stamp messages" along with her Valentines.

Stamps upside down — *I love you, or Kiss me*
Two stamps, side by side — *I love you twice as much*

Two stamps, one over the other — *Let's meet*
A stamp cut in half — *the right side: Our love is over*
the left side: You've broken my heart
A stamp at the bottom right of the envelope — *Oops, we've been found out!*

And don't forget the traditional line of hugs and kisses, Xs and Os, on your valentines. XXXOOOXXXOOOXXX.

SWEETS FOR THE SWEET

What would Saint Valentine do without sweets? Your child will love a special Valentine treat bag with cinnamon red-hots, chocolates, and those wonderful little pastel heart candies printed with mottos. You might make a heart-shaped cake or red jello for dessert on this special "I Love You" day.

THE VALENTINE BOX

Most schools, play groups, and organized children's classes have a Valentine Box where children exchange Valentines. Always try to get a list of names (first names will do) ten days or so ahead of Valentine's Day, so you and your child can make or cut out Valentines for EVERYBODY. It's always a great morale booster for timid or unpopular children, who may not always be included in group activities.

Make and deliver Valentines to all your child's special friends. Don't forget the neighbors, your babysitter, your librarian, the grandparents.

All Fool's Day — April 1 _____

April Fool's Day is for jokers. Anything, well almost anything, goes, until noon. It's called "Doll Day" in Japan, "Fish Day" in Spain, and "Cuckoo Day" in Scotland. Tell some of your favorite jokes, have a Backwards Day, and make Toe Puppets.

RIDDLES

What part of a fish weighs the most?   The scales
What has teeth, but doesn't eat?   A comb (or saw, or rake)
What is full of holes and holds water?   A sponge
What letters frighten a burglar?   I-C-U (I see you)
What has everybody seen that will never be seen again?   Yesterday

BACKWARDS DAY

Do everything contrariwise. Get up at an odd time, have dinner for breakfast, and breakfast for dinner. Wear your clothes inside out or backwards or upside down. If you play Tee Ball at the park, run to third base instead of first. OUT means SAFE and runs don't count. Greet visitors with: "So glad you had a good time, do come again." Say "goodbye" for "hello" and "hello" for "goodbye." A Backwards Day is a great time to read nonsense poetry by Edward Lear, Ogden Nash, or Lewis Carroll.

TOE PUPPETS

Everything is bizarre today, so why not decorate your toes? Get out the face paint or makeup (or use nontoxic acrylic paint) to paint puppets on big toes. Tip over a small table to make a puppet stage, lie back, and stick your toes up over the edge.

WHEN YOU TRICK SOMEONE

If you successfully trick someone, you say:

Up the ladder, down the tree,
You're a bigger fool than me!

WHEN IT'S OVER

All tricking is supposed to come to an end at noon on All Fool's Day. If someone plays a prank afterwards, you call:

April Fool has come and passed
And you're the biggest fool at last!"

Kite Festival

Create a neighborhood Kite Festival at the park to welcome spring. Gather everyone together to show the kites they made or bought. Award simple prizes, like a sticker that says CONGRATULATIONS on a piece of card, for every kite. You might want to make special mention of The Kite With the Longest Tail, The Biggest, The Smallest, The Highest Flyer, The Most Decorated, or whatever else shows up. Watch out for power lines and kite-eating trees.

MAKE AND FLY A SIMPLE KITE

String together drinking straws to make a tetrahedron (pyramid) shape. All four sides should be equilateral triangles. Cover two sides of the tetrahedron with tissue paper or a cut-up plastic shopping bag. Attach a string and watch it soar! You can string several tetrahedrons together to make a larger kites as long as two sides of each tetrahedron are covered.

IME NINO

Ime Nino is a Nigerian festival to celebrate masquerades. It is a village competition, held on the two days before Easter, where everyone dresses up and dances before the chiefs and elders of the village. Have the children dress up in costume and dance for your Kite Festival. Bring a boom box and some favorite tapes along to the park to provide the music.

Easter

EASTER EGGS — PISANKI

While Easter eggs now are a symbol of the Easter holiday, decorated eggs have been found throughout the Ukraine from thousands of years before the Christian era, with many of the same motifs in current use. The traditional designs are elaborate, geometrical, and multicolored.

If you are going to decorate hard-boiled eggs, make absolutely certain that you use nontoxic dyes. Otherwise, decorate the eggs, then blow out the contents after decorating. If you aren't certain of the dye that you used, throw away the contents of the egg.

There is a traditional language of colors and symbols used on these lovely eggs:

Orange — *friendship, attraction*
Red — *love*
Blue — *health*
Purple — *power*
Green — *money*
Black — *remembrance*
Dots — *stars*
Flowers — *love and charity*
Sun — *good fortune*
Stag — *health and prosperity*
Hen — *fulfilment*
Yellow and white — *traditional colors.*

Select clean, white, uncracked eggs. Prepare your dyes. Light a candle and assemble a steel pen with interchangable nibs. Divide the egg by placing a taut elastic band around the egg, lengthwise. Dip the pen nib into melted candle wax and trace a straight line along the elastic. If desired, rotate the elastic 90° and make another line. You can also move the elastic to around the egg's equator and divide it again. Dip the egg into the lightest color dye you plan to use and leave it until it is the desired color. Remember, the dye will dry slightly lighter. Wax your design for the next color and dip it in the next darker color. Continue until your egg is as you want it. To get a true black, paint half the egg with India ink, let it dry, then paint the other half.

To remove all the wax from the egg, warm a dry, folded cloth against a hot iron. Rub the egg with the hot cloth, refolding and reheating it until all the wax is removed. Polish the egg with the warm cloth, so the egg is spread with a final thin, glossy film of wax.

(While this is *not* how the most elaborate eggs are made and decorated, this will give you a good approximation, for use with your child.)

BLOWING EGGS

To make beautifully decorated, long-lasting eggs, use blown eggs. Make a small hole at one end of the egg with a sharp darning needle. Make a slightly larger hole at the other end. Pierce the yolk sac several times with the needle. Holding the larger hole over a bowl, gently blow the egg out of the shell through the smaller hole. Make sure you get all the egg out of the shell. Decorate and wax eggs before blowing them.

If you use a blunt needle, or hold the egg too firmly, the shell will fracture. It's also best to buy farm-fresh eggs, as the shells of supermarket eggs are sometimes flimsy.

EGG TREE

If you use a lot of eggs for baking or scrambled eggs, blow out and save the eggshells. Dye the shells or paint them with watercolor paints, and glue or tape on a bit of string for hanging. Have your child decorate an Easter Egg Tree outside.

EASTER EGG HUNT

Hide decorated Easter eggs or jelly beans. If you hide hard-boiled eggs, breakfast afterwards is easy. After all the decorated eggs are found, it's traditional to Crack Eggs together.

CRACK EGGS

Each person holds her egg, point forward. Two players crack the points of their eggs together, and the egg that stays whole the longest is the winner for the first piece of Kulich, the traditional Easter bread. Bets and side bets are sometimes placed on who has the strongest egg.

KULICH BREAD

Kulich is a wonderful sweet bread made with raisins, candied fruit, almonds, lemon rind, and lots of eggs and butter. It is often iced and taken to church to be blessed the evening before Easter morning. Sometimes, candles are placed on top.

Kulich is baked in a tall can to make the traditional onion-shaped spire on top. It contains all the foods that were forbidden during Orthodox Lent. The Cyrillic letters "X B," standing for Christos Voskres (Christ is Risen), are formed with strips of dough on top of the Kulich before being iced. To serve Kulich cut it across in circles.

To make a Kulich, add 1/2 cup sugar, 1 cup candied fruit, 1/2 cup raisins, 1/4 cup sliced almonds, 2 beaten eggs, and 1/4 cup melted butter to your favorite bread recipe. Thoroughly grease clean cans (labels removed), fill approximately 2/3 full of the dough, allow to rise, and bake.

Vacations and Travel _____

CAMPING

When Jenny was three, she begged and pleaded: "I want to go camping, I want to sleep in a real tent." I took her, and we loved it! Dad was a hold-out, but the next spring he agreed to come along for one night. He stayed for the entire long weekend! Now we all camp out frequently, and Jenny and I also camp out for at least a week during the summer.

Camping equipment encompasses a whole spectrum; from austere backpack, sterno stove, sleeping bag, and maybe a mountain tent at one end, to a fully equipped recreation vehicle with running water, electricity, plumbing, dishwasher, and VCR at the other end. I have a large tent, a portable two-burner propane stove, a huge cooler, and good air mattresses and sleeping bags.

For your first camping trip with your child, choose a campground not too far from home. Watch the weather, and don't go for more than two nights. Find a campground where you can be close to a comfort station and drinking water. Allow plenty of time to set up your campsite before dark, and take activities to entertain your child while you set up camp. She can help by handing you the tent pegs.

Preparation and planning is essential for any camping trip. Make complete lists of everything you need, including food. If necessary, do a "dry run" with all your equipment in the back yard or at the park. Once you're at the campground, a missing tent peg or a naptha lantern that you can't use, can spell disaster.

Last summer, I took Jenny and Jord camping for ten days at a conservation area about 125 miles north of the city. Dad came up the first weekend to help set up camp. Weekdays were strictly for the kids and me, but on the final weekend Linda, Dave, and Paul drove up on Friday evening for the weekend. We had a grand time.

What did the kids use? Field guides on every topic imaginable, dip nets, magnifying glasses, bug bottles and bug books, binoculars, their comfort toys, blankets and pillows, tapes for the boom box, crayons, markers, pencils, activity books, and piles of paper. They each had a backpack, their own water bottle, and a flashlight.

I reserved a specific campsite four months in advance of our trip, so we had a high, dry spot next to a primitive comfort station with running drinking water. The main lavatory, with showers and a laundry, was 300 yards away.

We went swimming, hiked, dip-netted in the marsh, identified numerous birds, critters, plants, bugs, mammals, and creepy crawlies. We collected rocks and threw them in the water. We watched stars, listened to loons, listened to bird calls, wrote in journals, cooked over campfires, toasted marshmallows. The kids attached themselves to the naturalists at the park for nature hikes and listened to legends of the native Ouendat people. The one and only time the kids fussed occurred when we had to go to town for an extra propane tank and some milk.

By the way, it rained seven of the ten days, and it didn't make a bit of difference. I had sealed every seam with sealant and the tent and camping gear stayed dry. We had raincoats and good rubber boots, and had a tremendous time!

Essential: Make it absolutely clear to your child that she is to stick to you like glue. Introduce her to the park rangers when you register, so they will know each other. Ask the ranger, each and every time you go camping, to outline to her in detail what to do if she gets lost. You may want to pin an emergency whistle onto her clothes. In most parks, they recommend that a child who realizes she is lost should stay still in one place, call out every couple of minutes, and wait to be found. Have her wear brightly colored clothes so you can spot her easily.

THE COTTAGE

My friend Jan says that going to the cottage is just like tenting, except that you stay dry at night. When I asked what they do in bad weather, she said they go into town and see a movie. When the weather is good, Sarah and Lauren ride on inner tubes, tell stories, have scavenger hunts, catch frogs, go fishing, try to scoop minnows with their hands, look for deer or moose tracks, turn over rocks, look for snakes, play in a rubber dinghy tied up to shore (with life jackets on) and look at the starry sky. They also do all the same things that we do camping.

Our family goes to a cottage way up north in the James Bay Frontier. We spend ages in the boat, wearing life jackets of course, searching for the moose, osprey, loons, mink, martens, otters, mergansers, and other wildlife that share the nearly uninhabited twenty-mile long lake. We go out exploring, with detailed maps, and fishing too.

Since our nearest movie is twelve miles away by boat and over a hundred miles by car, that really isn't a rainy day option for us. We take along huge piles of books, crayons, activity books, pads of paper, games, and favorite tapes. You need extra sets of batteries, if you are away from electricity.

CAR TRAVEL

Car travel is usually hardest for the first couple of hours. The driver isn't into the routine yet, and "Are we there yet?" can start as you back down the driveway! Small children have little sense of time.

Adjust your child's car seat so she can see the scenery. When possible, plan your route to include some interesting scenery, and stop frequently to enjoy it. Take along music to play on the tape deck, or have your child listen to a small personal recorder. Sing along to the music.

Watch for certain colored cars. If you have another adult along, make lists of where license plates come from. Talk about everything you see along the way. Show your child how to pull an imaginary whistle cord so she can ask tractor-trailer drivers to blow their air horns. Play I Spy. Take along magnetic puzzles, magnetic tic-tac-toe, and magic slates. Be sure to bring her blanket, pillow and special cuddly toy. (Warning: Reading and writing, in the back seat especially, can cause motion sickness in some people.)

Bring along a thermos of cold juice and plenty of healthy snacks. Fresh fruit, foil-wrapped cheese, healthy cookies and muffins travel well. Give your child a bag with her own water bottle, snacks, games, and toys. Stop frequently for drinks, snacks, restrooms, and a stretch.

When possible, combine these stops with sightseeing. If you see a historical marker, you may learn about an obscure fragment of history; if you stop at an interesting picnic ground along a river, you may see some shore birds, if you stop in a town, you might spot an interesting public building to explore.

You may want to follow back routes for a few miles now and then, to get away from expressway driving. Slow your pace and plan a short visit to a zoo, a historical site, or a special event along your way.

If your trip takes more than one day, stop early enough in the evening to explore a little before you collapse. Hotels with room service, indoor pools, and games rooms are nirvana. Take lots of breaks and take it easy when you travel by car with your child.

FLYING

Flying with your child is an experience that is either nerve wracking or marvelous; there seems to be no middle ground. I've had both experiences. By planning ahead, you can try to minimize many of the hassles. Money should never be your main consideration when flying with your child. Book a nonstop flight if you can. The next best choice is a direct flight, which does stop, but you don't get off the plane. If you must take connecting flights, look for good connections, because if you have bad connections, you'll be hanging around strange airports for hours. If you do get caught, walk around, visit the gift shops, watch the planes, and invest in a new activity book.

Try to avoid peak hours, especially the Friday and Sunday night crush. By leaving early in the morning, you avoid the crowds and start off fresh. Let your travel agent know that you are traveling with a child. Request seats with the most leg room, by the bulk heads, or near the washrooms, and make sure you have at least one aisle seat so it's easy to get up and wander around. Specify your needs at the time of booking your flight, including dietary needs; most airlines serve special children's meals. Often, airline staff call families to board and deplane first. Pare your luggage down to a minimum, especially if you are changing planes. Have at least one change of clothing per person in your carry-ons, along with moist wipes, activity books, markers or crayons, juice boxes, favorite snack foods, a couple of favorite books, and a favorite cuddle toy or blanket.

Check in early to ensure that all family members are able to sit together. Rent headphones for music. Your child will love flipping the dial around to sample all the different types of music. Some airlines even have a children's channel. If you're lucky, the airline will be showing a movie that interests your child.

While airline staff are there to be of assistance, and may provide a puzzle or coloring book, or even a visit to the flight deck, never rely on them to babysit or provide entertainment for your child. On your way in, check with the stewardess or purser to find out if they want you to deplane

first, or last. If it is after the other passengers, wait in your seats with your activities still out. Standing up and waiting, waiting, waiting, to get off the plane is very boring and may just overwhelm your tired child.

THE TRAIN

According to Jan and Susan, my experts on train travel, there is both an up side and a down side to train travel with children. Both of them agree, however, that it's much easier than going by car.

First, the bad news. Trains can run out of essential kid food, like milk, early in the journey. The club car can be inadequate and expensive. Air conditioning can break down and there are frequent delays. Once, Sue and her kids were caught in an ice storm; the train barely crept along, and all the food was gone! Surprisingly, the best place for kids may be the smoker because fewer people are smoking now, so there is more room, and the air conditioning is sure to be working.

Now, the good news. The highlight of train travel for all the children was going to the bathroom and getting drinks. Children can run around on the train and stretch their legs. Sometimes, the porter sets up a gamesroom in the lounge car before the bar opens. Kids can go up to the observation car to look at the passing landscape. Sarah once spotted a moose from the dome car! Kids love walking between cars and making new friends with other traveling children.

What to Bring and Do: Bring along a huge thermos of drinks and your own food. It's fun to take trips to the snack bar or club car as well, to buy what is available. Magnetic puzzles, tic-tac-toe, and storybooks are great. The conductor will sometimes provide coloring books and cutouts about train travel. Bring along that essential comfort toy and some new ones: tiny cars, dolls, buses, small bits of Lego (that you won't mind losing), farm animals, dinosaurs, zoo creatures. When you select your seats, try to get the ones in the corner, so you can turn them around to face each other. If you have a sleeper, bring toys that your child can use on the small floor space of your compartment. Bring along kids' tapes for a personal tape recorder, magic slates, drawing pads, tracing books and pencils. Your child always loves to carry her own backpack, so put some of the supplies in that.

THE BUS

I have talked to many mothers who have traveled long distances on a bus with small children. None do it enthusiastically.

If you must travel by bus, make sure there is a washroom on board, bring plenty of snacks and drinks, and seat your child next to the window, if at all possible. Bring along small toys and an individual tape recorder with earphones to help pass the time. Motion sickness seems to be the major problem on buses, so books, activity books, and reading together are not a good idea. Play out-the-window games, like I Spy, Let's Count the Red Cars, or What Type of Bird is That?

If you're lucky, your child might fall asleep. One mother who must travel by bus often always takes a late-night bus to ensure that just about everyone sleeps except the driver. The only time that didn't work was after a major sporting event when everyone was partying, except her grumpy child.

Staying Home _____

LEISURELY AFTERNOONS AT THE PARK

Summertime and holidays can be just great spent at home, using your park. We use our park with the wading pool in the early afternoon, taking along blankets, activity books, water squirters, crayons, snacks and towels. We meet up with whoever is in town that week and have a great time. The kids run around and the grownups gab over a thermos of tea. Occasionally a playground supervisor comes by with craft materials and new ideas or someone will bring along a tee ball, bat and tee for practice.

EVENINGS

During quiet summer evenings we go to a small park at the end of our street. Usually the dads are out, coaching Tee Ball or Lacrosse, and keeping an eye on the new two-wheelers in the adjacent empty parking lot. It's a great time to bring along a picnic, climb a tree, and use the playground equipment.

FAMILY DAYS FOR THE NEIGHBORHOOD

We've arranged several events in our park. We've had field days, miniolympics, a kite day, and a wonderful circus. We've also thought about a pet show, a puppet show, a musical day, a talent show, a space day, and a pioneer day, complete with square dancing and a sing-along. Of course, you can be seasonal and have a winter carnival, a spring fling, a summer fair, or an autumn harvest festival. One of the streets close by obtains a street-closure permit every year and has a family street festival that everyone in the neighborhood attends. Working together to create a special family day is a great chance to get to know the people living in your neighborhood. You might even be able to do a little fund raising to improve your playground facilities.

Hallowe'en _____

Hallowe'en is the most important festival for most preschoolers. Ghosts, skeletons, goblins, Jack O'Lanterns, witches, and dressing up in costume are a big part of the day. Arrange an afternoon get-together with your friends to have a costume parade. If you live in a safe neighborhood, you may want to take your child out Trick or Treating. If you go, make it early.

TRICK OR TREAT RULES

Give your child a meal before going trick or treating, and have her take along a snack. Tell her she is not allowed to eat *any* food she receives until you carefully inspect it at home. Throw away everything that isn't sealed in a package. Only Trick or Treat in neighborhoods you know or at friend's houses where the outside lights are on. Use lightly colored costumes, so you can be seen in the dark by passing motorists. Use face makeup and wigs. Masks can slip and obstruct vision.

Never let your child Trick or Treat alone. Buddy up with friends and go as a group, preferably with at least two adults carrying flashlights. Walk down one side of the street, then cross over at a crosswalk or traffic light, and come back down the other side. Never run back and forth across the street. Have her carry a flashlight inside a bright yellow or white plastic bag (or an old white pillowcase) so she can be seen. Make sure you go home before everyone gets tired.

When you offer treats, think of nonfood items. A few coins, crayons, a simple activity book (perhaps a couple of photocopied pages), a sealed toothbrush, a few balloons, markers, or a pencil are equally good a treat as candy and junk food. Stuff newspaper inside old clothes and decorate a pumpkin head for a dummy to spook visitors. Play a tape of spooky music. Jenny and I Trick or Treat, while dad stays home, dispensing treats. Many preschoolers are happy to dress up and stay home. They get a special treat and then they get to dispense treats to the kids who come by.

NICKY, NICKY, NINE DOORS

You may meet some wag who asks for a Trick. Nicky, Nicky, Nine Doors is the classic, at least since the days of outhouses. Only play it on someone who has asked for a trick, or a truly understanding friend. Simply bang on the door loudly, then run and hide before someone comes. Repeat several times. Explain that you never do this to an elderly person or a stranger.

HALLOWE'EN PARTY

Many parents, with good reason, prefer to have their children stay at home and have a party for friends on Hallowe'en. Play plenty of games and serve Hallowe'en snacks:

- Bat wings (blue corn chips served with dip)
- Spider web and bug salad (carrot shreds mixed with raisins and moistened with orange juice)
- Eyeballs (peeled or cut grapes)
- Purple passion punch. (Mix 1 pint of vanilla ice cream with 1 quart of gingerale and one can of grape juice. If possible, obtain a chunk of dry ice and place it in a large cauldron with some water. Put the punch in a smaller pot and place it, double-boiler fashion, in the smoking cauldron. Be careful not to leave it too long, as the punch might freeze.)
- Bob for apples
- Eat donuts suspended by strings
- Ice cupcakes (or cookies) with orange frosting. Decorate with a bit of green icing and chocolate chips.

OLD GRANNY WITCH

Old Granny Witch is a great game any time of year, but it's especially wonderful at Hallowe'en parties. Get a grownup to dress up in a witch's costume. She asks each child, "Whose little child are YOU?" The children answer, and hang around teasing Granny Witch. After a while Granny says, "No, you're all mine, and I'm going to turn you into a stew!" and gives chase. As she captures children, she puts them in her woodshed where they have to remain until another child can free them. If the witch manages to capture all the children, she runs and the children try to capture her!

OLD MOTHER WITCH

Mother Witch stands in the middle of a "ditch," a designated area about fifteen feet wide. The players line up on one side of the ditch. The object is to get to the other side of the ditch without mother catching them. They chant:

"Old Mother Witch, may we cross your ditch?"

Mother Witch procrastinates: "There's a dragon in my ditch," "My newts will eat you," or "Watch for the mandrake root," but at some point she says something that has a color, for instance, "My black cat won't like it." Any child wearing that color gets safe passage across the ditch. All the rest of the players must scramble across, and Mother tries to capture as many as possible. The children taunt her:

"Old Mother Witch, fell in a ditch, picked up a penny and thought she was rich."

POISON

On the ground, draw a circle and two Xs or a skull and crossbones to make a poison symbol. Have the children huddle around the symbol, but avoiding stepping on it. Everyone pushes a bit, trying to force another inside, so that person will become the Poisoner. The Poisoner is IT for tag, and anyone who is poisoned becomes another Poisoner. Establish a SAFE or TIMES spot for a quick rest to the count of twenty-five. The game continues until everyone is Poison.

Witch

Witch, witch, where do you fly?
Over the moon, and under the sky.
Witch, witch, what do you eat?
Little black apples from hurricane street.
Witch, witch, what do you drink?
Vinegar, blacking and good red ink.
Witch, witch, where do you sleep?
Up in the clouds, where pillows are cheap.
(Anonymous)

Witches' Charm

The owl is abroad, the bat and the toad,
And so is the cat a-mountain;
The ant and the mole both sit in a hole,
And frog peeps out o' the fountain.
The dogs they do bay and the timbrels play,
The spindle is not a-turning;
The moon it is red, and the stars are fled,
But all the sky is a-burning:
The ditch is made, and our nails the spade:
With pictures full, of wax and wool,
Their livers I stick with needles quick;
There lacks but the blood to make up the flood.
Quickly dame, then bring your part in!
Spur, spur, upon little Martin!
Merrily, merrily, make him sail,
A worm in his mouth, and a thorn in's tail,
Fire above and fire below,
With a whip i' your hand to make him go!
(Ben Jonson)

In a Dark, Dark Wood

(Recite in an ever-diminishing voice, until the last word)

In a dark, dark wood,
There was a dark, dark house,
And in that dark, dark house,
There was a dark, dark cupboard,
And in that dark, dark cupboard,
There was a dark, dark shelf,
And on that dark, dark shelf,
There was a dark, dark box,
And in the dark, dark box,
There was a _____!

(Shout out: MONSTER, GHOST, WITCH, VAMPIRE, BAT, JACK-O-LANTERN, TRICERATOPS, or whatever.)

(Traditional, North America)

Hallowe'en

One adult whispers, and one child responds with a small echo. Everyone else chants loudly: "Hallowe'en, Hallowe'en."

Witches on broomsticks
(echo)
Hallowe'en, Hallowe'en
Black cats, black cats
(echo)
Hallowe'en, Hallowe'en
Rattling skeletons, rattling skeletons
(echo)
Hallowe'en, Hallowe'en
Jack-o'-lanterns, Jack-o'-lanterns
(echo)
Hallowe'en, Hallowe'en
Spooks in the night
(echo)
Hallowe'en, Hallowe'en
Creepy crawlies, ghosts and ghoulies
(echo)
Hallowe'en, Hallowe'en

All together shout: "It's Hallowe'en at last!"

(Traditional, Canada)

KEEP WITCHES AWAY

There are some proven methods to keep witches away from your house. They may not work on Hallowe'en, of course, but for the rest of the year they will probably be quite effective.

- Place a bowl of salt or a broom outside your door. The witch will have to stop to count every straw in the broom or every grain of salt. She has to be home by dawn and so won't have time to come inside your house.
- Place a horseshoe over your door (with the ends up so the luck won't fall out). The witch will have to follow every path the horse has taken.
- Put a patch of true blue on your door. Blue is the color of the daytime sky, and witches like the night.
- Wear a penny in your shoe.
- Always put the salt on the table first, and take it off last when you set the table.

SPECIAL MUSIC

I love Robin Williamson's *Songs for Children of All Ages*, Pig's Whisker Music. His entire Celtic repertoire is great, but "Witch's Hat," "Brian O'Linn," and "Raggle Taggle Gypsies" are especially wonderful for Hallowe'en.

HALLOWE'EN STORIES

Here are some good Hallowe'en and monster books to read before Hallowe'en.

The Rabbi and the Twenty-nine Witches, A Talmudic legend retold and illustrated by Marilyn Hirsh, Holiday House
The Very Busy Spider, Eric Carle, Philomel
Where the Wild Things Are, Maurice Sendak, Harper Trophy
The Bunyip of Berkeley's Creek, Jenny Wagner, Picture Puffin

A Woggle of Witches, Adrienne Adams,
    Atheneum
The Ghost-Eye Tree, Bill Martin, Jr. and John
    Archambault, Henry Holt and Company
The Spooky Old Tree, Stan and Jan Berenstain,
    Random House Beginner Books
Spooky Riddles, Marc Brown, Random House
    Beginner Books
For Adults: *The All Around Pumpkin Book*,
    Margery Culyer, Holt, Rinehard & Winston

Diwali — The Festival of Light

Our city has many unique neighborhoods; there is an East Indian Bazaar near our favorite library! Diwali, the festival of light, is one of the great Indian festivals. It takes place early in winter and is the festival of the lighting of lamps. The lamps signify the triumph of jubilation and joy over the forces of darkness.

In some ways, Diwali is a New Year's Day as it is a time for settling debts and beginning a new financial year. Everything, from households to accounts, is tidied up. Lights are on everywhere to welcome Laxmi, the goddess of wealth. The festival is also sacred to Rama.

Diwali occurs on the second day of Kartika, in October or November, at the time of the new moon. Everyone wears new clothes and plays games of chance, if only to guess the luck coming in the new year. If you don't gamble on Diwali, you come back to earth as a donkey in your next reincarnation! It is a festival of light, sound, color, sweetness, gaming, feasting, joy, sparkle, meeting and greeting friends. Fireworks ward off evil spirits. Glass bowls of colored water are placed in front of candles and lamps. Sweets, often made with vegetables and milk, are decorated with edible silver or gold foils.

BURFI

One of the yummiest of confections, Burfi is easy to make.

Grease an 8" square cake pan with clarified butter (ghee), set aside.

Grind 1 cup of blanched almonds and 1 cup of pistachios until fine. Add 1/2 cup dessicated coconut and 1/2 cup raisins. Set aside.

In a heavy saucepan, bring 4 cups of milk to a boil, reduce heat to a low simmer, and cook until the milk is the consistency of heavy cream, stirring frequently. Add 1 cup granulated sugar and cook for 10 minutes more. Stir frequently. Add the nuts, coconut, and raisins, keep stirring, and cook for about 10 minutes more. Add 1 tsp rosewater (available at your drugstore), 1 tbsp ghee, and a pinch or two of powdered cardamon.

When the mixture pulls away from the pan, spread it in the cake pan, using a spatula or knife. Allow to cool, and cut into diamonds. Decorate each confection with edible silver or gold foil (available from an East Indian grocery), rose petals, blanched sliced almonds or pistachios, or crushed cardamon seeds. (If you can't find the edible foil, use silver dragées.)
Hint: If the milk doesn't thicken well, stir in a few spoonfuls of instant powdered milk.

The Christmas Season _____

From ancient times, festivals at the winter solstice have occurred virtually everywhere in the world. The Romans celebrated Saturnalia, sacred to Mithras, with light, food and drink. The Norse celebrated Yule, with yule logs, candles, evergreens, and mistletoe. The Jewish faith celebrates the Festival of Light, Hannukah, with latkes, the spinning of dreidles, and the lighting of lamps; and Christians celebrate the birth of the baby Jesus.

Share the season of the winter solstice with your child. Treat Christmas as the season from the beginning of Advent until at least Twelfth Night. Take the time to bake cookies, make gifts and ornaments, listen to the wonderful music of the season. Make mini-Christmases around Saint Nicholas Day (December 6) and St. Lucia Day (December 13); recover on St. Stephen's Day (December 26). Carry on your celebrations until Twelfth Day (January 6) or Eastern Orthodox Christmas (January 7th). Slow down, and give your child the most precious gifts of all; your time and attention at this special season of the year.

MUSIC

Fill your home with the music of the season. Your child will love *Raffi's Christmas Album*, Troubadour Records, and Rick & Judy's *Christmas is Coming*, J & R Records. Play your own favorite Christmas music, from the King's College Cambridge *Christmas Reading of the Lessons*, to Handel's *Messiah*. Look around for the Kingston Trio's *The Last Month of the Year* and The New Christy Minstrel's *Merry Christmas*. If you have Rick & Judy's *Family Album*, play "Jogging Along With Me Reindeer" from the best British Music Hall Tradition. You might want to listen to the "Little Match Girl" on the Rovers *Children of the Unicorn* album, Attic Records, and read Hans Christian Andersen's fairy tale as well.

Attend special Christmas carol concerts and services. Stop and listen to the Salvation Army brass bands in the shopping malls. Open your mouths and sing out the joyful music of the season!

O Christmas Tree

O Christmas tree, O Christmas tree
How lovely are thy branches
O Christmas tree, O Christmas tree
How lovely are thy branches
Not only green in summer's heat
But also winter's snow and sleet
O Christmas tree, O Christmas tree
How lovely are thy branches.
(Traditional, Germany)

I Saw Three Ships Come Sailing In

I saw three ships come sailing in,
Come sailing in, come sailing in,
I saw three ships come sailing in
On Christmas day in the morning.

And what do you think was in them then,
Was in them then, was in them then.
And what do you think was in them then,
On Christmas day in the morning.

Three pretty girls were in them then,
Were in them then, were in them then,
Three pretty girls were in them then,
On Christmas day in the morning.

One could whistle and one could sing
And one could play on the violin.
What joy there was at my wedding,
On Christmas Day in the morning.
(Traditional, English)

If you enjoy beautiful trained voices, listen to Kathleen Battle's version of this song on her *A Christmas Celebration* album, EMI Angel.

THE NUTCRACKER

The *Nutcracker* is for children. There's a huge party, a growing Christmas tree, dancing children, battling mice, magic scenery and the Sugarplum Fairy. What an introduction to the world of ballet, stage, and Tchaikovsky's wonderful music! Dress up in your best party finery, and hope that they have some of the chocolate-dipped strawberries left at intermission.

If you can't see a live performance, rent a video of *The Nutcracker*; there are four or five absolutely great performances in the Christmas section of your video store. Veronica Tennant, former Sugarplum Fairy with the National Ballet of Canada, has recorded a marvelous tape of *The Nutcracker*, Kids' Records.

You may want to invest in *The Nutcracker*, by Jane Kendall (David R. Godine, Publisher). It's a marvelous cutout book, complete with the cast of characters, scenery, stage, and props.

THE PANTOMIME

"Panto" is for the whole family. The "Oh no I didn't" — "Oh yes you did!" interchange between the villain and the audience is traditional. With music, special effects, dancing, overacting, parody, and a chance to cheer the good guys and hiss the villain, the pantomime guarantees a side-splitting time for all. Plays like *Aladdin & the Magic Lamp*, *Jack in the Beanstalk*, *Dick Whittington and his Cat*, *Mother Goose*, *Goldilocks and the Three Bears*, *Snow White*, and *Cinderella*, performed in the best British variety show tradition, are sure to be the highlight of the Christmas season.

Some children may need reassurance about the special effects, especially in front rows where actors run through the audience. Tell your child that the good guys will win and the villain will reform at the end. Read the story to your child before you go, even though the play may be totally different.

CHRISTMAS STORIES

In addition to children's books such as *The Olden Days Coat*, Margaret Laurence (McClelland & Stewart) and *Seasons of Delight*, Tasha Tudor (Philomel Books), introduce your child to some classic Christmas tales.

Read a shortened version of Charles Dickens's *A Christmas Carol*, and watch it on television or rent the video. You might want to introduce Selena Hastings' version of *Sir Gawaine and the Green Knight* (Walker Books), a medieval tale that is part of the Arthurian legend.

SAINT NICHOLAS DAY (DECEMBER 6)

Saint Nicholas is the most popular and venerated saint in Christian churches in central Europe, both in the Eastern and Western orthodox traditions. He saves children from mortal danger and deposits infants down chimneys. Rich himself, he leaves gifts secretly in the middle of the night, provides dowries for poor girls, and brings children presents on his name day.

Saint Nicholas is accompanied by Black Peter, also called Grampas, who is the devil incarnate, complete with horns, hooves and rattling chains. Saint Nicholas wears the clothes of a mitred and sceptered bishop, and rides a white horse. Black Peter carries a sack so he can carry off evil children, and birch switches so he can beat them. He carries a huge red ledger where all the good and evil deeds of children have been recorded throughout the past year.

Have your child put out her boots, wooden shoes, or stockings, filled with hay or a carrot for Saint Nicholas's horse. If she's been good, Saint Nicholas will fill her shoes with sweets, apples, nuts, Lebkuchen, and perhaps a beautifully decorated birch switch, given as a warning to remain good throughout the coming year. If she's been bad, Black Peter will fill her shoe with switches. If she's been awful, Black Peter will wake her up for a beating. If she has been truly evil, Black Peter will pack her into a sack and take her away to Spain, where Saint Nicholas and Black Peter live.

Saint Nicholas was one of the first saints in the New World. He was the figurehead on Henry Hudson's ship. Christopher Columbus named the port of Saint Nicholas on Haiti on December 6, 1492.

Lebkuchen

Originating in Poland, this recipe has been in my friend Susan's family for generations.

Mix together and bring to a boil:
  1/2 cup honey and 1/2 cup molasses
Let cool thoroughly, and add:
  1 beaten egg
  1 tbsp lemon juice
  3/4 cup brown sugar
Sift together and add to liquid mixture:
  2 3/4 cup flour
  1/2 tsp baking soda
  1 tsp cinnamon
  1/2 tsp allspice
  1/2 tsp nutmeg
  1/4 tsp cloves (optional)
If desired, add:
  1/3 cup chopped nuts or candied fruit

Chill well, roll, and cut with your favorite cookie cutters. Decorate with almonds, candied fruit, or raisins. Bake for 10 minutes, maximum, in a 350°F oven. Do not overcook, or they will be hard. Glaze while hot, and store in a sealed cookie tin.

Glaze: Boil 1 cup sugar and 1/2 cup water about 10 minutes, stirring constantly. Stir in 1/4 cup icing sugar, and brush over the cookies while still hot. If the glaze gets too thick, add a drop or two of water.

BAKING

Start filling your home with the smells of Christmas cooking starting the week before Advent begins (we call it Stir-up Sunday), and continue until Twelfth Night. Search out your old family recipes and look for traditional ones in magazines and cookbooks. Look for: Stollen, Marzipan, Lebkuchen, Speculas, all kinds of cookies, Springerle, Shortbreads, Fruitcake, Plum Pudding, Bûche de Noël, Tortière.

COOKIE PARTY

Jenny and I have had a Cookie Party for two or three small friends for several years. I have bowls of premixed dough in the fridge, and we usually mix up a bowl or two on the spot as well. Sometimes, one of the other parents will send along a favorite batch of dough, already mixed and chilled. The object of the party is to make and decorate as many cookies as possible.

I have collected a wooden Springerle rolling pin, a huge assortment of cutters, and a cookie press. We use the dining room table so there's lots of room. I put out pastry cloths and rolling pins, baking sheets, sprinkles, colored sugars, peppermint drops, gumdrops, lifesavers, a batch of icing, a pastry bag, silver dragées, chocolate chips, and whatever else I can think of. Once we're finished, we divide up the loot and everyone has a batch of cookies to take home.

COOKIE SWAP

I make apricot jam thumbprint cookies, Susan makes Lebkuchen, Rikie makes Speculas, Kathy makes chocolate chip, Linda makes gingersnaps. We get together to trade even dozens of cookies and get a huge variety. It's a great way to collect favorite family recipes from your friends, too. Make copies of all the recipes you get for your child's recipe file.

DECORATE, DECORATE, DECORATE

Fill up your home with Christmas decorations.

Candy Cane Reindeer

Using white glue, place two google eyes on the front of a cellophane-wrapped candy cane. Fold a pipe cleaner around the top of the bend of the cane and twist it to form antlers. Tie on a decorative bow.

Cup Bells

Decorate a styrofoam cup using white glue, glitter, stickers, and other Christmas art supplies. Attach a bell to one end of a pipe cleaner, stick the other end through the styrofoam and bend in a hook.

Ping Pong Balls

Decorate ping pong balls and attach them to your tree using paperclips or ornament holders.

Paper Chains

Glue together strips of paper, six inches long and about an inch wide. Make a pattern using strips of different colors. You might want to make a mobius chain (p 140).

Tissue Bits

Cut or rip tissue into small squares. Lay a square over the eraser end of a pencil, dip it into a bit of diluted white glue, and place it on your decoration. Lots of squares close together give a lovely ruffled effect. You can cover cardboard tubes for "crackers," donut-shaped wreath forms, or wooden clothespins to make costumes for nutcrackers or sugarplum fairies.

Candy Tree

Cover a styrofoam cone with foil or festive paper. Stick gumdrops, lemon, orange, or lime candy slices, and spearmint leaves onto the tree with toothpicks.

Snow

Make "snow" to ice windows, cardboard, or winter scenes. Using your wire whisk or eggbeater, whip together two cups of pure laundry soap powder or flakes with 1/4 to 1/2 cup of water until it's the consistency of thickly whipped cream. Mold with damp hands, use a pastry bag or cookie press for fancy effects, or spread it with a knife. This mixture dries to a porous texture and will last quite a while if treated gently. Try it as a fingerpaint on black construction paper. Use less water and roll it into soap snowballs.

Della Robia Wreaths

Using white glue or a hot glue gun (you use the hot glue), make a wreath using different-sized nuts (hazelnuts, brazil nuts, walnuts, pecans, peanuts in the shell), and pinecones. You could also make a horseshoe for luck, instead of a traditional wreath.

Gumdrop Chain

String gumdrops into a chain for your tree, with a tapestry needle and dental floss. Stale popcorn, cranberries and dried apples make lovely chains, too, and after the holidays, you can hang them out for the birds.

Gift Bags

Decorate white paper bags or large sheets of newsprint for hard-to-wrap gifts.

CHRISTMAS CARDS AND PAPER

Make your child's very own special Christmas card list. Include her friends, coaches, relatives, and the naturalists at your camping area. Make cards using Bristol board, stamps, stencils, cookie cutters, glitter, pretty papers, tinsel, gummed stars, and stickers. Mail her creations to her favorite people.

Have your child stamp Christmas designs on white shelf paper using sponge stamps or cookie cutters. Make stencils, cut out of styrofoam meat trays, in Christmas shapes. Add glitter sprinkled on glue for an extra-special festive touch.

THE CHRISTMAS TREE

Does anything smell more wonderful than a fresh Christmas tree inside your home? You may want to go to a tree farm to cut your own tree, or you may want to purchase a potted tree you can plant outside after Christmas. If you purchase a tree at your corner lot, thump it on the ground; it shouldn't shed needles. Make sure you have a sturdy stand or bucket of water or wet sand, and keep the tree away from all heat sources: stoves, televisions, fireplaces, refrigerators, heaters. Never use candles near the tree; use electric lights and check them carefully before putting them on the tree. Always unplug your tree at night or when you go out.

Make as many of your own decorations as possible, and start a collection of special ornaments for your child to keep when she grows up.

GIFTS

There's nothing more special than a child's handmade gift, given with love. She can make Jacob's Ladders for friends (p 34), woven pot holders (p 104) and corked hot mats (p 89) for grandmas and aunties, and bird feeders (p 129) for neighbors. T-shirts, fireplace starters, and yule logs make wonderful gifts for just about everybody.

T-SHIRTS

Wash a new T-shirt to remove the sizing, and when it's dry ask your child to draw a picture on it with fabric markers or crayons. Puff paints and glitter paints add highlights. If you use fabric crayons, use an iron to set the dyes. Grandpas especially love decorated T-shirts that say "I love you."

FIREPLACE STARTERS

Roll large pine cones in slightly cooled melted wax, tie them with a bow, and give them to friends to use as fire starters. It's a great way to use up candle ends and crayon bits.

THE YULE LOG

A huge log is burned all night on Christmas Eve to ensure good luck. If you don't have a fireplace, drill four holes in a birch log, using an auger, and insert four candles. Light one candle for each Sunday in Advent. Buy an extra-long taper candle and leave it burning on Christmas Eve for good luck. Decorate the log with holly and ivy, or other greenery, and use it as a centerpiece on Christmas day. The wonderful chocolate cake, meringue, and whipped cream Christmas Log, the Bûche de Noël, is an edible version of the Yule Log.

CHRISTMAS EVE

Never, ever, go into stables, barns, cowsheds, or pigstys at midnight on Christmas Eve. The animals are given the power of speech and horrible things will happen to you if you hear them talking. Of course, you never gossip in a stable at any time, because horses carry tales (tails).

You should also avoid sitting outdoors under pine trees on Christmas Eve, just in case you happen to hear the angels sing. It foretells an early death.

The place to be on Christmas Eve is indoors after carol service, beside a warm hearth, the yule log burning brightly, stockings hung, waiting for Santa Claus, and eating tortière.

Old Sante Claus

Old Sante Claus with much delight
His reindeer drives this frosty night.
O'er chimneytops and tracks of snow,
To bring his yearly gifts to you.

The steady friend of virtuous youth,
The friend of duty, and of truth,
Each Christmas eve he joys to come
Where love and peace have made their home.

Through many houses he has been,
And various beds and stockings seen,
Some, white as snow and neatly mended,
Others, that seem'd for pigs intended.

Where e'er I found good girls and boys,
That hated quarrels, strife and noise,
I left an apple, or a tart,
Or wooden gun, or painted cart.

To some I gave a pretty doll,
To some a peg-top, or a ball,
No crackers, cannons, squibs, or rockets
To blow their eyes up, or their pockets.

No drums to stun their Mother's ear,
Nor swords to make their sisters fear;
But pretty books to store their mind
With knowledge of each various kind.

But where I found the children naughty,
In manners rude, in tempers haughty,
Thankless to parents, liars, swearers
Boxers, or cheats, or base tale-bearers,

I left a long black, birchen rod.
Such as the dread command of God
Directs a parent's hand to use
When virtue's path his sons refuse.
(*The Children's Friend*, No. III, pub. 1821, New York)

NISSE

Nisse is a barn elf from Scandinavia, who is mischievous, but benevolent. Put out a bowl of porridge for him on Christmas Eve. All children eat a bowl of porridge, too, flavored with sugar, cinnamon and a pat of butter. Hide an almond in your child's bowl; that means she gets a piece of Marzipan candy and good luck for the coming year.

CHRISTMAS DAY

Fill the special day with many traditions and enjoy it with all the members of your family. Make telephone calls to those who are away. Feast on a special meal that you and your child have planned and prepared. Listen to wonderful music, perhaps try to catch the Queen's greetings or the Pope's message. Celebrate the wonderful occasion of the birth of a child.

ST. STEPHEN'S DAY — BOXING DAY

Boxing Day is the day the alms boxes are opened to give to the poor. In England, it's the day for the great hunts, because St. Stephen is the patron saint of horses and huntsmen. It's the time to give gifts to all those special people who have served you all year. It's also the time to visit your rector, for his gift of bread, cheese and ale to the congregation. St. Stephen's Day is a good day to gather your friends and neighbors together to go out wassailing.

Good King Wenceslas

(Everybody sings)
Good King Wenceslas looked out
On the Feast of Stephen,
When the snow lay round about,
Deep and crisp and even:
Brightly shone the moon that night,
Though the frost was cruel,
When a poor man came in sight,
Gathering winter fuel.
(Only men sing)
"Hither, page and stand by me,
If thous know'st it telling,
Yonder peasant, who is he?
Where and what his dwelling?"
(Only women and children sing)
"Sire, he lives a good league hence,
Underneath the mountain,
Right against the forest fence,
By Saint Agnes' fountain."
(Only men sing)
"Bring me flesh and bring me wine,
Bring me pine logs hither:
Thou and I will see him dine,
When we bear him thither,"
(Everybody sings)
Page and monarch forth they went,
Forth they went together:
Through the rude wind's wild lament
And the bitter weather.
(Only women and children sing)
"Sire, the night is darker now,
And the wind blows stronger;
Fails my heart I know not how;
I can go no longer."
(Only men sing)
"Mark my footsteps, my good page,
Tread thou in them boldly:
Thou shalt find the winter's rage
Freeze thy blood less coldly."

(Everyone sings)

In his master's steps he trod,
Where the snow lay dinted;
Heat was in the very sod
Which the Saint had printed.
Therefore, Christian men, be sure,
Wealth or rank possessing,
Ye who now will bless the poor,
Shall yourselves find blessing.

(Traditional, Christmas Carol)

SHARING

Christmas becomes truly meaningful when you share your love and good fortune with others. Have your child help you gather baskets of non-perishable canned goods and take them to food banks. Perhaps she will share some of her toys and warm clothes with children who are less fortunate than she. You can visit a children's hospital and take along some activity books and crayons. Visit a nursing home with a group to sing Christmas carols, or just visit quietly, listening to stories of Christmases long ago.

UNDERWEAR BUNCHIN'

I told my friend Linda about Goof-off Day, our special family holiday where we take a complete break from our daily routines.

She told me about her family's "Underwear Bunchin'." Once a week, nobody gets dressed or goes out. It's a day for sleeping in, catching up on all the family news, and just being together at home, being a family.

MERRYTHOUGHT

Hey, ho, 'tis nought but mirth,
That keeps the body from the earth.

("The Knight of the Burning Pestle"
Francis Beaumont, early 1600s)

INDEX

ART

WORD PLAY

FACTS AROUND A THEME — SPACE